PEASANT NATIONALISM AND COMMUNIST POWER

Peasant Nationalism and Communist Power

THE EMERGENCE OF REVOLUTIONARY CHINA
1937–1945

Chalmers A. Johnson

STANFORD UNIVERSITY PRESS

STANFORD, CALIFORNIA

1962

Stanford University Press
Stanford, California

London: Oxford University Press

© 1962 by the Board of Trustees of the
Leland Stanford Junior University

Library of Congress Catalog Card Number: 62-16949

Printed in the United States of America
Published with the assistance of the Ford Foundation

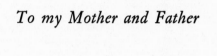

To my Mother and Father

Preface

This study of Chinese Communism during the Sino-Japanese War has two distinct goals. On the one hand, it is intended to illuminate certain aspects of the so-called Yenan period of Chinese Communist history. On the other hand, it seeks to interpret the phenomena uncovered by historical research in terms of a general analysis of mass nationalism.

The subject of the purely historical inquiry is the resistance movement of the Chinese peasants against the Japanese invaders. The general outlines of the wartime Chinese resistance are well known; many foreign observers who found themselves in Yenan or Chungking popularized the exploits of the Chinese guerrillas throughout the world. Writers like Edgar Snow and Evans Carlson have already given us pictures of the heroic dimensions of the peasants' struggle against the Japanese. What they did not explore were the political and military characteristics of the resistance and the influence of the resistance movement upon the course of Chinese politics. This study, drawing chiefly upon the archives of the Japanese Army and the Kōain (Asia Development Board), seeks to describe the extent and consequences of the political and military confrontation that occurred between the Chinese peasants and the Japanese army.

The wartime picture that emerges from a reading of the Japanese Army archives is one of widespread guerrilla warfare—warfare which thwarted Japanese political objectives in China and against which the Japanese never developed an effective response. This resistance was by and large led by the Chinese Communist Party and drew its manpower from the war-mobilized peasantry. The alliance between Party and peasantry not only had a negative effect upon the Japanese war effort, but also helped initiate the peasantry into an expanded role in Chinese political life. The 19 guerrilla bases established behind the Japanese lines were training centers where the pre-political peasantry was introduced to the concept and goals of the Chinese national community. The circumstances in which the peasants and the Communist Party collaborated, as well as the nature of the rear-area governments that they jointly established, are therefore major subjects for investigation.

It is in interpreting the Communist-peasant resistance movement that the focus of the study necessarily widens. One must confront the fact that, as a result of the Communist Party's leadership of the resistance, the Party obtained a mass following that it subsequently used to conquer all of China. When we review the vicissitudes of the Chinese Communist Party since its founding in 1921, one fact stands out in striking relief: the link between the Party's wartime popularity and its postwar triumph. This link between the wartime activities of the Communists and their postwar authority has never been fully explored despite its obvious relevance to the meaning of mid-century Communism in China and elsewhere. An investigation of precisely this connection is the second major goal of the present research.

In studying the rise to power of an elite organization such as the Communist Party, one must give primary consideration to the circumstances under which it achieves a mass following. In some Communist-ruled countries—namely, in those Communist states created by the Soviet Red Army—the Party has never held a clear title to mass loyalty. In the Communist states in which the Party achieved power independently of the Soviet Union—i.e., in China, Yugoslavia, and North Vietnam (possibly, also, Cuba)—it did so as a result of winning the allegiance of a significant portion of the population. In two of these states, China and Yugoslavia, the Party became a mass movement in the context of resistance to a foreign invader during World War II. Thus, the relationship established between the Party and the masses in the course of the Chinese and Yugoslav resistance movements is central to an evaluation of the postwar political authorities established in those two countries.

Many interpretations of the Communist rise to power in China have been advanced in the decade since 1949. All of them deal directly with this question of the appeal of Communism to the Chinese peasantry in the period following the Long March (1934–35). Some analysts emphasize the economic distress of the Chinese peasantry and the attraction of Communist proposals for alleviating this distress. Others contend that the question of the appeals of Communism is irrelevant because Communist parties are self-serving conspiracies and are indifferent to the attitudes of the populations under their control. The latter view emphasizes the techniques of mass manipulation, developed in model form by the Bolshevik Party, which were allegedly used by the CCP to "seize" power. Still other writers argue that Chinese Communist success is to be laid to military superiority alone, and they discount the political environment during the war as being of secondary importance in producing a Communist victory. According to this view, the masses simply followed the winner. All these interpretations reflect certain actual features of Chinese society and political history. However, as complete hypotheses that purport to unravel the causes of Communist success and, at the same time, to account for the extraordinary work ethic that has developed among the Chinese masses, they are clearly deficient.

On the basis of a study of wartime resistance in China, the view advanced here is that the Communist rise to power in China should be understood as a species of nationalist movement. Nationalism, as is well known, is a poorly defined and much misused concept. There are numerous accounts of it as an ideological, colonial, intellectual, linguistic, European, racial, or religious phenomenon; and the Communists themselves have an extensive literature on nationalism as a manifestation of "bourgeois" society. At the same time, many Western writers on Communism have found cases in which Communist leaders have made use of non-Communist nationalist symbols in order to advance the interests of the Party. Our concern is not with these traditional descriptions of nationalist movements, nor with the use of nationalism that may have been made by the Chinese Communists. We are concerned, rather, with giving definition to the Chinese Communist movement, using nationalism as a meaningful tool of social science research.

This study employs a functional definition of nationalism—in other words, one which identifies specific physical pressures that by acting upon given political environments give rise to nationalist movements. With the aid of this definition, plus a specific comparison with the Yugoslav Partisan movement, the study thus seeks a fresh perspective on the foundations of the Chinese Communist Party's authority. In essence, the Party is seen as the leader of a war-energized, radical nationalist movement; while the Chinese Communist version of Marxist-Leninist ideology is viewed as an adjunct to Chinese nationalism—that is, as a "national myth" serving the newly created Chinese nation state. According to this formulation, the Chinese masses, the peasants, were unified and politicized as a concomitant of the drastic restructuring of Chinese life that accompanied the Japanese conquest of north and east China. Participation in the popular guerrilla base governments, together with the numerous other projects for national mobilization undertaken by the guerrilla leadership, gave an entirely new political perspective to the Chinese peasantry. This wartime awakening became the basis for a new order in China following Japan's collapse: the wartime leaders of the resistance were confirmed by their followers in positions of legitimate national authority.

It might be supposed that the sources employed in this study—principally, the military and political archives of the former Japanese government—contain a built-in bias that might be reflected in the conclusions. This is partly true and partly false, and a preliminary comment upon the nature of these materials is needed in order to clarify this point. Many of the "Japanese" sources used below are actually of Chinese origin. In the prosecution of their war against China, the Japanese captured, compiled, and translated an enormous quantity of documents, newspapers, handbooks, and the like issued by both the Chinese Communists and the Kuomintang. In addition, the Japanese themselves made investigations into Chinese conditions and prepared analyses of the situation in the occupied areas. Both types of materials were then published in "secret diaries" and other highly classified periodicals, which have provided the primary sources of information for this book. Are these Chinese materials genuine and how accurate are the Japanese studies?

With regard to captured materials and on-the-spot investigations, two considerations lead to the conclusion that they are reliable. First, the archives in which they are collected (those used in this study) are all inscribed "secret"—that is, they were not employed for propaganda purposes, but, rather, for a realistic appraisal of military and political developments in China by Japanese leaders. Second, they are internally consistent and are corroborated by other non-Japanese sources of information. As for Japanese analyses of the situation, a summary statement may be made here that will be elaborated in the text. The Japanese regularly underestimated or ignored their own role in producing conditions of anarchy and popular discontent in the occupied territories. After the period of initial fighting was over, however, the Japanese clearly recognized that such anarchic conditions did exist; and they did not obscure the fact—in classified summaries —that the Communists were turning these conditions to their own advantage. Since, in all likelihood, we shall never have the secret files on this period of either the Communists or the Nationalists, it does not seem premature to undertake a study of 1937–45 developments in China using the rich, and on the whole accurate, archives of the third active participant.

Finally, I should like to stress my essential neutrality with regard to the general merits of Communism in China. There is an unfortunate tendency in Western educated circles to suppose that nationalism outside of Europe is axiomatically good, or at least "natural," and to condemn Communism as evil, regardless of its popular *bona fides.* It must be pointed out, therefore, that in characterizing the Chinese revolution as nationalistic I am making no attempt to influence anyone's opinion in favor of the Communist regime. Conversely, those who persist in making a rigid distinction between Communism and nationalism in China in order to discredit the present government must also be disavowed. The object of this study is to establish a basis upon which contemporary Communism in China may be understood as a particularly virulent form of nationalism. If this point is accepted, then the so-called "liberal" question of whether or not one is favorably disposed toward nationalism and opposed to Communism becomes meaningless. On the general question of making a judgment on the merits of a particular nationalist movement, Professor Kedourie's conclusion cannot be improved:

> To welcome a change or to regret it, because one set of rulers has gone and another has come, is something which we all do, for some rulers are more likely to look to our own welfare than others; but these are private preoccupations for which such private justification is reasonable. Public justification requires more; to welcome or deplore a change in government because some now enjoy power and others are deprived of it is not enough. The only criterion capable of public defense is whether the new rulers are less corrupt and grasping, or more just and merciful, or whether there is no change at all, but the corruption, the greed, and the tyranny merely find victims other than those of the departed rulers. And this is really the only question at issue between nationalism and the systems to which it is opposed.*

In the execution of this study, I should like to acknowledge the valuable criticisms I have received from Professors Robert A. Scalapino, Ernst B. Haas, and Joseph R. Levenson, who have all read the manuscript in various stages of its completion. I owe a special debt to Professor Scalapino, who is responsible for securing the Kōain materials on microfilm for the East Asiatic Library, University of California, Berkeley, and who first recog-

---

* Elie Kedourie, *Nationalism* (London: 1960), pp. 139–40.

nized their great relevance to the Chinese Communist movement. In addition, I should like to mention the many courtesies extended to me by Colonel Abe Kunio, War History Compilation Officer, Japanese Self-Defense Force. Colonel Abe kindly made available to me copies of *Kaikōsha kiji,* which have been used in this study, and he spent many hours in conversation with me at the War History Office, Japanese Defense Agency (Bōeichō Senshishitsu), Tokyo. I would also like to thank the Center for Chinese Studies, University of California, and the Ford Foundation for financial assistance that enabled me to conduct the research for this work, both in Berkeley and in Tokyo. Finally, I must acknowledge the aid I have received from Sheila K. Johnson, my wife, who has contributed to the book in hours of argument with me about its substance, in drawing the maps, and in her implacable insistence that a clear prose style is a necessary ingredient of clear thinking. Needless to say, no one but myself should be held responsible for any of the views expressed or conclusions reached in the following study.

C. A. J.

Contents

Maps

PEASANT NATIONALISM AND COMMUNIST POWER

ONE

Peasant Nationalism in China

The Communist government of China was formally proclaimed on October 1, 1949, and it is this date that is celebrated today as the national anniversary of its accession to power. However, to regard 1949 as the beginning of Communist government in China obscures the fact that the Communist Party actually ruled a large part of China for at least ten years before that time. Following the outbreak of the Sino-Japanese War in 1937, the Communist Party enlarged the territory under its control to a degree previously unimagined even by the Communist leaders themselves. This enlargement took the form of "guerrilla bases," which were established in rural areas behind the Japanese lines. Before Japan's capitulation in 1945, one-fifth of the population of China was living in these guerrilla bases and following the leadership of the Communist Party. Thus, it is from the early stages of the Sino-Japanese War that we should date the Chinese Communists' true rise to power.

The Communists' success during the war was in marked contrast to their experiences in the decade preceding the war, when they first undertook seriously to organize the peasantry. Although the Communists were in effective control of various small enclaves in the Chinese countryside from 1927 on, their painful efforts during that period to set up rural "soviets" were incomparably less successful than their activities during the blackest period of the Sino-Japanese War. The Party's prewar failure was not the result of a lack of effort. From the first Communist-led jacqueries in 1927 until the beginning of the Long March in 1934, the Communists utilized every available economic, ideological, and military tool to establish a durable political order in the territories defended by their army. In 1938, however, using essentially the same organizational techniques they had used in the past, the Chinese Communists were successful in rural

China as they had never been before. An understanding of the factors that brought about this development is crucial to an assessment of Chinese politics today and to an appreciation of what a "Communist" China means in the twentieth century.

PEASANT MOBILIZATION

The critical difference between the two periods was that the Communist Party failed to obtain mass support in the Kiangsi period, but did achieve such a following during the Resistance War.[1] Prior to 1937, although the peasantry collaborated half-heartedly with the Communists (the Communists purchased peasant support of the Red Army with their anti-landlord economic policy), the relationship established between the two was contingent upon Communist military successes and the failure of other contenders to make the peasants a better offer. As we know, the Communists were not successful militarily in the Kiangsi period, and the Kuomintang did make the peasantry at least an equally good offer.[2]

However, after the outbreak of the war the situation changed; it became much more fluid, much more dynamic. The politically illiterate masses of China were awakened by the Japanese invasion and its aftermath; wartime conditions made them receptive to a new kind of political appeal—namely, the defense of the fatherland. The war presented the peasantry with a challenge to its security of such immediacy that the peasants could not ignore it. Prewar pressures on the peasantry—such as economic exploitation, Communist ideology, warlord wars, and natural calamities—had never been sufficiently widespread or sufficiently intense to give rise to a peasant-based mass movement. But after July 7, 1937, the peasants spontaneously created resistance organizations in many areas of China; and they felt a heightened sensitivity to proposals for defensive organization throughout the entire occupied area. There were several specific influences that promoted this new activity among the peasants.

First, as the armies of the Central Government retreated from north China and the lower Yangtze Valley after the Japanese invasion, and as the majority of the officials and other agents of the existing establishment retreated with them, anarchy settled on the Chinese villages. The U.S. War Department has described the situation in the occupied areas as follows:

> While the Japanese set up a Chinese puppet administration, and through this and their army authorities maintained a measure of order in their occupied zones in North China, the rural areas around these

zones fell prey to ravaging hordes of Japanese soldiers engaged in grain confiscations and "mopping up" operations against Communists and remnants of Chinese provincial forces, roving units of disorganized Chinese soldiers who had turned bandits, and bandit groups formed out of peasants who had collected arms on various battlefields.[3]

The rural villages responded to this situation by establishing self-defense forces and, in some cases, guerrilla corps. In their efforts at defensive organization, the villagers welcomed whatever capable military and political leadership they could find—Communist, Nationalist, Sacrifice League (Shansi), secret society, KMT Army remnants, or purely local leaders. Hundreds of new, anti-Japanese popular governments were set up behind the Japanese lines at the basic level of Chinese local government—the hsien, or county.[4] These rear-area governments, led by local men or Partisans of battle-proved integrity, filled the vacuum left by the retreat of the former authorities. Such governments provided for self-defense, education, agricultural cooperation, support for full-time guerrillas, and other needs of the villages; most important, they served as instruments for helping the rural masses attain a political understanding of the war to serve as a gloss on their personal experience. While mining a road, or guarding a village, or attending a meeting of one of the mass associations (some of the many activities sponsored by the guerrilla governments), the rural "common man" learned that his peril was also China's peril.

Many of these governments were, of course, sponsored by or under the influence of the Communist Party; but, as William G. Carleton has put it, "Under Communism, the mass of Asiatics in some countries may come into close contact with their governments for the first time in their history; and this contact, because of the many functions exercised by Communist governments, will be far more intimate than the contacts of the mass of Europeans with their national governments in the days when European nationalism was emerging."[5] These wartime governments were not democratic (there was virtually no opposition), but the masses did participate on an enormous scale in "governmental" activities via the so-called "mass movement" (*min-chung yün-tung*). The feeling of belonging and of having a stake in government that grew up in this period was entirely novel to the Chinese masses; and it brought with it an exhilarating sense of self-determination. At the same time, villages in which the population decided to cooperate with the Japanese generally suffered for their decision, and this also had its educative effect. Thus, the very setting of the war proved favorable to Communist propaganda.

A second factor that influenced the peasants after 1937 was the propaganda and educational effort launched by the Communist Party. This propaganda was remarkably free of a "Communist" quality; it stressed *chiu-kuo,* or national salvation. The Communists had, of course, used patriotic and anti-Japanese appeals in their propaganda since the Manchurian Incident (1931). What was actually new in the propaganda field after 1937 was that the Japanese Army had created a huge ready-made audience for Communist propaganda as a result of its conduct of the invasion. The Communists themselves took no chances on repeating their failure to unite the masses in the Kiangsi Soviet; they eschewed their old slogans of class warfare and violent redistribution of property in their post-1937 propaganda and concentrated solely on national salvation. As one example of the wartime orientation of this propaganda, here is part of a leaflet prepared by the CCP-dominated Shansi Sacrifice League and captured by the Japanese Army in Chiehhsiu hsien, Shansi, in September 1938.[6] It reads:

> Exterminate the Traitor Peace Preservation Committees! Comrades! Japan has invaded our Shansi, killed large numbers of our people, burned thousands of our houses, raped our women in countless numbers, robbed us of our food and wealth, trampled on the graves of our ancestors, forced our wives and children to flee, destroyed our famous places, . . . and made the joy of peace impossible. . . . Everybody! Rise up and join a guerrilla self-defense unit! Exterminate the Peace Maintenance Committee which sells out the nation! Defend our anti-Japanese patriotic people's government! Assist the all-out resistance of Commander Yen [Hsi-shan]! Act in unison with Army and people to overthrow Japanese imperialism![7]

This is merely one sample of the propaganda—itself only one tool of the total Communist effort—employed by the Party behind the lines to help the peasantry help themselves, and also to obtain from them assistance for the Communist Army in its efforts to hamper the invasion. These activities promoted mobilization in the countryside and, at the same time, fed upon the spontaneous peasant unrest. Nationalistic propaganda from Communist sources fell on fertile ground, where it both furthered the mobilization of the masses and helped determine the form this mobilization took.

Still another component in the complex of forces that assaulted the Chinese peasant after 1937 was the policy of Japanese reprisals. Because the Japanese Army was suffering from Communist military pressure and from a situation in which it could not distinguish a guerrilla from a villager, the Japanese and puppet forces took ruthless action against the rural population, action that resulted in the depopulation of several areas.[8] The effect of this policy—as in Yugoslavia under similar circumstances— was to arouse even the most parochial of village dwellers to the fact that politics could no longer be ignored. The "mop-ups" (Chinese *sao-tang;* Japanese *sōtō*) tended to confirm the charges made against the Japanese by the Communists, notably that there was no way of accommodating to Japanese rule short of slavery. Peasants who survived the mopping-up campaigns were forced to conclude that their only hope lay in resistance, and the Communists were widely regarded as the most competent organizers of resistance. The question of whether or not Communist activity provoked Japanese reprisals will be considered in a later chapter; the point to be stressed here is that the peasants of the occupied areas faced the continuous threat of military attack from the Japanese Army throughout the eight years of the Sino-Japanese War. The dislocations produced by the invasion itself were relatively minor compared with the destruction caused by the mopping-up campaigns, for example those of 1941 and 1942 in Hopei and Shansi provinces.

All these forces—the evacuation, the establishment of *ad hoc* governments, Communist propaganda, and Japanese reprisals (plus other influences, such as the policies of the puppets and the incipient KMT-CCP civil war, which we shall discuss subsequently)—broke the hold of parochialism on the Chinese peasant. Before the Japanese invasion the Chinese peasantry was indifferent to "Chinese" politics, being wholly absorbed in local affairs. The war totally destroyed the traditional rural social order and sensitized the Chinese peasantry to a new spectrum of possible associations, identities, and purposes. Foremost among the new political concepts were those of "China" and "Chinese nationality" (as distinct from one's normal identity as a mere resident of the warlord satrapy of, for example, Han Fu-ch'ü). During the war, the peasants began to hear and use such terms as *Han-chien* (Chinese traitor), *wei-chün* (bogus army, i.e., the puppet forces), *wan-chün* (reactionary army, i.e., the KMT forces as seen by Yenan), and *Jih-k'ou* (Japanese bandits). The intrusion of these terms into the peasants' vocabulary signified the spread of a force that hitherto was prevalent only among the intelligentsia and city-bred people —namely, nationalism.[9]

Like all illiterate populations in such circumstances, the Chinese masses themselves—the peasants[10]—have left no record of the transformation wrought in their lives and thoughts when they were assaulted from the east by the Japanese and invaded from the west and north by the Communists. This study attempts to reveal the nature of that transformation as it is unwittingly disclosed in the archives of the Japanese government. Later on in this chapter I offer an abstract explanation, in terms of a theory of nationalism, of what the Chinese peasants experienced during the war; and in succeeding chapters I shall detail the actual experiences that support such a theory. Before we proceed to these subjects, however, it is necessary to discuss the Communist victory, which was one of the products of the transformation of the peasant masses.

If one were to make a diagram of the fortunes of the Communist Party of China in terms of its popular following, the result would be an undulating line. Starting with the Party's foundation in 1921, a slowly ascending curve rises to 1927; then, with the Nationalist-Communist split and the Kuomintang's purge of the Communists, the line descends precipitously. Next comes the ascent from approximately 1929 to 1934, representing the growth of the Kiangsi Soviet, followed by the sharp dive when the victorious Kuomintang armies drove the Communists from south China. Starting after the period of the Long March, the line begins again from the bottom of the graph, ascends slowly to the peak of 1940, dips sharply in 1941 and 1942 (recording the effect of the Japanese mopping-up campaigns) and then rises from an already fairly high level up and off the top of the page. In the first hump, the Party made a strong economic appeal to the urban workers and shared with the Kuomintang the leadership of the early anti-imperialist, anti-Japanese nationalist movement among the intellectual and urban classes. In the second period, the Party sought to profit from the endemic land hunger of the Chinese tenants and farm laborers and promised them a radical redistribution of farmlands. In the third period, the Party joined its experienced guerrilla cadres with the violently uprooted peasants of the Japanese-occupied areas in tactical alliances against the invader and his puppets. This last period was the one in which the Chinese Communist Party won the Chinese masses to its cause.

Again, we might view this 25-year history in terms of a metaphor from the laboratory. If we think of the Chinese population as a culture plate and of the Communist Party as a colony of viruses growing on its surface, we may suggest various ways in which the Party and the population influenced each other. In the periods before the Japanese invasion, the culture nourished the Communist virus scarcely at all and only sustained the life of other viruses in specific and atypical patches. The Party attempted to adapt itself to its environment and in the process displayed the entire spectrum of Leninist and Comintern disguises, in addition to a few that it created itself. However, it failed and was in its worst straits just prior to the Japanese invasion. After the invasion of 1937, large patches of the culture plate that had previously inhibited political growths of any variety became highly receptive to a particular kind: one that was anti-Japanese, possessed organizational and military abilities, and recognized that a change had occurred in the culture. In other words, from 1921 to 1937 Communism failed in China because the Chinese people, in general, were indifferent to what the Communist Party had to offer. After 1937, it succeeded because the population became receptive to one particular kind of political appeal; and the Communist Party—in one of its many disguises— made precisely that appeal: it offered to meet the needs of the people for leadership in organizing resistance to the invader and in alleviating war-induced anarchy in the rural areas.

A similar process brought the Yugoslav Communist Party to power at the end of World War II, and a study of the better documented and more realistically observed Yugoslav revolution accordingly offers us useful comparative insights into the dynamics of the Chinese revolution. (The Yugoslav comparison is taken up in detail in Chapter Six; for the present we are interested only in the general similarities.) There were two forms of Communist territorial expansion in the 1940's. The first was by means of the Soviet Red Army (Czechoslovakia, although not invaded, was included in the sphere of influence created by the Red Army); the second was by means of Communist-led, rural-recruited partisan armies united under the banners of defense of the fatherland and anti-fascism.

There are only two cases in which the second method was employed successfully: China and Yugoslavia. The rise to power of the YCP was remarkably similar to that of the Chinese Communist Party. The Yugoslav Party enjoyed only a limited base of popular support in the 1920's and 1930's, and this situation became reversed during World War II. Forces similar to those in China operated to bring about a situation favorable to the Yugoslav Communists. The German invaders carried out unenlightened occupation policies. The war offered an opportunity for the Communist Party to discredit the "legal" wartime government of Drazha

Mihailović, first by gaining access to the realm of nationalist sentiment in which the Chetniks had claimed a monopoly, then by emasculating the Chetniks' remnant claims to the mantle of nationalism, and finally by denouncing them as traitors. And, above all, the political role of the peasantry was drastically increased—a result of the dislocations produced by invasion and of Communist engineering. As in China, the Yugoslav Partisans participated in the resistance movement as defenders of Yugoslav national integrity and set aside, for the duration of the war, elements of Marxist dogma that would have conflicted with the interests of the mass movement. As one of the leading non-Communist analysts of the Yugoslav revolution has observed:

> The Yugoslav Communists appealed to the peasants with slogans that were not economic but purely patriotic. The peasants had no idea what would happen to them in the event of a Communist victory. For example, in the locality of Srem [the region between the Danube and the Sava in Serbia], one of the most fertile regions, they fought valiantly in the ranks of the Partisans without ever reflecting that the next day their property might be redistributed or collectivized by Tito.[11]

Thus Communism and nationalism were fused in wartime China and Yugoslavia as a result of the identification of the CCP and YCP, respectively, with the resistance movements of the two countries—movements that the Communist parties themselves were not primarily responsible for setting into motion. The result of this fusion was the creation of Communist nation-states that were not subordinate to the Soviet Union, specifically because the traditional party allegiance to Moscow counted for less than the national unity created between the agricultural masses and the Party by their close cooperation in wartime. Milovan Djilas stresses the difference between the Yugoslav-Chinese experience and the cases of the Soviet satellites in his discussion of national Communism:

> The differences between Communist countries will, as a rule, be as great as the extent to which the Communists were independent in coming to power. Concretely speaking, only the Communists of three countries—the Soviet Union, China, and Yugoslavia—independently carried out revolutions or, in their own way and at their own speed, attained power and began "the building of socialism." These three countries remained independent Communist states even in the period when Yugoslavia was—as China is today—under the most extreme influence of the Soviet Union; that is, in "brotherly love" and in "eternal friendship" with it. In a report at a closed session of the Twentieth

Congress, Khrushchev revealed that a clash between Stalin and the Chinese government had barely been averted. The case of the clash with Yugoslavia was not an isolated case, but only the most drastic and the first to occur. In other Communist countries the Soviet government enforced Communism by "armed missionaries"—its army.[12]

The fact that wartime alliances between uprooted peasants and the pre-existing Communist parties of China and Yugoslavia brought the second and third independent Communist governments into being presents many different problems of analysis. Our primary concern in this study is with the origin of the alliances themselves and particularly with the peasants' side in these alliances. To place such concerns in their correct context, however, it is first necessary to consider what this particular mode of political success meant to the Communist movement, and to discuss certain aspects of postwar Communist government that cause many people in the West to doubt that the Chinese or Yugoslav governments could possess a popular basis of support. Among the various problems that require mention are those of the "Leninist party," Comintern direction, and the United Front. We might call the first problem that of "totalitarianism and legitimacy."

In both China and Yugoslavia, Communist governments came to power after the collapse of the Axis governments and proceeded to implement a broad program of national reconstruction. Although this was undertaken in the name of Communist ideology and the historical mission of the Communist parties as the vanguard of the working class, both parties' popular basis of support in fact derived from peasant armies whose chief and almost sole concern had been successful resistance against fascist invaders. Did the peasants, therefore, regard their postwar governments as a betrayal of the wartime alliances with the Communists? There is every indication that they did not. Although it is true that the Communist parties eschewed Marxist-Leninist dogmatism in their efforts at wartime mass organization, they nevertheless transmitted their ultimate objectives and their world view to the population by means of propaganda and education, particularly in the later periods of the war, when victory was in sight. This ideology was, in turn, given legitimacy by the fact that the Communist parties were proving their ability to lead and govern during the resistance. The peasants thus did not question the nature of their postwar governments, because the Communist parties had achieved not only power but also authority.

A relation between ruler and subject based solely on power implies nothing more than the possession of superior coercive instruments in the hands of the ruler, regardless of the attitudes of the ruled. A relation based on authority is another matter: here a dialogue of mutual interest exists between ruler and subject. Superior means of coercion may still be present (in fact, such means are part of the definition of a "state"); but a government possessing authority can execute its policies without an overt show of force because the citizens feel that it is to their advantage to follow governmental directives, and because they feel that the government itself was legitimately placed in its position of command. On authority in general, Max Weber has written: "The motives of obedience to commands . . . can rest on considerations varying over a wide range from case to case; all the way from a simple habituation to the most purely rational calculation of advantage. A criterion of every true relation of imperative control, however, is a certain minimum of voluntary submission; thus an interest (based on ulterior motives or genuine acceptance) in obedience."[13]

What were the interests of the Chinese masses at the time that they accepted the leadership of the Chinese Communists? Their interests lay with plans and abilities that offered a means to cope with conditions of mass destruction and anarchy. The Chinese Communists had such plans, had veteran guerrilla cadres to put them into effect, and possessed the imagination to offer their leadership to the peasants. By 1945, the peasants of north and central China had experienced at least six years of life and work in the Communist-led anti-Japanese guerrilla bases. With the victory, for which the Communists logically took credit, the interest of the masses in continuing Communist leadership was further strengthened. The Communists had proved their abilities through years of difficult war; far from questioning the value of the Communists' newly unfurled ideology, the peasant felt that his own experience during the war indicated a need for him to learn the new ideas which promised so much and which, viewed retrospectively, had already succeeded in defeating the Japanese Army.[14]

The distinction here is between the usurpation of power and the achievement of a position in which power is exercised in pursuit of goals shared by the entire community. War provided the means by which the Communist Party re-entered Chinese political life; its war record made its Communist ideology legitimate (although the ideology itself may have been altered in major respects in the process—a subject to which we shall return later). In what sense "legitimate"? In the sense that the Chinese

Communist Party came to power on the basis of a loyal constituency of about 100,000,000 peasants *during* the war, and that this constituency was still further expanded as a result of Japan's capitulation and the Communists' successful discrediting on nationalist grounds of the semi-exiled government of Chiang Kai-shek during and after the war. (Many peasants of north China were scarcely aware of the Chungking government's existence during the war; or they confused it with the Nanking puppets, who also called themselves the "Kuomintang.")

All this is not to ignore that the Chinese Communist government is totalitarian—i.e., that it is committed to the wholesale reorganization of society under conscious direction from above, and that it has enlisted all the institutions of the society (particularly the state) in the service of this single aim. Moreover, as we shall see, even during the war the Chinese Communist Party showed its Leninist virtuosity in organizing mass associations for ensuring total involvement of the peasants in the war effort and for isolating dissenters. The point, however, is that the Chinese masses—at least during the war and at the beginning of the regime—placed themselves at the disposal of the Communist Party to be used for nationalistic purposes. The travesties of individual human dignity perpetrated by totalitarianism were accepted during the war and in the first years of the regime (no one can speak authoritatively of contemporary internal conditions) as the necessary labor pains of China's renaissance. It was not totalitarian instruments of mass manipulation that originally led the Chinese masses into their pact with the Communist elite; it was, rather, the effects of the war and the national awakening that the war induced. Regardless of how well a Communist party masters Leninist theory, it is destined to remain a minor party without a mass following unless at some point it brings its interests into correspondence with those of the people (even if it subsequently reorients the interests of those people). Communist "organizational weapons" are important, but they scarcely account for the entire dynamic of a Communist society, or for that matter any other totalitarian society.

Totalitarianism is not incompatible with legitimacy, or nationalism, or the self-appraised interests of the masses; in fact, totalitarianism usually seems to depend upon the existence of these factors. As George Lichtheim has observed, "Since it is of the essence of a totalitarian regime to be dynamic, it cannot function in an atmosphere of public indifference."[15] We run the danger in contemporary Western studies of Chinese Communism of elevating "organization"—the party structure, communes, the cult of Mao, brainwashing, and so forth—to the level of a sociological secret weapon and, as a result, of accepting the "manipulation hypothesis" as a satisfactory explanation for the entire Chinese Communist work ethic. The present study is not concerned with the policies of the Communist government in power; but as for the *origin* of Communist power, this was simply the mutual interest of the Party and the masses in fighting the Japanese, and this interest developed in a normal fashion to the point at which the Party's directives were obeyed as those of a legitimate authority.

There are those, of course, who believe that the Communist rise to power in China can be explained without reference to the peasantry. Such persons pay little attention to the problems of the mass basis of Communist power and focus directly on Moscow's leadership of the international Communist movement. According to this view, if one possesses a knowledge of the "classical" Comintern-directed (i.e., Moscow-directed) Communist revolution, the formulas for which have been given wide publicity, the idea that indigenous forces could bear any responsibility for the revolution becomes absurd. As Jules Monnerot has described it, "What is happening . . . can be compared to what the situation would have been in the Roman world of the third century if there had been *international* and *preconcerted* synchronization between the Christian refusal of obedience and the successive thrusts of barbarian invasion; in other words, if a *single general staff,* devoted to the ruin of the ancient world, had had command of both the Christian church and the barbarians."[16] Clearly, the emphasis here is upon a "general staff" that plans the entire operation. To extend the analogy, the Chinese peasantry, which supported the Communist armies with men and provisions but denied them to the Nationalists, would be the Christian subversives in the grip of a foreign religion, while the Soviet's Far East General Army under Marshal A. M. Vassilievsky, which invaded Manchuria on August 9, 1945, becomes the barbarian horde. The general staff, needless to say, is the Comintern and its successors.

One of the difficulties of this theory is in proving that communications existed between the two control centers, Moscow and Yenan.[17] It may be argued, of course, that whether contacts existed or not the Chinese Communist leaders were still Communists. Although the success of the Communist Party may have been based upon an alliance with a nationalistically aroused peasantry, this does not—in and of itself—make the Communist Party any less Communist. Article I of the Party statutes of 1928 states that, "The Chinese Communist Party is a part of the Communist International"—that is, subject to Moscow—and the Party did not repudiate this tie during the period under study. It may also be advanced that the essence of Leninist theory and of Maoist practice is the use of professional revolutionaries to capitalize on mass discontent, regardless of its origin. Thus, one may ask, what difference does it make whether or not the Communists manipulated the symbols of nationalism or of any other sufficiently widespread ideology, so long as they were successful? They were and still are Bolsheviks.

The major feature of the Sino-Japanese War which supports the contention that the Communist Party acted as a Soviet tool was the creation of the KMT-CCP "United Front" against Japan. As is well known, the United Front tactic was ordered at the Comintern Congress in 1935 and was successfully implemented in China following the Sian Incident.[18] But one can scarcely regard the United Front as the vehicle by which the Communists came to power. In the first place, the United Front between the KMT and CCP was clearly a sham after the establishment of the blockade against Shen-Kan-Ning in 1939, and ceased to exist after the New Fourth Army Incident of January 1941. Despite this, Communist forces continued to expand their territories and popular following. Moreover, this expansion was not into areas in which the United Front had been strongest, such as the Hankow area, or into areas in which the façade of the United Front was still maintained (it is doubtful whether the publication of the Communist *Hsin-Hua jih-pao* in wartime Chungking can be credited with converting anyone to the Communist side, except possibly some Western journalists). The expansion was, instead, into areas that the Japanese armies had overrun.

In the second place, use of the United Front tactic in China had developed prior to and independent of the Seventh Comintern Congress; in the pre-1937 period it was predominantly an anti-KMT device used in the cities.[19] Party propaganda of that period was not an actual call to the colors for war with Japan, but a way of developing popular pressure on Chiang to call off his Communist-suppression campaigns. Least of all was the United Front used to legitimatize the Communist Party in the eyes of the peasantry—the only group whose support was of lasting importance to the Communists.

In actual fact, the United Front was irrelevant to the peasantry. The so-called "three-thirds" system—the practice whereby the Communists occupied no more than one-third of the posts in the guerrilla area governments—was not a "United Front" in any functional sense, i.e., in the sense of its being necessary for peasant support. Unity between the peasants and the Party was not based upon the three-thirds system, because the peasants actually supported the Communists through the mass organizations and the army.[20] The three-thirds system was a device for incorporating local non-Communist leaders, landlords, rich peasants, and other well-known people into the regional governments; it was similar to the system of "democratic parties" adopted in post-1949 Communist China.

The only concrete benefit obtained by the Communist Party as a result of its implementing the Moscow line on the United Front was that it permitted the recruitment, for a short period of time, of comparatively large numbers of students from urban areas. These students, after completing the course at Yenan's Anti-Japanese Military-Political University (K'ang-jih Chün-cheng Ta-hsüeh, abbreviated K'angta), generally served in the Communist forces as lower-level political officers. The existence of the United Front thus gave one important advantage to the Communists. However, other features of the United Front that the Communists viewed as desirable prior to 1937, such as the calling off of Nationalist attacks on Communist areas, all evaporated with the advance of the Japanese armies.

In short, we must conclude that the United Front was not the basis upon which the Communist Party built its strength in China. It did not prevent continual armed clashes between KMT and CCP troops; it did not facilitate the large-scale supply of arms by the Western Allies to the Communists; and it did not allow the Communists to subvert the legitimate government from within (as in Spain). Most important, it did not promote acceptance of Communist Party leadership in the north China guerrilla bases (north China was a traditionally conservative area where even the KMT was almost unknown); yet it was in the guerrilla bases of north China that the Communist Party came to power.

THE ECONOMICS OF THE COMMUNIST-PEASANT ALLIANCE

Among the many scholars who have recognized that the ranks of the victorious Communist armies were filled with peasants, there exists a great deal of confusion about the nature of the Communist-peasant partnership. Much of this confusion derives from the view that Communism should be understood solely or chiefly as an economic doctrine and that the peasant-based Communist revolutions should be regarded as a rural analogue of the Marxist proletarian revolution. This view has promoted two different kinds of erroneous interpretations. On the one hand, some writers see the impoverishment of the Chinese peasantry as the primary motivating force that drove them into alliance with the Communists, who are, in turn, regarded as agrarian reformers. On the other hand, those who regard the twentieth-century Communist movement as an elitist conspiracy primed to capitalize upon any crisis or fissure in the society that it hopes to capture are at pains to expose how little Communist parties promote the class interests of their followers. Although the latter theorists object, correctly, to regarding the Chinese Communist revolution as a "peasant rebellion," they ignore the possibility that the peasants had other motives than the economic interests of their class; and they insist that the Communists won over the peasantry by manipulation and fraud.

This failure to consider the basis of the wartime Communist-peasant alliances reflects the general lack of attention paid to the wartime resistance movements (by which the Communists of China and of Yugoslavia actually came to power) and the lack of inquiry into the origins of the nationalistic policies pursued by the Communist governments that achieved power independently of the Soviet Union. As examples of these policies, one need mention only the Soviet-Yugoslav dispute beginning in 1948 and the Sino-Soviet controversy of the early 1960's. We shall return in a later chapter to the problems of "national Communism"; for the present we must deal at greater length with the question of economic determinants in the Communist-peasant wartime alliances.

"Pure" peasant rebellions, in the sense of sporadic outbursts against local misery, are commonly met with in the histories of agricultural societies. Rarely, however, have they had any significant political effects. Thus, when the interpreters of the rise of Communism in China refer to the Communist revolution as a "peasant rebellion," they do not mean by that term merely a spontaneous demonstration or a local rebellion. The reference in the following remarks by Professor Mary Wright is not to a small-scale effort or to a movement lacking purpose or direction. She observes:

> The Chinese Revolution of which the Communists have secured leadership was and is a peasant revolution. . . . There [in the countryside prior to 1930] Mao Tse-tung's group survived because it found the key to peasant support and control, land reform and a host of subordinate policies designed to mobilize the peasantry, improve agrarian production,

and secure its fruits. . . . Communists do not have to fabricate figures to prove the poverty of the Chinese peasant. In actual fact, conditions are intolerable, and peasant revolt has long been endemic.[21]

The inspiration for these remarks comes predominantly from a knowledge of Chinese social history. Large-scale peasant rebellion in response to intolerable conditions of land tenure, food shortage, natural calamities, excessive taxation, usurious moneylending, and general misery in the villages has long been identified as the crucial event in the spectacular upheavals associated with changes of regime in China. The most recent of these disturbances occurred slightly more than a century ago, when the Taiping Rebellion erupted across south China as a reaction to population pressure and to the great famines of 1847 and 1849. That rebellion combined a quasi-Christian religious movement with a movement for agrarian reform. The result was a revolutionary effort of such scale that its ultimate failure seems more remarkable today than its successes. Professor Wright characterizes the Taiping Rebellion as an "agrarian revolution," i.e., one in which economic conditions were the primary determinants, and places it squarely in the history of the Communist revolution: "Today's agrarian revolution began a century ago when the Chinese peasantry rose against the existing order in the great Taiping Rebellion."[22] Even if Mao's effort does not actually span the century and link with the "long-haired thieves" (*ch'ang mao tsei*) of the Taiping leader Hung Hsiu-ch'üan, persons who agree with the peasant-rebellion theory argue that the Communist Party of China, after slowly coming to an appreciation of the potentialities of rural revolution, abandoned its futile attempts at urban insurrection and won the support of the peasantry by transforming itself into the scourge-of-the-landlords. Certainly Mao Tse-tung's Communism was as adaptable to this purpose as Hung's Christianity.

The essence of this analysis is the identification of rural economic distress as the cause of peasant rebelliousness. Although this may have been the crucial inducement to rebellion during certain periods of Chinese history, it fails to explain the success of the Communist-rural coalition of World War II. During the war the Communists did not contemplate the redistribution of land or any other class-oriented measures that would have radically altered the pattern of land ownership. Instead, the economic policies implemented by the Communist Party during the Sino-Japanese War were designed to create maximum unity—"to protect everybody from everybody else."[23] As Mao has put it, "The agrarian policy is a dual policy of demanding that the landlords reduce rent and interest, stipulating that the peasants pay this reduced amount of rent and interest."[24] This moderate wartime policy did not, of course, necessarily alienate the peasantry; but the Communists' success in winning peasant support cannot be attributed to their carrying out an "agrarian revolution."

It is in fact very difficult to apply economic criteria to either the Taiping or the Communist revolution. No answer can be given to a specific question dealing with the course of these revolutions in terms of economic forces alone. In the case of the Taipings, the desperately poor Hakka and Miao inhabitants of south China, who were the first to join Hung, came not out of economic motives but as converts to his religion.[25] The majority of peasants joined him as the rebellion gained momentum and after traditional rebels and local leaders had allied themselves with the Taiping objectives. Economic motives certainly underlay specific decisions to rebel, but they can be understood only as necessary, not as sufficient, causes. Relative economic deprivation came to a head in the Tao-kuang period (1821–50) and was a constant circumstance in various areas of China thereafter; however, it influenced but did not direct rebellion. The economic variable does not account for particular targets of rebellion (the dynasty, foreigners, invaders, or traitors); and it does not explain why rebellion occurs in one area, and then in another, but not in all places that have grievances and have given expression to them in the recent past. Underlying economic pressures also existed during the resistance war and exist today, but again an analysis purely in terms of economic forces leaves most political questions unanswered. Why is it that the peasantry did not support the Japanese and their puppets after 1937? Why did huge numbers of north China peasants volunteer for the Communist armies only after the Japanese invasion? Obviously, an argument based solely on the economic situation in China ignores the influence of the Japanese invasion, and thereby misinterprets the role of the Communist Party as leader of the anti-Japanese peasant armies.

This is not to argue that if the Japanese invasion of China or the German invasion of Yugoslavia had not occurred, the prewar governments could have continued to exist unassailed or that the process of social change associated with the Communist governments would never have begun. If the invasions had never occurred, a severe economic catastrophe in the future, or a prolongation of the rural depression of the 1930's, might well have produced revolutionary mobilization. But a constant, or slowly evolving, rate of economic deprivation would still have constituted only a conditioning factor in the subsequent revolutionary movements; and it is unlikely that such revolutionary movements would have confined themselves to economic reforms, just as the Chinese Communist government aims at more ambitious goals than the relief of rural misery. The movement of Fidel Castro in Cuba, for example, can hardly be accounted for by reference solely to the economic conditions of the Cuban peasants—conditions that have existed for decades. An economic analysis alone offers no insights into the potentiality of success of a revolutionary movement, and commonly distorts attempts at political analysis of the policies pursued by postrevolutionary governments.

There are other critics of Professor Wright's views, but, paradoxically enough, they seem to accept her idea that economic hardship is the only logical motive for peasant rebelliousness. Their argument with her turns on the question of whether the Chinese Communists were true agrarian reformers; they accurately point out that the CCP did not offer to advance the economic interests of the peasants during the war. Thus, they conclude (very like those who consider Chinese Communism the result of a Moscow-directed conspiracy), the Communists cynically manipulated the peasantry, and the peasants had no stake, real or imagined, in Communist leadership. Professor Franz Michael, for example, has stated:

> The fact that the Communist armies were enlarged by recruiting from the peasantry does not make them any more or less peasant armies than the nationalist troops with which they are contrasted and which drew their recruits from the same source. That the Communists had a land policy which in different forms favored the small peasants does not alter the fact that the Communists and not the peasants commanded the army. The term "peasant armies" implies an expression of the peasant will and peasant control which obviously did not exist, and the term "peasant leader" implies a man who represents the peasants rather than the Communist Party and its policies.[26]

This type of analysis does not, of course, explain what the basis of the Communist-peasant alliance was, nor does it in any way account for the development of national Communist states. Professor Michael implies that the peasantry played no role in the revolution other than to provide soldiers and services for the armies of either the Kuomintang or the Communists (ignoring, among other things, the fact that the KMT had to utilize conscription from March 1936 on, whereas the Communists, in the main, relied upon volunteers both for their regular forces and for what was surely the world's largest militia system).

The major difficulty, as Professor Michael sees it, is the lack of correspondence between the "peasant will" and the "Communist Party and its policies." This use of the term "peasant will," and the implication that the peasant will is not equatable with Communist policies, suggests a confusion between the Communist Party's acting on the *side* of the peasantry and their acting for the *sake* of the peasantry. "For the sake of the peasantry" refers specifically to Communist policies that appealed directly to the economic interests and class-consciousness of the landless farm laborers, and that were directed against landlords and middle and rich peasants. This type of land policy was on the statute books in the Kiangsi Soviet Republic, but it was unsuccessful in creating a mass basis for the Party. The Party faced a dilemma in Kiangsi that became more difficult as the Party tried to deal with it. If the "radical" agrarian reform law were strictly implemented, it would alienate all but the poorest section of the peasantry, thereby defeating its purpose, which was to gain general rural support. On the other hand, if it were honored in the breach, as was the common practice in Kiangsi, it not only failed to gain supporters, but also left the Communist Party open to invidious comparison with the Kuomintang's announced land program.[27] The failure to resolve these questions of mass support was one of the strategic weaknesses of the Kiangsi Soviet, and thereby contributed to its military failure.

During the Anti-Japanese War period the Party abandoned the "radical" land program altogether and carried out a policy designed to create maximum unity for national defense.[28] All plans for agrarian reform were abrogated during the war while a mild policy of rent reduction and general rationalization of debts was carried out. Despite this, the Communists achieved their greatest popular following precisely during the period in which their unity policy was in effect. Clearly, their acting on the *side* of the peasantry—i.e., their successful opposition to the Japanese invaders—had become more important than their actions for the *sake* of the peasantry. In retrospect, the Communist Party was successful only when it ceased acting solely for the sake of the peasantry and began acting on the side of the peasantry instead. The interesting question, of course, is how the peasantry came to have a side at all.[29]

MASS NATIONALISM IN CHINA

It is the thesis of this study that the rise to power of the CCP and YCP in collaboration with the peasantry of the two countries can best be understood as a species of nationalism. A definition is necessary here because so many different usages for the term "nationalism" exist. In the past "nationalism" has been employed to refer to the postfeudal monarchies of western Europe, to certain romantic doctrines of the nineteenth century, and to the underlying dynamic of Communist Russia. The word has been equated with "a daily plebiscite," "political *bovarysme*," and a form of tribalism; persons as different as Theodore Roosevelt, Mahatma Gandhi, and Fidel Castro have been called "nationalists." Thus, in order to avoid confusion, it is necessary to consider at some length the meaning of nationalism in general and, more particularly, of nationalism in China during the period under investigation.

The first distinction to be made in the use of the term involves its altered scope over time. There has been a long-range trend toward the expansion of the numbers of persons subject to nationalism; and, as a result, the use of the term in 1960 is very different from its use in 1789. E. H. Carr's periodization of this expansion is standard: originally, national "populations" consisted of only the ruler and the nobility, and "the first period begins with the gradual dissolution of the mediaeval unity of empire and church and the establishment of the national state and the national church."[30] The second period occupies the century of the "Third Estate" (1789–1914), during which nationalism spread to the bourgeoisie; the contemporary third period is characterized by "the bringing of new social strata within the effective membership of the nation, the visible reunion of economic with political power, and the increase in the number of nations."[31] Contemporary studies of nationalism are concerned with mass nationalism, i.e., the third period; in China, this means peasant nationalism. A successful nationalist movement today—one that succeeds in founding a nation state—must be a mass movement; and a regime that rules a people indifferent to or unaware of government, such as that of Chiang Kai-shek or of the late Rafael Trujillo, cannot properly be called "nationalist."

A second distinction must be made between two analytical uses of the term nationalism: nationalism understood as a condition already in existence, and nationalism understood as a process of coming into being. An example of nationalism understood as a condition occurs in the work of the historian Carlton J. H. Hayes. He writes: "I would define nationality as a cultural group of people who speak a common language (or closely related dialects) and who possess a community of historical traditions (religious, territorial, political, military, economic, artistic, and intellectual)."[32] Many students of nationalism would take exception to this definition, particularly to the insistence upon linguistic homogeneity; however, the important point here is that Hayes considers nationalism as a static condition —namely, as consciousness of nationality.[33] How people become conscious of their national characteristics, or what their self-image was before they were conscious of nationality, is not considered.

The deficiency of this definition lies in its lack of differentiation between "national movement" and "nationalism." Hayes's definition will not help us to explain why, for example, the Japanese were more nationalistic in 1930 than in 1830, since at both times they spoke the same language, held roughly the same religious views, and painted the same kinds of pictures. Professor Hayes mentions the importance of political, military, and economic traditions; but by not asking what lies behind these traditions or why certain traditions are honored over others, he is considering only the plumage of nationalism. For purposes of studying the spread or onset of nationalism, we must identify the forces that cause populations to form nation states and isolate the circumstances under which groups of human beings are transformed into national citizens. Also, in order to understand why the particular traditions and characteristics mentioned by Hayes are valued by a given national community, we must relate these elements of "national plumage" to a functional model of the nation.

Karl W. Deutsch has summed up the failure of writers to use functional concepts in early studies of nationalism: "The dangerous result was that nationalism came to be widely accepted as a mere 'state of mind' with *few tangible roots*."[34] Deutsch himself has done much to correct this deficiency by developing a functional definition of nationalism—one that is helpful in understanding nationalism among the peasantry in China. Deutsch's central concept is that of a "people," which he defines in the following way:

> The community which permits a common history to be experienced as common is a community of complementary habits and facilities of communication. . . . A large group of persons linked by such complementary habits and facilities of communication we may call a people. . . . All the usual descriptions of a people in terms of a community of languages, or character, or memories, or past history, are open to exception. For what counts is not the presence or absence of any single factor, but merely the presence of sufficient communications facilities with enough complementarity to produce the over-all result.[35]

Thus Deutsch regards the ability of members of one large group to communicate with each other as the basic "root" of nationalism. "The essential aspect of the unity of a people . . . is the complementarity or relative efficiency of communication among individuals—something that is in some ways similar to mutual rapport, but on a larger scale."[36] The important question is how does such a mutual rapport (identity of interest, intermingling of wills, sharing of responsibility, and so forth) come into existence among a specific population at a given time and place?

"Social mobilization" is the shorthand term generally used to describe the dynamic process whereby pre-national peoples enter into political community with their fellows. This is the primary conceptual tool in contemporary studies of nationalism.[37] Social mobilization refers to the pressures that cause populations to form political communities—in other words, the changes that cause people of towns, villages, and regions to knit together into new political orders which transcend these areas as their inhabitants realize that their mutual interests extend beyond daily contacts. The pressures that cause social mobilization may be evolutionary, revolutionary, or both. Deutsch, in his study of social communication, is concerned primarily with how national communities developed out of European feudal society; he points particularly to the importance of the growth of towns, the shift from a subsistence economy to an exchange economy, and the enlargement of basic communications grids in promoting this development. However, although the evolutionary growth of physical links was an important mobilizing agent in early modern Europe, it is not the only source of effective social mobilization; and towns, regional communications, and markets all emerged in China many centuries ago without producing a nation state. In the twentieth century, evolutionary pressure has been accelerated and supplemented by more immediate and violent ways of mobilizing a population.

E. J. Hobsbawm in his study of pre-national mass movements (particularly among peasants) describes some of these other, more immediate, forces that may mobilize populations:

> [Pre-political] men and women . . . form the large majority in many, perhaps in most, countries even today, and their acquisition of political consciousness has made our century the most revolutionary in history. . . . They come into it [the modern political world] as first-generation immigrants, or what is even more catastrophic, it comes to them from outside, insidiously by the operation of economic forces which they do

not understand and over which they have no control, or brazenly by conquest, revolutions and fundamental changes of law whose consequences they may not understand, even when they have helped to bring them about.[38]

Among the forces listed by Hobsbawm, foreign invasion and internal resistance organization have taken, in recent years, a predominant role in mobilizing pre-political populations. World War II, in particular, unleashed forces of mass awakening in countries such as China and Yugoslavia, where previous "national movements" had appealed only to educated elites. War-induced anarchy and the organization of guerrilla resistance gave the Chinese and Yugoslav peasant masses new experiences and a new history. Their common action in defending and governing large areas of occupied territory and in solving specific political, economic, and military problems laid the foundation for social communication.[39] That is to say, the masses of China and Yugoslavia were socially mobilized by the war.

In making this observation we are not overlooking the prewar movement in China that centered upon the Kuomintang. Nationalism in China did not, of course, make its first appearance during the Sino-Japanese war; at the time of the invasion a nationalist movement had already existed for at least forty years. However, the National Movement (with capital letters) that began with Sun Yat-sen and developed among the students and educators in Peking after May 4, 1919, was not a mass movement; it was confined almost entirely to the socially mobilized but unassimilated intelligentsia and to the small middle classes that grew up in the treaty ports. Sun himself acknowledged the popular weakness of his party when he sought alliance with the CCP, and when he initiated the KMT reorganization as an elite association in 1924. Early Kuomintang nationalism bears a strong resemblance to nineteenth-century nationalism among central European intellectuals and to the formative periods of colonial or non-European nationalism in this century—for example, the movements in Egypt, Tunisia, and Turkey. Because of this similarity, the term "nationalist" has commonly been used to characterize the activities of intellectuals in their creative search for doctrines of national identity and uniqueness. Although this usage has been bolstered by general acceptance, it must be clearly understood that nationalism among intellectual elites and mass nationalism are two distinct, if related, phenomena.

Such early intellectual nationalism in China was peculiarly the product of Westernized, or cosmopolitan, educated Chinese. They sought a new understanding of Chinese culture and history that would facilitate the acceptance of China into the modern world and rationalize their own discontent at China's backwardness. It is not surprising that the various doctrines to emerge from this intellectual ferment were amalgams of Western revolutionary thought, violent reactions to contemporary Japan, and drastic revisions of traditional Chinese philosophy.[40] For a century Chinese culture had been under continuous assault both from abroad by missionaries and merchants and from within by native iconoclasts; during this time Chinese intellectuals consulted a broad range of social theorists (from Henry George to Japanese militarists) in order to explain and to overcome China's political backwardness. Equally important, prewar intellectual nationalists were concerned with the obstructions to China's reform created by imperialism and the unequal treaties. The wars, humiliations, and material and territorial losses suffered by the Ch'ing empire and the stillborn Republic during the century of contact with modern imperialist states were continuous sources of outrage and inspiration to the new nationalist ideologues.

For all the political activities of the prewar Chinese educated elites, theirs was a nationalist movement with a head and no body. The Chinese peasantry was isolated from the long-standing Chinese nationalist movement, having neither a stake in Chinese literati culture nor any direct contact with the imperialists. The humiliations to China were largely meaningless to the agricultural masses; and when imperialism did impinge upon their lives in a direct way, as at the time of the Boxer Rebellion, their reaction was essentially nativistic and pre-political.[41] The peasants did not share the intellectuals' idealized vision of the Chinese state; they had no theory of tutelage by which it should be achieved, no "Three Principles of the People" which, if fully implemented, would restore China to a position of equality as a sovereign nation.

If this indifference of the Chinese masses to prewar politics is ignored, a realistic appraisal of the Nanking Government (1928–37) cannot be made. That is to say, if we characterize Chiang Kai-shek's government as nationalistic, we overlook the opportunistic alliances among military leaders that underlay Chiang's power, and we disregard the ceaseless efforts made by Nanking to unify the country after 1928 by direct military action. Prior to 1937, nationalism in China was a powerful sentiment among many leadership groups, but the social milieu in which they acted was not nationalistic. When, during the war, the peasants were mobilized and the Communist Party identified itself with Chinese nationalism, the Nationalist Government was slow to recognize the implications that this development had for its own future. The failure of the wartime KMT to understand that its own claims to nationalist leadership were not accepted by the whole population and that it was vulnerable to an attack on purely nationalist grounds contributed directly to its defeat by the Communist-peasant alliance.

Mention of the fact that prewar Chinese nationalism was primarily an ideological phenomenon restricted to educated elites raises further questions in the definition of nationalism. In the past, particularly in the nineteenth century, nationalist activities appeared to be confined exclusively to the sort of ideological controversy that we associate with the May Fourth period in China. Nationalist intellectuals sought, in their polemical and creative activities, to identify the peculiar characteristics of a particular people (usually their own) or to establish a historical, linguistic, or racial tradition that would support a claim for these people to form a nation-state—for example, early German claims of linguistic unity, Slavic claims of religious uniqueness. As a result of the predominance of ideological disputation in nationalist movements, the study of nationalism has often become the province of the intellectual historian; and the establishment of an intellectual claim to "self-determination" (or to "manifest destiny") was often thought to constitute all that was meant by nationalism.

An exclusive concern with nationalism as nationalists themselves define it is of almost no use for purposes of general analysis; and it ignores the question of timing in the onset of a particular search for nationalist doctrine by given intellectual circles. Today such nationalist activity is understood as a product of the social mobilization of nationalist intellectuals—usually prior to the mobilization of the general population and as a result of causes different from those that affect total populations. Education, or foreign residence, is a common mobilizing agent among intellectual elites —particularly when colonial domination, racial discrimination, or other circumstances prevent the people concerned from achieving a social status commensurate with their education. The origins of the early twentieth-century Chinese nationalists, in these terms, are well known: Sun Yat-sen's intimate association with overseas Chinese and his extensive foreign travel, the creation of the T'ung Meng Hui among Chinese students in Japan, the peculiarly elevated position of Peking University students at the time of World War I, and the extensive European travel and education of the early Chinese Communist leaders.[42] Thus, in recognizing the existence of a nationalist movement in China before the wartime peasant mobilization, we are not recognizing a different kind of nationalism, but only one that was prior to the mass movement, restricted to specific types of people, and energized by different but analogous forces. It is perfectly possible that an intellectual nationalist movement will not ever possess a mass nationalist following; or that a later mass nationalist mobilization will unseat a pre-existing nationalist elite and install its own leadership; or that intellectual nationalists may guide and control, particularly by education, the subsequent development of mass nationalism. China offers an example of a mass nationalist movement unseating a previously mobilized and installed nationalist elite.

So far in this discussion of the meaning of nationalism, we have stressed the central importance of the process by which a people become a nation. We have labeled this process "social mobilization," and we have indicated that a variety of forces may be responsible for bringing it about—particularly a social cataclysm such as war, or the collapse of a colonial government, which acts as a catalyst for more general pressures of social change. Many years ago Max Weber noted the important fact that nations and nationalism do have a beginning and suggested the need for studying the activating forces in nationalism. His observation, interestingly enough (although erroneously) based on a Chinese example, was: "Only fifteen years ago [from c. 1914], men knowing the Far East, still denied that the Chinese qualified as a 'nation'; they held them to be only a 'race.' Yet today, not only the Chinese political leaders but also the very same observers would judge differently. Thus it seems that a group of people under certain conditions may attain the quality of a nation through specific behavior, or that they may claim this quality as an 'attainment'—and within short spans of time at that."[43] Despite the fact that Weber, along with Sun Yat-sen and many other Chinese, was to be disappointed by the 1911 revolution, his point is very valuable. Social mobilization, as we have used it, corresponds to Weber's "certain conditions" under which a given people attain the quality of a nation; on the basis of evidence presented in subsequent chapters, it is advanced here that the peasants of the occupied areas in China were socially mobilized by war and resistance organization, and thereby became a national population.[44]

However, social mobilization itself is not all that is meant by nationalism; it is, rather, the crucial occurrence in the onset of nationalism. There is another constituent in mass nationalist movements, which usually appears simultaneously with or shortly after mobilization; this is ideology. Following upon a given national mobilization, the newly mobilized people will commonly receive from their leadership a more or less elaborate doctrine that serves to idealize the activities undertaken by the people in common. In model form, such a doctrine will provide an ideological framework within which the mobilized people may understand and express their behavior as a nation. Often it will portray the given nationalist movement as undertaken in behalf of an ultimately triumphant cause; and it will draw upon allegedly universal religions or philosophical systems for "proof" of the justness or inevitability of nationalist activities.[45] Such a national myth usually exalts the leadership elite that directs the work of the mobilized population and places an ideological support under the claims to legitimacy that the elite enjoys.

The content of these national myths ranges widely over the entire spectrum of human thought; "racial science" or "geopolitics" may support certain national communities, enlightenment philosophy supports others. Buddhism is enlisted in the service of Burmese nationalism, Islam in the Middle Eastern states, Catholicism in Ireland, and an undifferentiated protestantism in the United States. Professional exponents of particular religions as well as *bona fide* scientists may, and often do, object to the use of religion or science in the service of nationalist doctrines. It must be understood, however, that national myths drawn from nonnationalist systems of belief or analysis do not have the effect of placing the nation-state under the guidance of popes or scientists; rather, they are intended to reinforce the legitimacy of the nation by incorporating the legitimacy of priests, scientists, or philosophers into it. In other words, myth draws from doctrines that are independently respected in society and reinterprets such doctrines so that they will tend to mobilize popular imagination in support of a national government—a government that in all probability is already supported on the basis of interest.

Although national myth is constructed by nationalist intellectuals from among all the diverse historical, religious, and philosophical influences present in a people's past, a given myth is not, of course, selected at random. The study of both the transmission of myth to nationalist ideologues and the current intellectual and philosophical trends that dictate "choice" among national myths is of great importance. As Professor Hatfield has observed in connection with Nazi myth, "Did these dogmas actually determine events, or were they a mere ideological façade? Even if they were only that, it would remain a matter of some importance to discover why one façade was chosen rather than another, and why it impressed so many people, not all of them Germans, by any means."[46] This observation is true, but it must be clearly understood that the subject of ideological inquiry is a national myth overlaying the social mobilization of a given people. Failure to bear this in mind has produced, for example, the plethora of uniformly ineffectual anti-Marxist books that aim at "meeting Communism on its own terms"; and it likewise explains the weakness of the counter-ideological approach to Communism—for example, that of Moral Rearmament.

With regard to the question, raised by Professor Hatfield, of a functional role for myth in determining events, this is found as a general rule not to be the case. Myth is most often an *ex post facto* revision either of written history or of the nonnationalist ideology that is being used as the basis of the myth. This is not to say that national myth does not exist prior to the victory of a mass nationalist movement; of course it does. But ideology itself—whether fascism, communism, or only a belief in a glorious ancestral history—does not in and of itself mobilize either intellectual elites or nationalist masses. Such mobilization is produced by other more immediate and less abstract pressures, as discussed earlier. Myth exists before mass mobilization because the elite is usually mobilized before the masses. A nationalist elite will acquire or create a fairly well developed "explanation" of its "mission," looking to the time when mass mobilization might occur. However, as the two cases of China and Yugoslavia strongly suggest, the prewar elite ideology itself will probably undergo an extensive process of renovation and "nationalization" at the time when elite mobilization is translated into mass mobilization. Thus we commonly find that the ideological history of an elite group prior to the time it comes to power is largely irrelevant to its subsequent ideological activities and pretensions. In such cases, it is convenient to distinguish pre-mobilization ideology and post-mobilization ideology as two separate entities—for example, to distinguish the Yugoslav Communist Party's Stalinism of 1939 from its Titoism of 1948 and after.

This general idea of national myth following upon and supplementing social mobilization is useful in understanding the political history of the national Communist states. When we assert that the Chinese and Yugoslav Communist movements can best be understood as a species of nation-alism, we have in mind other considerations than just the two movements' wartime origins. Most important of these considerations is the marked eccentricity displayed by China and Yugoslavia in their relations with the other eleven Communist governments.[47] This eccentricity goes beyond the possibility that China and Yugoslavia merely consider Moscow's leadership to have been faulty in particular instances; both states have broken with the USSR in response to different types of Soviet leadership, and the Soviet Union has been unable to reconcile its differences with the two nations by either enticement or discipline. Although it is possible to maintain that national Communism in China and Yugoslavia represents simply a reac-tion to national Communism in the USSR, one must still account for the fact that only the Chinese and Yugoslav parties have successfully given expression to their resentment.

We observe the emergence in both China and Yugoslavia of indigenous brands of Communism. The propounders of these new formulations claim that Chinese and Yugoslav revolutionary experiences, respectively, consti-tute an advance over Soviet revolutionary tradition, and at the same time insist that they are squarely in the line of development predicted by "scien-tific socialism." In view of the existence of the wartime resistance move-ments in both Communist China and Yugoslavia, as well as the subsequent development of national Communism in both states, it is necessary to re-examine their particular histories from the point of view of nationalism. It appears today that China and Yugoslavia, from the time of the invasions to the present, offer typical examples of mass nationalist movements in which Communism serves as an official rationale for nationalist policies.

Communism, in the sense of the philosophy of Marx and Lenin, is re-markably well suited to the role of national myth. In addition to proclaim-ing the inevitability of success in the work of national construction under Communist auspices, it also partakes of the single most widely accepted ideology of the present age—science. With the necessary revisions, Com-munism legitimatizes the totalitarian rule of the national directorate ("the vanguard of the working class"), and it provides a Manichaean identifica-tion of the nation's enemies ("the imperialists") to be used as an ever-present scapegoat in case of nationalist setbacks.

Although we often read that the "Chinese Communists have stood Marx on his head,"[48] we rarely consider why Marxism has such a grip on the Chinese. We do not consider how revised Marxism eases the tremendous sacrifices required for national construction, or how it reinforces the desire of many Chinese to make China a powerful nation. We do not contemplate the demands of Chinese nationalism or the place of Communism in its support; as a result, we are astonished when the Communist leaders resort to ideological pedantry to explain reverses in the development program. The defense of Chinese Communist ideology is as important to Chinese nationalism as the successful raising of bumper crops. It is because he is a nationalist that the Communist leader claims Marxist legitimacy: "While revising Marxism in accordance with the national environment and his own beliefs . . . the local leader always claims that he is not revising Marxism, but is only 'applying it creatively.' Furthermore, he usually asserts that his interpretation of Marxism is the only correct one and might well be imitated by other countries. For this reason, national Communists refuse to admit that they are national Communists."[49] Obviously, if a national Communist declared that his revisions diverged from Marxism as a consistent system, he would forfeit the advantage he obtains from being a Marxist—the participation in a widely accepted theory that underwrites his actions as "scientific."

In a later chapter of this study we shall review certain of the nationalist manifestations in Chinese and Yugoslav Communist ideology. For the present, my intention is only to introduce the concept of national myth as complementary to social mobilization in the present use of the term "nationalism." In essence, I understand a mass nationalist movement as a combination of the concepts of social mobilization and national myth. My purpose in advancing this hypothesis is not to offer a general theory of nationalism describing the basic circumstances in which all nations have been formed. It is, rather, to seek an understanding of the remarkable change in fortunes experienced by the Chinese Communist Party during World War II—a question that has been ignored in the past largely because of insufficient data. On the importance of the war, Fitzroy Maclean, Commander of the British mission to the Yugoslav Partisans, once wrote: "At the bottom of their dispute with the Kremlin lay Tito's claim that 'the Jugoslav brand of Communism was not something imported from Moscow but had its origin in the forests and mountains of Jugoslavia.' "[50] Similarly, I suggest that the origins of the Sino-Soviet dispute are to be found in the plains of central Hopei and in the mountains of Shantung at the time of the Japanese invasion.

TWO

The Japanese Role in Peasant Mobilization

The role played by the Japanese Army in bringing the Chinese Communists to power has never been fully appreciated by foreign observers. In addition to their mopping-up campaigns and reprisals against the civilian population, which accelerated the process of rural mobilization, there were other activities of the Japanese that further strengthened the position of the Chinese Communists. For example, the Japanese unwittingly advanced the Communists' claim to national legitimacy by singling out the Communists as their special enemies and by giving puppet regimes the special task of Communist "extermination." Conversely, the cavalier treatment of the Chungking government in Japanese propaganda tended to weaken Chungking's attempts to guide and control the resistance behind the Japanese lines; and thus it also aided the Communist cause.

Still another ingredient of the political situation in the occupied territories was the disillusionment that seized the traditionally more conservative northern Chinese. Prior to 1937, the population of north China was more willing than the Chinese of other areas to countenance a Japanese-sponsored government; the Japanese actually possessed such a potential for popular support in the rural areas that, according to Michael Lindsay, they could have succeeded if they had only taken the trouble to shoot a few hundred of their own officers![1] In actual fact, the devastation and exploitation that accompanied the Japanese invasion produced a radical change in the political attitudes of the northern Chinese. The peasants of north China gave very strong support to Communist organizational initiatives during the war, and the largest number of Communist guerrilla bases was located in the rural areas of the north.

In order to understand why the Chinese Communists were successful in their attempts to organize the population of the occupied areas, it is essential that the conditions created by the invasion and by Japanese occupation policies be fully appreciated. Let us, therefore, go back to the time before the invasion and review the circumstances that led to Japan's military adventure in China.

Hostility to Japan by Chinese nationalists dates at least from the Twenty-One Demands of 1915, and particularly from the seizure of Manchuria in September 1931. It was not until after 1931, however, that this hostility became so widespread among many different Chinese elite groups that it presented a serious obstacle to Japanese ambitions. In the period 1931–37, Chinese unity behind Chiang Kai-shek and patriotism among urban elements throughout the country developed more rapidly than the simultaneous efforts by Japanese officers to set up pro-Japanese puppets in China's five northern provinces. It is this circumstance more than any other that solidified the determination of Japanese leaders to use the incident of July 7, 1937, as a pretext for invasion.

Prior to 1937, Japanese initiatives short of war to establish Japanese agents in Hopei and Chahar provinces had met with but moderate success. The two puppets in Hopei were General Yin Ju-keng, head of the East Hopei Autonomous Government (November 24, 1935), and General Sung Che-yüan, leader of the Hopei-Chahar Political Council (December 1935). Despite the similar status of the two men, there were major differences between the Yin and Sung governments. General Yin's regime was the product of a series of agreements extorted from China by military force following the occupation of Jehol (1933) and the T'angku truce (May 31, 1933).[2] On the other hand, General Sung's Hopei-Chahar Political Council was accepted by Nanking as a stopgap measure to forestall complete subjugation of north China in accordance with the well-known schemes of General Doihara Kenji, the "Lawrence of Manchuria."[3] Sung was therefore less under the control of the Japanese military than General Yin; in fact, it was Sung's 29th Army that made the first resistance to the Japanese invasion after July 7.

Despite these modest successes, the Japanese were most alarmed by the growing strength of popular pressure upon Nanking to abandon its policy of appeasing Japan. The Sian Incident of December 1936, which gave birth to the anti-Japanese United Front, was both the culmination of these popular efforts to influence the Central Government and the symbol of urban China's refusal to tolerate further Japanese interference. Moreover, Chiang

Kai-shek's change of outlook at Sian was not the only ominous sign to the Japanese; the fact that the Chinese Communists were in secure occupation of a large section of Shensi province—part of an area that the Japanese were beginning to regard as their future sphere of influence—was equally alarming. An illustration of Japanese insight into these events occurs in a small pamphlet published by the Army Ministry in November 1936. It gives a detailed account of the course of the Long March and predicts the unification, in the near future, of Government and Communist forces.[4] Japan's worst fears were realized only one month afterward at Sian; and when, in early 1937, the Japanese observed some one thousand youths departing for Yenan to enroll in K'angta (Anti-Japanese Political-Military University) and another large group of students in the Peiping area joining Sung Che-yüan's 29th Army, they felt the need to revise their policies accordingly.[5] Japan thus chose to seek her objectives in China by direct military action.

THE INVASION OF CHINA

On the night of July 7, 1937, a company of Japanese soldiers—part of the China Garrison Army authorized by the Boxer Protocol (1901)—was fired upon by elements of General Sung Che-yüan's 29th Army near the Marco Polo Bridge (Lukouch'iao); and it responded in kind. The Commander of the Japanese garrison at Tientsin, Lieutenant General Katsuki Kiyoshi, subsequently demanded that Sung's 29th Army be withdrawn from Hopei province, and when Sung temporized he decided to expel the 29th Army by force. Although the central authorities in Tokyo did not send their approval of Katsuki's decision until July 26, reinforcements for the Japanese garrison were already under way from the Kwantung Army and from Korea by that time.[6] Three divisions were also mobilized in Japan to join the China Garrison Army. Meanwhile, in Shanghai the deaths of a Japanese naval lieutenant and of a seaman on August 9 (the Ōyama Incident) provided the pretext for dispatching the Shanghai Expeditionary Army (main force: two divisions, the Third and the Eleventh). The war thereby spread to the Yangtze area. The onset of full-scale invasion may be dated from September 4, when the commander of the newly formed North China Area Army, General Terauchi Hisaichi, arrived at Tientsin from Tokyo.[7]

In north China the Japanese began their advance from T'angku, the port for Tientsin, along three major rail lines: one force moved westward along the Peiping-Suiyüan railroad and invaded Shansi; another proceeded to the southwest along the Peiping-Hankow railroad; and the third advanced in a southeasterly direction along the Tientsin-Pukow railroad toward Nanking. Initial resistance in the Peiping area was made by the 29th Army, commanded by Sung Che-yüan. His force was attacked by the China Garrison Army on the morning of July 28 at Nanyüan; and by nightfall it had retreated in confusion, leaving many dead. Colonel Evans Carlson later commented that the 29th Army showed high morale and good fighting qualities, but that it was hampered by poor leadership.[8] Although the Central Government sent reinforcements to fill the void created by the 29th Army's collapse, this was not enough to stem the Japanese advance, which was proceeding rapidly in all directions. The Japanese forces that were advancing westward along the Peiping-Suiyüan railroad turned at Huailai* and advanced southwestward to invade Shansi. At the same time, a force from the Kwantung Army advanced into Suiyüan, capturing the capital, Paot'ou, on October 6. Both of these Japanese columns then drove southward into Shansi; and the provincial capital, T'aiyüan, fell to the Japanese on November 9, 1937. On the other two north China fronts, Japanese forces had moved down the Peiping-Hankow line to within a few miles of the Yellow River by the end of 1937 and, on the Tientsin-Pukow railroad, as far as T'aian in Shantung.

The advance down the Peiping-Hankow railroad by the Japanese First Army had an unforeseen result that illustrates the new political and military atmosphere created by the invasion. During the Chinese retreat from Paoting (seized by the Japanese on September 24), the commander of one regiment and some of his men found their escape route closed and went into hiding in the countryside of Ankuo hsien. The commander was Lieutenant Colonel Lü Cheng-ts'ao; his unit was the 683d regiment, 129th division (Chou Fu-ch'eng), 53d Army (Manchurian). Lü, a native of Liaoning, had been driven from Manchuria in 1931, but had continued to serve in Wan Fu-lin's 53d Army (part of the former Tungpei Army, reorganized in 1932). Following the rout of Chinese forces at Paoting, Lü and some of his troops united with local militia in Ankuo hsien and on their own initiative established a "people's self-defense corps." During that same fall and winter of 1937, Chinese Communist forces began their penetration of the occupied areas. At the time Lü was creating his enclave, General

* See Appendix (pp. 189–91) for the location of the hsien mentioned in this study.

Nieh Jung-chen, Vice-Commander of the 115th division, Eighth Route Army, was setting up the famous Communist guerrilla base in the mountainous border region between Hopei and Shansi (the Chin-Ch'a-Chi Border Area). General Nieh sent one of his deputies to make contact with Lü and to incorporate his forces into the Eighth Route Army. Lü accepted with alacrity, and by June 1938, when the Kuomintang tried to reclaim his services (Lu Chung-lin, the new KMT governor of Hopei, made contact with him), he was the head of both the Central Hopei Military Area (Communist) and the Third Column of the Eighth Route Army.[9] This course of events in setting up the guerrilla base in central Hopei established a pattern that was soon to be repeated all over north China.

In central China, the battle for Shanghai was not as one-sided as the Sino-Japanese clashes in north China; fierce fighting between Chiang's best troops and the Japanese was continuous in the Shanghai area for three months (August 13–November 12). The first Japanese contingent to be engaged in the battle at Shanghai was the Special Naval Landing Party (4,000), which took up offensive positions shortly after Lieutenant Ōyama Isao was killed on the evening of August 9. Following the naval forces into Shanghai was General Matsui Iwane's Shanghai Expeditionary Army from Japan, which landed at the mouth of the Whangpoo on August 23. In mid-October, in order to guarantee the still doubtful success of Matsui's attack, the central authorities dispatched another powerful force to Shanghai. This was the 10th Army (under Lieutenant General Yanagawa Heisuke), composed of more than three divisions, which made the famous unopposed landing at Hangchow Bay on November 5 and thereby outflanked the Chinese defenders.[10] The Chinese began a general retreat on November 12; and the Japanese, having received the order to capture Nanking, pursued them closely. The Chinese were unable to regroup their forces in time to defend the city effectively, and Nanking fell on December 13. Immediately after the capture of the capital, the 10th Army proceeded against Hangchow; and it was occupied on December 24.

During the first few months of 1938, Japanese forces in central China remained quietly in place while they awaited the outcome of the T'ungshan Operation—the attempt by the North China Area Army to recoup its lost prestige after part of its Second Army suffered a major defeat at the hands of the Nationalist Generals Sun Lien-chung and Li Tsung-jen. This defeat, on April 1–5, 1938, came at T'aierhchuang, a small town on the Grand Canal in southern Shantung near the Tientsin-Pukow railway line. Although the battle of T'aierhchuang was far from being decisive, its sobering effect in Japanese military circles influenced the whole character of the China Incident. After this defeat, officers of the Japanese command in north and central China were summoned to Tokyo where, on April 7, they received orders to destroy all Chinese forces in the vicinity of T'ungshan (a suburb of Hsüchou), the point at which the strategic north-south and east-west rail lines cross and the area in which the victorious Chinese armies were concentrated. In addition, the commander of the Second Army was relieved, and on April 3 Lieutenant General Prince Higashikuni Naruhiko was appointed in his place. The view of the Chinese situation that prompted this strong reaction by the Japanese was described years later by Japanese staff officers:

> [The Chinese] . . . judging that the Japanese forces were absorbed in the stabilization and pacification of the occupied areas and that they had exhausted their fighting strength and were unable to continue the offensive, and believing that they [the Chinese] had won a signal victory in the battle near T'aierhchuang, the morale of the enemy increased tremendously and they began to talk boastfully about destroying the Japanese forces. An extensive propaganda campaign was conducted in China and abroad which *crystallized the anti-Japanese sentiments of the Chinese people* and prompted positive action in the form of an "aid-to-Chiang" policy by powers friendly to the Chiang Kai-shek regime.[11]

In the subsequent T'ungshan Operation, the Japanese took Hsüchou and T'ungshan (May 19); and the Chinese forces, retreating to the west, responded to the Japanese pursuit by destroying the banks of the Yellow River northeast of Chengchou, Honan, on June 12. The river altered its course toward the southeast and flooded the Huai River. It disrupted life in general in the area, but it did bring the Japanese pursuing operation to a close.

The actual significance of the T'ungshan Operation lies not in its military manifestations, but rather in the political decisions that accompanied it. At the time of the order for the attack on T'ungshan (April 7), Imperial General Headquarters also issued a directive entitled "Essentials for the Tactical Guidance of the Operation in the Vicinity of T'ungshan." Point 3 of this document commands the North China Area Army to "seize the Tientsin-Pukow railway north of T'ungshan (to include T'ungshan) and, after defeating the enemy, [to] occupy that sector north of the Lunghai rail-way which is east of K'aifeng."[12] The Central China Area Army was similarly directed to occupy the Tientsin-Pukow line south of T'ungshan and also the area around Hofei, in Anhwei province. These orders are important because they laid the groundwork for the subsequent overcommitment of Japanese forces on the Chinese mainland, a condition that contributed directly to the spread of Communism. The T'ungshan Operation actually marks the end of all attempts by the Japanese government to localize the China Incident. With regard to the orders cited above, it is doubtful whether even the whole Japanese Army could have effectively occupied and maintained order in the sector north of the Lunghai railroad and east of K'aifeng, since this area includes most of Hopei and Shantung provinces; the North China Area Army alone certainly was not able to do so. The result was anarchy, Communist intrusions, guerrilla warfare, and Japanese punitive expeditions—conditions that all contributed to Yenan's long-range success.

The ultimate proof of the Japanese decision to extend the war was the Imperial General Headquarters order of August 22 directing the attack on Hankow. Following this order, the Japanese forces, now entirely reorganized as the Central China Expeditionary Army under the command of General Hata Shunroku, proceeded to concentrate the large force of 14 divisions that would be used in the Wuhan campaign. (Wuhan is the general name for the three cities of Hankow, Hanyang, and Wuchang.) The military aspects of the campaign, which lasted from September 11 to October 28, 1938, are not unusual except for the severe epidemics of malaria and cholera suffered by both armies. But the political dispute between the Kuomintang and the Communist Party over the defense of the city is of interest, since it is one of the first major breaches in the United Front.

Following the Japanese seizure of Hsüchou, the Communist Party, which was operating publicly in Wuhan as a partner in the anti-Japanese United Front, advanced the slogan "Defend Wuhan to the death." Arguing from the analogy of the workers' defense of Madrid, Party leaders urged the government to arm some 100,000 to 150,000 workers, students, and townspeople, and to create an elite division of 5,000 to 10,000 youths "with the highest national revolutionary consciousness" to lead the armed civilians. Part of the Communist Party leadership obviously had not yet abandoned all schemes of urban insurrection. Ch'en Shao-yü, Chou En-

lai, and Ch'in Pang-hsien published a long article in the *Hsin-Hua jih-pao*
of June 15 on the subject of Wuhan's defense. It reads in part:

> Are we able to defend Wuhan or not? The answer is clear—we can!
> Recall the glorious example set by the Spanish people in the defense
> of Madrid. When the Franco forces, with the assistance of German and
> Italian fascists, advanced on Madrid, the greater part of the Spanish
> armed forces had revolted, and only a few troops plus armed workers
> and townspeople existed in the Republican Government and People's
> United Front. Yet they repulsed the attack of the rebel army and have
> maintained Madrid's defenses for two years to the present.[13]

Basing its recommendations on developments in the Spanish Civil War,
the article continues with a specific seven-point program, which it urges the
government to adopt.

This type of propaganda was damaging to the Kuomintang. If such
Spanish-style units had been set up, the Communists would have controlled
them and this would have created a dangerous situation. Therefore the
Kuomintang rejected the idea. Chiang realized that Wuhan could not be
held against an overwhelming assault and was already planning his retreat,
but he also realized that the Communists were attempting to discredit his
patriotism by their insistence upon a desperate defense. In 1938, during the
heyday of the United Front, the Communists had little effect upon Chiang's
reputation; but their machinations were harbingers of things to come as
the war wore on. Already, during August of 1938, the KMT was forced
to break up Ch'en Shao-yü's rapidly growing Wuhan Defense Committee
and to prevent temporarily the publication of the *Hsin-Hua jih-pao*.[14] These
events were later used by Communist political workers as evidence of
Kuomintang treachery toward the United Front and toward China.

In south China, meanwhile, the Japanese occupation of Canton was
carried out simultaneously with the Wuhan operation; its objective was to
cut the supply routes serving the Nationalists in Chungking. Reassured by
the Munich Agreement (September 29, 1938) of British unwillingness to
obstruct Japanese actions near Hong Kong, the 21st Army (under Lieutenant General Furushō Mikio) carried out the invasion on October 12,
1938. The occupation of Canton was largely uneventful. In 1939, the 21st
Army further occupied such localities as Swatow and Hainan Island to
tighten up the blockade.

Like the seizure of Canton, the attack on Hainan had a certain routine quality about it. Little did the Japanese or anyone else suspect that so unlikely a place as Hainan Island would soon become a Communist guerrilla base. A Japanese brigade invaded Hainan on February 10, 1939, and had completed its mission by the 23d. The Chinese force on the island was estimated by the Japanese at 3,600 troops; many were killed in the Japanese attack, and the remainder fled into the mountains. The Japanese high command imagined that they had eliminated all opposition, until on March 4, 1940, the Hainan Island Detachment requested part of the 18th division to carry out a mopping-up of "enemy bandits" in the northeastern section of the island. This became the first of several operations against one of the least-known Communist guerrilla bases—the Ch'iung-Yai liberated area, set up in 1939.[15]

By mid-1939, the Japanese Army was finding it difficult elsewhere in China to govern the large territory that had proved so easy to invade. Problems of maintenance of peace, military government, the establishment of puppet authorities, and control of guerrillas began to occupy more and more of the attention of Japanese staffs. This aspect of the Japanese impact on China during the war, which we shall turn to now, was as important as the invasion itself in bringing about rural mobilization. The invaders may have been safe in their cities, but five miles out of town it was another story.

TABLE 1

ORGANIZATION AND LOCATION OF CHINA EXPEDITIONARY ARMY,
OCTOBER 1, 1939

Headquarters, China Expeditionary Army	Gen. Nishio Juzō	Nanking
North China Area Army	Gen. Tada Hayao	Peiping
First Army	Lt. Gen. Shinozuka Yoshio	T'aiyüan, Shansi
Twelfth Army	Lt. Gen. Iida Sadakata	Tsinan, Shantung
Eleventh Army	Lt. Gen. Okamura Yasuji	Hankow
Thirteenth Army	Lt. Gen. Fujita Susumu	Shanghai
Twenty-first Army	Lt. Gen. Ando Rikichi	Canton

TABLE 2

JAPANESE HIGH COMMAND IN CHINA, 1937–1945

NORTH CHINA—NORTH CHINA AREA ARMY		CENTRAL CHINA—CHINA EXPEDITIONARY ARMY	
Dates of Service	Commander	Dates of Service	Commander
July 7, 1937–July 11, 1937*	Lt. Gen. Tashiro Kan'ichiro (Army known as China Garrison Army)	Aug. 23, 1937–Nov. 7, 1937	Gen. Matsui Iwane (Army known as Shanghai Expeditionary Army)
July 11, 1937–Aug. 31, 1937	Lt. Gen. Katsuki Kiyoshi (Army known as China Garrison Army)	Nov. 7, 1937–Feb. 14, 1938	Gen. Matsui Iwane (Army known as Central China Area Army)
Aug. 31, 1937–December 1938	Gen. Terauchi Hisaichi	Feb. 14, 1938–December 1938	Gen. Hata Shunroku (Army known as Central China Expeditionary Army)
December 1938–Sept. 23, 1939	Gen. Sugiyama Gen	December 1938–Sept. 23, 1939	Gen. Yamada Otozō (Army known as Central China Expeditionary Army)
Sept. 23, 1939–July 7, 1941	Gen. Tada Hayao	Sept. 23, 1939–March 1941	Gen. Nishio Juzō
July 7, 1941–Nov. 22, 1944	Gen. Okamura Yasuji	March 1941–Nov. 22, 1944	Gen. Hata Shunroku
Nov. 22, 1944–end of war	Gen. Shimomura Sadamu	Nov. 22, 1944–end of war	Gen. Okamura Yasuji

* General Tashiro died of illness at Tientsin, July 11, 1937.

THE ESTABLISHMENT OF PUPPET GOVERNMENTS

By late 1939 and early 1940, many influential spokesmen for the Japanese cause in China were beginning to draw attention to the serious situation that had developed in the occupied areas. General Nishio's Chief of Staff, Lieutenant General Itagaki Seishirō, admitted at an army briefing that the Chinese Communist forces had filled a power vacuum in northern Shansi, in Hopei, in most of Shantung, and in north Kiangsu.[16] Reports in the Kōain's political affairs journal were even more alarming. One of the numerous articles on Communism pointed out that, "Since the establishment of the KMT-CCP alliance, the Communist Party has plagiarized the slogans of [Sun Yat-sen's] 'Three Principles of the People,' i.e., nationalism, livelihood, and individual rights, and has hidden behind the slogan of KMT-CCP cooperation to the point that it has anesthetized the masses; actually, it is implanting Communism."[17] Another, more analytical, writer for the Kōain went so far as to place the blame somewhat closer to where it belonged: "The Communist Army's consciousness of opposition to the enemy is quite intense. The explanation for this consciousness is to be found in a certain clumsiness [!] in the China Incident on our part as well as in a comparative decline in the consciousness of the Nationalists. We have been unable to dispel fear concerning our policies during and after the war. At present, the fact of an intense anti-Japanese attitude on the part of the Chinese armies and masses is beyond dispute."[18]

The Japanese reaction to this situation took two forms: the establishment, in 1940, of a Japanese-controlled central government to rival both Chungking and the guerrilla bases in the struggle for mass support, and the extermination of "Communist" bases by mopping-up campaigns, "rural pacification" drives (*ch'ing hsiang*), the construction of fortifications, and the like. The puppet government technique was more sophisticated politically and had greater hope for success; its eventual failure was as much a result of the growth of rural nationalism as it was of Japanese bad faith. It is, therefore, worth while to consider the strengths and weaknesses of the puppet regimes, which were important ingredients in the Chinese political mixture upon which Communism thrived.

Immediately after the initial phase of the Japanese occupation was over, puppet interim governments were set up in both north and central China, and also in Mongolia. These early puppet regimes were the Provisional Government of China, established at Peiping, December 14, 1937; the

Mongolia Federal Autonomous Government, established at Kalgan (Wanch'üan), September 4, 1937; and the Reformed Government of China, established at Nanking, March 28, 1938. They were all the frank tools of the Japanese Army on the model of the old East Hopei Autonomous Government; the staff of the Provisional Government, for instance, was drawn largely from the former Hopei-Chahar Political Council. The three governments also coincided neatly with the spheres of influence of the three major branches of the Japanese Army in China—branches that were never brought under centralized control. The Manchurian-based Kwantung Army supported the Wanch'üan regime; the North China Area Army dealt with the situation in Peiping; and Nanking headquarters controlled the Reformed Government. This regional orientation of the Army, combined with the traditionally greater Japanese interest in north China, at first ruled out the establishment of a single, unified government at Nanking.[19]

By 1939-40, the political situation in China had outgrown the abilities of the early puppet governments to deal with it effectively. The development of the rural resistance movement and the spread of Communism were threatening to make the invasion an endless military operation, and were interfering with Japanese exploitation of China's material wealth. It was in response to these developments that authorities in Tokyo undertook a reorientation of their policy toward China. The chief requirement of the new policy was that it harmonize Japanese economic demands on China with the obvious need to establish a regime that the Chinese could and would support. The new Japanese policy included vigorous military operations against Communist areas and the total blockade of Chungking, but its basic feature was the establishment of a new central government.[20] The mopping-up campaigns and the occupation of French Indo-China and Burma would all be for nothing if the China Incident could not be ended and the country reunified under a pro-Japanese government. It was toward this end that on March 30, 1940, the new National Government of China was established at Nanking, with Wang Ching-wei as its president.

The Nanking government and the philosophy of Asian solidarity that lay behind it held the greatest potential for securing a settlement of the China Incident favorable to Japan. The government at Nanking offered the possibilities of peace and of mutually advantageous economic relations with Japan; even more important, it also possessed the potential ability to unite the forces of Chinese nationalism behind it in opposition to Western domination. Several observers in the occupied areas noted that anti-British propaganda by Nanking and the Japanese was much more popular and better received than the "new citizen" or revival-of-Confucianism campaigns.[21] Prior to the outbreak of war with the United States, there can be no doubt that the ideology underlying the Nanking government appealed to many Chinese. In essence, it substituted an anti-Western-oriented Asian nationalism for an anti-Japanese-oriented Chinese nationalism. Despite these potentialities, the Nanking government failed completely either to attain leadership of nationalist sentiment in China or to bring about a peace favorable to Japan. In fact, as we shall see, the balance sheet of Nanking's influence on China's wartime policies actually shows a credit for the Communists. First, however, it is necessary to underscore some of the reasons why the Nanking regime never gained popular support.

The most pronounced characteristic of the Nanking regime was its inability to demonstrate its claim to a legitimate existence independent of the Japanese Army. Part of this was due to Wang Ching-wei's personal reputation and abilities. Wang was not the first choice of the Japanese: they had been unable to secure the services of the old warlord Wu P'ei-fu— a kind of Chinese Pétain—and had to settle instead for a species of Pierre Laval. The Japanese never gave Wang the kind of independence that he needed in order to succeed, probably because Wang lacked the kind of conservative background in which the Japanese could place their wholehearted trust. Moreover, without Wu P'ei-fu (who died in December 1939), Japanese Army circles in the north were unwilling to transfer all prerogatives to Nanking, and, as a result, north China remained a semi-autonomous enclave run by the North China Area Army, although nominally under indigenous, centralized control. The unusual relationship between Nanking and Peiping is demonstrated by the fact that Wang Ching-wei did not make an official visit to Peiping until October 27, 1942, when he attended the Third National Convention of the Hsin Min Hui (New Citizens' Society), the north China collaborationist political party.[22]

At Nanking itself there were many other manifestations of the new Central Government's subservience to Japan. Virtually all the foreign relations of the new state were dominated by Japan—even those concerned with foreign representation in China. After the capitulation of Germany, for example, it was the Japanese Foreign Office that notified the German and Hungarian consulates in Shanghai to close their offices, despite the fact that they were accredited to the Central Government of China.[23]

Japanese economic exploitation of China also continued after the creation of the Nanking government, albeit under the rubric "joint anti-Comintern defense." The basic document ("The Fundamental Principles for the Readjustment of Relations between Japan and China") drawn up in Japan in 1940 to guide the new government included the following points: "IIb. Japan and China will jointly carry out anti-Comintern defense. To this end, Japan will station troops in areas deemed necessary"; and "IIIa. In regard to specific resources in north China and Mongolia, especially ore deposits necessary to national defense, Japan and China will cooperate in their exploitation *to effect joint anti-Comintern defense* and economic cooperation, and in regard to their utilization, special concessions will be granted to Japan upon due consideration of the *requests* of China."[24] This was a very thin veneer for what amounted to a Japanese carte blanche in the occupied areas, particularly when "joint anti-Comintern defense" came to mean simply the razing of peasant villages by Japanese and puppet armies.

In late 1942 and early 1943, Japan did make certain moves designed to eliminate the most glaring inequalities in the original status of the Nanking regime. In November 1942, the Japanese ambassador to Nanking, Shigemitsu Mamoru, inaugurated a series of negotiations between Wang and the authorities in Tokyo which led to a larger measure of Chinese independence. Japan relinquished her imperialist concessions in China and the right of extraterritoriality, in return for which Nanking declared war on Great Britain and the United States (January 9, 1943). Most agencies concerned with the welfare of Chinese civilians were turned over to Nanking at that time. By 1943, however, it was no longer possible to generate enthusiasm for Nanking by bolstering its authority, since it had already lost a great part of the rural population to the Communists.

One of the difficulties that the puppet regimes encountered in attempting to convince the masses of their legitimacy and independence arose in connection with the massive immigration of Japanese civilians into China. These immigrants replaced the Chinese in many professions and exploited the population in every manner possible; but they were not restrained by either the Japanese Army or the puppet government. This situation, which was observed daily by Chinese in the occupied cities, confirmed the people's belief that China was to be treated as a conquered nation whether the Nanking government existed or not. According to Japanese estimates,[25] there were ten times as many Japanese nationals living in China in 1944 as there had been in 1937—a civilian invasion of some magnitude.

If this influx were not enough to dispel any illusions about the basis of political power in the occupied zones, the Japanese also inaugurated labor conscription in 1943. All males in Shansi province between the ages of 17 and 40 were to be organized into a labor army (named the Self-Sacrifice Construction Corps) with a three-year term of service. According to radio reports, the Japanese Army aided in the organization of the corps, which could be used inside or outside of Shansi.[26] A similar labor force was also set up in Shantung in February 1944.[27] Under such conditions, neither the façade of Chinese sovereignty surrounding the Nanking government nor the public celebration of Confucius's birthday by puppet officials (August 28) was sufficient to keep the populations of the occupied areas docile and working. Japanese oppression served to mobilize and to alienate the Chinese masses; and once they had determined on a course of resistance to the Japanese, they welcomed Communist leadership in guerrilla warfare and in the establishment of bases. However, Japanese "carpet-baggers" and labor conscription were relatively minor irritants compared with the effects of the rural pacification movement. That aspect of the occupation will be discussed later in this chapter.

It is useful here to examine briefly certain comparable developments in the Yugoslav revolution, developments that illustrate clearly the role of puppets amid conflicting claims to nationalist legitimacy. In Yugoslavia, civil war between the Chetniks (representatives of the Royal Government exiled in London) and the Partisans (military formations of the Yugoslav Communist Party) took place simultaneously with the struggle against the German invaders. In the early part of the war, the Chetniks had been the first to resist the Germans, but the development of the "Communist menace" drove them to coordinate their activities with other anti-Communist forces. Because considerations of fidelity to Yugoslav nationalism were of equal importance to those of Communist affiliation in the minds of war-mobilized guerrillas, Mihailović (the Chetnik leader) was made to look like a traitor when he cooperated with puppets and Germans. Although Mihailović described the Chetnik and German anti-Communist measures as "accidental parallel action," he was clearly compromised on nationalistic grounds.[28] It became impossible for him to mobilize resistance either to the Communists or to the Germans, and the Allies could no longer continue to support him. Much of the population simply moved to the Partisan side by default.

The role of the puppets in the discrediting of Mihailović as a nationalist was crucial. The puppets worked unceasingly to draw Mihailović's Chetniks—the non-Communist nationalists—into an anti-Communist front against the Partisans. The puppets' motive for this behavior was that an anti-Communist front, if realized, would justify their having sided with the invader in the eyes of the Yugoslav masses, who were presumed to be opposed to "Communism." The greater the number of non-Communist nationalist groups that joined the anti-Communist front, the more likely it was that this justification would be realized. It developed, however, that for the duration of the war the Partisans had replaced their Communist allegiance with loyalty to Yugoslav nationalism (a change that subsequently modified their own Communism), with the result that the puppet-sponsored front against Communism looked like a German move to divide the Yugoslav resistance. At the same time the Partisans' position was bolstered by German brutality and reprisals that were not directed solely or even primarily against the Communists.

Thus the group occupying the middle ground—the non-Communist nationalists—was under attack from both sides. If the Chetniks became as nationalistic as the Partisans (i.e., by carrying out positive resistance against the Germans and their puppets), the Germans would respond with reprisals that would drive more peasants into the resistance. This would, in turn, give rise to a contest between Chetniks and Partisans for leadership of the ever-expanding revolution—a challenge the "legitimate" nationalists could not accept, since it would have admitted the existence of a truly Yugoslav rival. On the other hand, when the Chetniks opposed the Communists, they forfeited their own claim to nationalism, since the Communists were demonstrably fighting the Germans. The first alternative was eliminated when civil war broke out between Chetniks and Partisans over questions of jurisdiction and right to command; the Chetniks joined the anti-Communist front and thereby transformed themselves into virtual puppets. This development swept away all opposition to the Partisans as leaders of the Yugoslav people in their war with the fascists. The puppets' major contribution to the wartime political struggle in both Yugoslavia and China was the emasculation of non-Communist nationalist groups by raising the question of Communism at the height of the battle against the invader. It gave the Communist forces something they could not have otherwise obtained: a claim, not simply to participation in the nationalist struggle, but to the *exclusive* defense of nationalism.

In China, the situation had not degenerated to the extent that it had in Yugoslavia; yet a similar challenge to the KMT's nationalistic purity had passed the embryonic stage by the time of Japan's defeat. The idea of joint puppet-Chungking operations against the Communists had strong support from people who regarded the Communists as a greater threat than the Japanese. It may be assumed that if full-scale civil war had actually broken out during the anti-Japanese war, such a coalition would have developed, even though Chungking would have risked the withdrawal of Allied support. At the same time, Nanking's calls for unity among all anti-Communist groups (Nanking, the Japanese, and Chungking) were valuable to Yenan's propagandists as tools for discrediting Chungking's patriotism. When it was reported that Ch'en Li-fu, Ho Ying-ch'in, Ch'en Ch'eng, and others in the KMT right wing had advocated military action against the Communists, the Communists responded by asking what the difference between Nanking and Chungking was—since both were anti-Communist.[29] So successful was this line that even after Japan's defeat Chiang could not openly collaborate with the puppets;[30] the dangers of ending up with nothing but puppet support were too great. Chiang himself was not at any time totally discredited as a nationalist (as was Mihailović); but among the unsophisticated rural masses of the occupied zones, the degree to which Nanking did any damage to Chiang's nationalist reputation benefited the Communists.[31]

Much of the damage to Chiang's reputation was the result of propaganda by the puppets rather than of any real collaboration between the two forces. Nanking propaganda subverted the KMT's claim to nationalist leadership in two ways. First, it described the Chungking government as the unwilling tool of the Communists and maintained that Chungking continued the resistance only out of obstinacy and opportunism, and not out of nationalism or patriotism.[32] Second, it emphasized that only the Communists stood in the way of puppet control of the entire country, and that the Communists were the only true enemy of the puppets and of Japan. Nanking did not speak of Chungking as the "enemy," but as the "traitor to Greater East Asia [*Tōa no hangyaku-sha*]"; the enemy was in Yenan.

A further complicating element in the propaganda struggle was that the Nanking and Chungking governments both had identical names and political parties. Even before it was established in 1940, the Nanking government ostentatiously described itself as the true Kuomintang and co-opted all of the KMT slogans and national paraphernalia. It must have been confusing to a peasant to see the same old "blue-sky, white-sun, red-earth" flag planned by Sun Yat-sen flying over both Chungking and Nanking, and at the head of both armies. In the early period of the war, Nanking flew a triangular pennant above the KMT flag, inscribed with the characters "peace, anti-Communism, and national construction," but even that was discarded in February 1943.[33] Details such as these made it more difficult for the Chungking Kuomintang to appeal to the loyalty of the people in the occupied zones, and thus made them more receptive to Communist initiatives.

Nanking's vociferous anti-Communist statements actually promoted Yenan's interests. People who had reason to hate the puppets and the Japanese on other grounds—particularly the peasant victims of invasion or of mopping-up campaigns—found confirmation of Yenan's claim to resistance leadership in Nanking's denunciations of the Communists. An example of Nanking's position on Communism is found in Wang Ching-wei's widely circulated book, *T'ung-sheng kung-ssu,* translated by the International Military Tribunal as *Sharing Our Fate.* In the article "Talk by President Wang on the First Anniversary of the Campaign to Purify the Land" (Nanking, July 1, 1942), Wang remarked:

> In July last year, the Nationalist Government gathered together its political and military strength and, delimiting districts in Kiangsu Province, executed its land-purifying program. Today, on the first anniversary of the land-purifying campaign, I wish to tell my impressions to all parents and brethren in the purified districts and all our friends throughout the whole nation. The purpose of land-purifying is, just as its name indicates, to wipe out Communist guerrilla troops, and to rescue the people from danger. The purport of land-purification . . . lies not only in sweeping away the Communist guerrilla troops, but also in completely repelling them and extirpating them and in making it impossible for them to return.[34]

Suffice it to say that if one were the victim of one of the "land-purifying" campaigns, whether or not one had been a Communist before it started, one might very well be after it was over. Considerations of nationalism made for strange bedfellows on the left, just as fear of Communism drove together the most disparate elements on the right.

MILITARY ACTION AGAINST THE COMMUNISTS: NORTH CHINA

The policy followed by the Japanese Army in attempting to win the allegiance of the Chinese masses by establishing the new Chinese National

Government was an obvious failure. It failed because the Nanking government was the handmaiden of Japan, and Japan had earned the hatred of the Chinese people. This hatred derived from Japanese attempts to subjugate the countryside by force more than it did from any other Japanese action. From 1938 until the very end of the war, the Japanese Army mobilized massive forces and sent them into areas believed to contain Communists, where they carried out extensive mopping-up campaigns. The importance of these campaigns to the growth and entrenchment of the Chinese Communist movement in the countryside cannot be overstated. The threat of terror and devastation was a constant ingredient in Chinese rural life for seven years; the party that met this challenge with an effective policy and the organizational ability to make this policy work won the support of the peasant population as no other political group has done in recent times. The actual source of the Communist Party's authority in China today dates from the wartime period when it led the mobilized masses of previously non-Communist areas in their struggles with the Japanese Army.

The Japanese Army itself explained the rural pacification drives as having been provoked by Communist activities. However, the belief that Japanese terrorism was only a response in kind to a provocative policy first undertaken by the Communists—one designed to force the hand of the Japanese at the expense of Chinese civilians—is only partially correct. It is true that the existence of any sustained Chinese resistance at all was due to the cooperation between the local peasantry and the Communist veterans of Kiangsi. However, this cooperation was largely the product of peasant mobilization—a process that was *initiated* by the Japanese invasion and by the conditions of rural anarchy following the evacuation of local elites. The Communists were the beneficiaries and not the main source of this mobilization; their contribution was the organization of the mobilized peasants, the establishment of rear-area bases, and the leadership of effective guerrilla warfare against the Japanese. These guerrilla campaigns did cause the Japanese to step up their reprisals (this was particularly true of the Japanese reaction to the Hundred Regiments Offensive), and this in turn broadened the rural mobilization. But the creation of the original situation that led the Japanese to resort to terrorism in the villages cannot be credited to the Communists.

Virtually all on-the-spot observers were agreed that Japanese treatment of all Chinese peasants, both the hostile and the cooperative ones, was disastrous to the long-range Japanese goals and favorable to the development of resistance on a mass scale. Michael Lindsay, for example, notes: "As the Chinese [Communist] leaders admit, the behavior of the Japanese has been the most important factor in uniting the population, but this has only provided the foundation on which the new political organization has been built." Again, he comments: "To win any sort of popular support the Japanese would have to stop *indiscriminate* terrorism, so that the ordinary peasant would know that he had nothing to fear from the Japanese unless he actively helped the guerrillas, and they would have to provide reasonably good government in the areas they controlled."[35] George Taylor has summarized the problem in a different way: "Put in its simplest terms, the struggle for government resolved itself into an attempt on the part of the Border Government [the Communist Chin-Ch'a-Chi guerrilla base] to arouse, and the Provisional Government [the Peiping puppets] to repress, peasant nationalism. The Provisional Government, therefore, was always at a disadvantage because peasant nationalism was not the type of movement which could be diverted into other channels; it simply must not exist. It was no accident that terrorism was the chief weapon employed against the villages of north China."[36] The mopping-up campaigns might never have occurred if the invasion had never occurred; but the invasion did take place, and in its wake the process of peasant mobilization.

Was there a real alternative to the policy of leading the mobilized peasants in positive resistance, even though such resistance invited reprisals? In some other countries occupied by the Axis powers during World War II, resistance forces waited for an allied counterinvasion before launching their uprisings, thereby mitigating the danger of reprisals. This policy was not possible in China for two reasons: first, the very nature of the Japanese invasion and of the subsequent exploitation of China (like the German invasion of Yugoslavia) caused the mobilization of the rural masses and the spontaneous development of self-defense forces; second, since there were two Chinese parties competing for the title to national leadership, the advocacy of a wartime policy of "waiting in preparation" by any one party was politically disadvantageous. Given the mobilization of the peasantry in the occupied areas, the Kuomintang—even if there had been no Communists—would have been compelled to champion the cause of positive resistance. Moreover, China's position within the anti-fascist alliance of World War II was dependent upon Chinese military action of all kinds to keep the China war alive, a consideration not relevant to most other occupied countries. As for the Communists, they naturally promoted the resistance: it was their entrée into Chinese political life following the defeat of the Kiangsi Soviet and the retreat to the northwest.

The general effects of the mopping-up campaigns are clear, but the reconstruction of the campaigns' specific details is a complicated process. In the first place, the organization of the rural pacification movement took several different forms, depending upon the area in which it was carried out and the forces employed in its execution. In the second place, the measures implemented in the pacified areas following the end of a mopping-up campaign varied considerably between north China and the Nanking-controlled areas. These differences must be carefully considered, since the success of the Communists often varied inversely with the measure of success achieved by the puppets in consolidating a pacified area. Some understanding may be gained of these problems by reviewing the occupation from the point of view of the Japanese military forces.

The initial Japanese instructions concerning the restoration of order in the occupied areas conformed to generally accepted precepts of military government. In the directive of September 23, 1937, for instance, the North China Area Army laid down as its policy that "administration of north China rear areas (including east Hopei) is to be carried out by Chinese administrative organs with the internal guidance of the Army Special Affairs Bureau."[37] For this purpose, Peace Maintenance Committees composed of local pro-Japanese sympathizers were set up at the municipal level, as well as hsien magistracies and, above them, Administrative Inspectorates that supervised the hsien governments.[38] The North China Area Army's instructions further specified that former enemies should be excluded from the administrative organs, that there should be no weapons allowed in the rear areas, and that the guiding principles of administration should be the maintenance of peace and order and the realization of Japanese-Manchukuoan-Chinese co-prosperity. A system of army control was created to correspond to the various levels of Chinese administration: there was a liaison officer to the hsien government and one to the Administrative Inspector's Office, as well as a Special Affairs Organ in contact with the Peiping and Tientsin Peace Maintenance Committees. All these officers reported to the North China Area Army Special Affairs Department (Kita-Shina Hōmengun Tokumubu). The initial instructions of September 23 do not mention Communism, nor do they specify any special measures to combat it; the Communists, of course, had not yet shown their hand.

By mid-1938, however, the North China Area Army was alarmed by the fact that Communists were appearing in widely separated parts of Hopei. They were also carrying out "persistent guerrilla attacks" in the areas northwest of Ihsien, west of Ch'ingyüan, and particularly in the vicinity of Laiyüan—all in a sector of Hopei adjacent to the Chin-Ch'a-Chi border region. The official Japanese explanation of this situation was that the withdrawal of their forces in order to take part in the T'ungshan Operation had opened the area to Communist infiltration. For example, all units of the 114th division in western Hopei had been pulled out in April and attached to the Second Army on the T'aierhchuang front.[39] However, these troops were not actually garrisoned in the rural areas, and not until March 1938 did the Japanese Army even begin to occupy some of the hsien cities of Hopei and Shansi. Even by April 1939, only about 80 out of 120 hsien cities in Hopei had garrisons. When the hsien were occupied, it was only the towns that had a few troops—the countryside was Communist territory. The failure of the Japanese to occupy the countryside early was of greater importance to the initial diffusion of Communist forces than the troop requirements of the T'ungshan Operation.

A fragmentary sampling of the innumerable Japanese staff studies on the Communist problem during this period reveals some weaknesses in the Japanese analysis of the situation. On December 21, 1937, the headquarters of the North China Area Army issued an "Instruction on Principles for Carrying Out Peace Preservation" which stressed the security aspect of the Communist question. "Peace preservation has as its aim the speeding up of complete stabilization in the areas occupied by the Army as well as the establishment of a new political authority, but its first objective is the safety of the Army's position."[40] Needless to say, this emphasis on security only increased the danger to the Army's position; more authority in the hands of the Chinese and some restraint on the part of the Army would have been more likely to create conditions of peasant imperviousness to Communism. Since the Japanese Army itself had already sown what the Communists would later reap, it was highly unlikely that the Army would have the perception to try to *prevent* the spread of Communism. For example, although the instruction mentions that propaganda methods are as important as military methods in Communist suppression, it quickly passes to the overrated menace of the foreign concessions as Communist hiding places.

The concessions in Tientsin and the protected residence areas of Peiping undoubtedly did harbor Communists and other elements regarded as undesirable by the Japanese. However, the Japanese directed attention to the concessions at the expense of the rural areas, where the real threat to their position lay.[41] Theodore White has essayed a partial explanation of this Japanese shortsightedness: "Japanese political and military intelligence in China was far and away the finest in the world, but it had concentrated on schisms and rifts, on personalities and feuds, on guns and factories. Its dossiers on each province, each general, each army, contained so much of the wickedness and corruption of China that the accumulated knowledge was blinding. The one fact that was obscure to them was that China was a nation."[42] Possibly this overstates the case somewhat, but there was a nation-in-the-making in the peasant villages. The Japanese seem to have been unaware both of the political awakening in the countryside and of the effect that their mopping-up tactics would have in bringing this new nation into being.

One final example of the Japanese analyses of the general Communist situation—this one made in late 1941—reveals a curious mixture of stereotype and insight. In an article for *Jōhō,* one of the Kōain's staff complains that destruction of Communism is a difficult business even in a country like Japan with its "indomitable national spirit [and] settled social life," but in a "semi-feudal, semi-colonial" country like China it is almost impossible. He cites as circumstances promoting Communism in China: the lack of a spirit of national unity, a "survival of the fittest" situation caused by neglect of the people's welfare, warlord rulers, corrupt police organs, and the like.[43] Although these conditions did exist in China and contributed to the success of Communism, they were certainly not the primary cause. This same writer goes on to compare the situation faced by the Japanese Army vis-à-vis the Communists in 1941 with the experiences of Chiang Kai-shek in the Kiangsi campaigns; and in this analysis—here reduced to five points—he clearly illustrates that the crucial difference between the two periods was the growth of Chinese nationalism:

(1) Chiang Kai-shek had the confidence and support of the entire people, and because of this he was able to mobilize the entire country for Communist destruction. On the other hand, the main anti-Communist forces today [1941] are the Japanese Army and the Nanking government, and they certainly do not possess the confidence of the broad masses.

(2) The size of the Red Area is different; Chiang Kai-shek dealt

with only part of Kiangsi, but today we face Communists in the north-west, in Shansi, in Hopei, in Shantung, in Chahar, in Suiyüan, in Ho-nan, in Anhwei, and in Hupeh, as well as pockets in Manchukuo, Jehol, and south China.

(3) The Red Army has greater strength today; the regular troops of the Red Army in 1934 were divided into 26 divisions and 2 independ-ent brigades, mustering a total of about 75,000 men. In September of this year [1941], Communist regulars amount to about 350,000, while village self-defense corps add another 100,000.

(4) Chiang Kai-shek could engage the majority of his troops in Communist suppression even after the Manchurian Incident, but Japan must divide its strength against the Chungking Army and against international enemies.

(5) The Red Army in the Kiangsi period was not necessarily an indigenous army, but today it champions army-civilian integration everywhere and is continuously organizing local armies. As a conse-quence, it is extraordinarily difficult to separate bandit from citizen in Communist destruction work.[44]

All these considerations, combined with the inescapable fact that the occupied areas could not be garrisoned adequately, contributed to the Japanese decision to launch assaults on the villages in the Communist areas. There were few pacification drives carried out in the north during 1938 (one at Foup'ing in March, one in east Hopei after August, and one at Wut'ai in the autumn); but in 1939, Imperial General Headquarters made "peace preservation" a first-line operation.[45] In response to Tokyo's 1939 general order to smash all Communist and anti-Japanese forces in the rear areas, the North China Area Army made the following operational assignments: the First Army (three divisions and three independent mixed brigades[46]) was given Shansi province; the Area Army itself (four divi-sions and two independent mixed brigades) took Hopei and Honan north of the Yellow River; and the 12th Army (two divisions and four inde-pendent mixed brigades) was assigned Shantung.[47] Operations were con-tinuous throughout the year; the First Army sent forces against the Com-munist Eighth Route Army in northern Shansi (March 1-22, 1939), into the 100-by-150-kilometer fastness of Wut'aishan (May 8-June 12, 1939), and all over southeastern Shansi (July 3-August 21, 1939). Similar actions were taken in Hopei and Shantung by the Japanese forces stationed there.

When, in the course of these operations, the Communist armies gave battle to the Japanese intruders, they inflicted serious damage; Japanese sources admit, for instance, "heavy casualties" suffered by a unit of the

Third Independent Mixed Brigade in Wut'ai before its retreat on May 14, 1939.[48] The usual report, however, was "no enemy force encountered" —a consequence of the Communist armies' strict adherence to the basic logic of guerrilla warfare: to fight only at times of the guerrillas' own choosing. Of course, the success of this tactic required that the Communists be ready to retreat on almost a moment's notice. As an illustration of their readiness in this respect, the Bethune International Peace Hospital located in the Wut'ai base, the largest of the guerrilla base medical centers (1,500 beds), could be evacuated on a half-hour's notice and was some twenty times.[49] What happened, however, to those villagers who did not move out along with the Communist Army?

The 1939 operations of the Japanese Army were not yet of the "drain the water" variety (the Japanese answer to Mao's aphorism that the relation between the guerrillas and the people was like that of fish to the sea), but they did arouse the population and make the work of the Eighth Route Army political organizers easier. For instance, in the Ankuo hsien area of central Hopei, where Lü Cheng-ts'ao had organized the peasantry, the Japanese Army seized and garrisoned the towns in September 1939. Fourteen months later, in December 1940, they withdrew and Lü's army quietly returned to Ankuo. In the year and a half that followed the withdrawal of the Japanese garrison, the people of central Hopei gave Lü the strongest possible support; even the Japanese referred to this time as the "golden period" of the Communist Army in central Hopei.[50] Evidently, the Japanese occupation had stimulated the residents of Ankuo to support Lü and his forces rather than to repudiate them and follow the puppets and the New Order.

This estrangement between the peasantry and the Japanese Army was confirmed in May 1942, when the Japanese garrisoned Ankuo for the second time. General Okamura's policy of "kill all, burn all, destroy all" (*sankō-seisaku*) was being implemented at this time, and Ankuo hsien was also one of those areas of Hopei in which tunnels were being used as shelters from the Japanese. These tunnels were hidden dugouts, which were used as a means of escape from Japanese encirclement, and they became a special target of Japanese terrorists. One example of the measures taken against the tunnels occurs in an attack on the village of Peihuan in Ting hsien—Ankuo's neighbor—on May 28, 1942. The Japanese surrounded the area with some 300 soldiers and then pumped poison gas into the tunnels; 800 Chinese were killed.[51]

This type of action was sanctioned by the Area Army as part of the *sankō-seisaku* adopted after the Communists' Hundred Regiments Offensive of 1940. The "three-all" policy, according to Fujita Masatsune, came into use in 1941 and 1942, and was based upon German practices. It was aimed at destroying the close cooperation that existed between the Communists and the populace.[52] The essence of the *sankō-seisaku* was to surround a given area, to kill everyone in it, and to destroy everything possible so that the area would be uninhabitable in the future. Instances of the policy's implementation were common: 1,280 persons were executed and all houses burned at Panchiatai, Luan hsien, east Hopei, in 1942; the largest-scale destruction occurred in the Peiyüeh district (21 hsien) of the Chin-Ch'a-Chi border region, where more than 10,000 Japanese soldiers carried out a mopping-up campaign between August and October of 1941. The results in that area were some 4,500 killed, 150,000 houses burned, and about 17,000 persons transported to Manchuria.[53]

In order to understand why such measures were employed in 1941 and not in 1939, it is necessary to examine developments in 1940 in some detail. By the end of 1939, the Communist guerrillas were inflicting real damage on the Japanese, particularly to railroads. No less a person than the former Chief of Staff of the First Army, Lieutenant General Hashimoto Gun, assessed the guerrilla situation at the close of 1939 in this way:

> The destruction of railway and communications lines was the most annoying part of the guerrilla activities. Besides cutting the railway and communications lines with tools and instruments, the guerrillas frequently blew them up and, as they became more skillful in the use of explosives, many trains were blown up by land mines. Such tactics rendered ineffective various protective measures which had been employed in the past, such as observation patrols. Therefore, the 110th division built screening trenches parallel with the Peiping-Hankow railway line in order to protect it from guerrillas. It also made efforts to mop up the occupied areas by searching every private home for guerrillas.[54]

Damage to railroads was only one of the serious military problems faced by the Japanese as a result of Eighth Route Army activities; another one was the Hundred Regiments Offensive.

There have been many explanations for the Eighth Route Army's Hundred Regiments Offensive of late 1940 and for the violence of the Japanese reaction to it. One theory maintains that the Communists wanted to prevent the Japanese from crossing the Yellow River and taking Sian;[55] another states that the Communists were reacting to General Tada's tactic of building blockhouses in the guerrilla areas.[56] Probably the most important consideration, from the Communist point of view, was that the deteriorating international situation, particularly in Europe, had given rise to a great wave of pessimism in Chungking and strengthened the pro-Japanese elements. Friction between Yenan and Chungking had become intense during 1940; and the Communists obviously feared a peace settlement between Chungking and Japan, which would be at their expense. One way to keep Chungking in the war was to keep the war alive, and the Hundred Regiments accomplished just that.[57] From the Japanese point of view, the Communist offensive was a sudden demonstration of how active the China war still was, just at a time when the Army was refining plans for an advance southward into Indo-China and beyond. A guerrilla offensive was most embarrassing and disturbing to Army officials. Moreover, the actual damage inflicted during the three-month campaign was so great as to necessitate drastic Japanese action to prevent further guerrilla offensives.

The Hundred Regiments Offensive was launched August 20, 1940, when 400,000 troops in 115 regiments of the Eighth Route Army simultaneously attacked the Japanese forces in five provinces of north China. The battle continued for three months and was divided into three phases. During the first period, August 20 to September 10, the main objectives of the attacks were the Chengt'ai (or Shansi) railroad, the Peiping-Hankow railroad, the Tientsin-Pukow railroad, the Peiping-Shanhaikuan railroad, the Peiping-Suiyüan railroad, and several other lines. The Chengt'ai line—the railroad connecting Shihchiachuang and T'aiyüan—was rendered almost useless by the attack, and the coal mine at Chinghsing, on the Chengt'ai line, was heavily damaged. This mine had been a major source of fuel for the Japanese forces. In the second period, which lasted from September 20 to early October, Communist assaults were directed against Japanese strong points and blockhouses that had been advanced into the guerrilla areas. The largest battle of this period was fought in the mountains of southeastern Shansi, where the Communists sought to destroy the Japanese road between Yüshe and Liao hsien (Tsoch'üan). Other important battles occurred in the Chin-Ch'a-Chi border area and in central Hopei, particularly in Jench'iu. The third period lasted from October 6 to December 5; during that time the Japanese First Army regrouped its forces and carried out large-scale mopping-up operations in all areas from the T'aihang Mountains of southeast Shansi to the area west of Peiping. The Communists responded to these intrusions with fierce counterattacks.[58]

The over-all effects of the Hundred Regiments Offensive were serious, as even the Japanese themselves admitted. Japanese reports stated that the Communists

> attacked the garrison troops along the Shihchiachuang-Yangch'ü [i.e., T'aiyüan] railroad and the northern sector of the Tat'ung-Fenglingtu railway [running north and south the length of Shansi], and at the same time blasted and destroyed railroads and communications facilities. The Chinghsing coal mine in the garrison area of the Eighth IMB [Independent Mixed Brigade] was attacked suddenly on the same night [August 20, 1940] and its facilities were completely destroyed. These totally unexpected attacks caused serious damage, and it was necessary to expend much time and money in restoration work.[59]

The Japanese estimated the size of the Communist forces that attacked the Chengt'ai railroad at 6,000 men, drawn from the 129th division (Liu Po-ch'eng), two regiments of the Chin-Ch'a-Chi guerrilla army, and students from K'angta. They also identified the Communist 129th division as the unit that cut the Peiping-Hankow railway between August 23 and 25, 1940.[60] As a result of these unprecedented developments, Japanese staff officers were compelled to re-examine the situation in the guerrilla areas and to make a new estimate of the danger posed by the Eighth Route Army.

Up to this time, Japanese military operations against the Communists had been concentrated on building roads and pillboxes to blockade and cut up the guerrilla areas so that they could be attacked without the guerrillas' escaping. This policy, associated with the command of General Tada, was an adaptation of Chiang Kai-shek's 1934 strategy in Kiangsi.[61] After the Hundred Regiments Offensive, and with the assumption of command of the North China Area Army by General Okamura (July 7, 1941), the scorched-earth or "three-all" policy was undertaken, along with even more extensive construction of fortifications.[62] The period 1941–42 was the most difficult that the guerrillas faced during the entire war: the population of the Communist areas in north China was reduced from 44 million to 25 million, and the size of the Eighth Route Army was cut from 400,000 to 300,000.[63] It was not accidental that the Communists' well-known *cheng feng* (rectification) movement and Army-assisted agricultural production movement were undertaken during this period. The need to establish the firmest possible determination among the leadership of the guerrilla areas was obvious, and the internal production movement was an effort to avoid famine in the blockaded bases.

In spite of the shrinkage of the guerrilla areas and the severe losses suffered in them, the Communists reaped certain advantages from the fact that there was now hardly a village left in Hopei or Shansi that was not half-burned or worse. The revolution spread and became irreversible in the years 1941–42. Instead of breaking the tie between the Eighth Route Army and the peasantry, the Japanese policy drove the two together into closer alliance. This alliance derived partly from nationalism (hatred of the invader), but to a large extent it was purely a matter of survival. We know that in Yugoslavia Tito's detachments were a refuge for peasants threatened with extermination by the Ustashe; the Partisans' adversaries served the Communist cause by forcing the people and the Party together, often for the first time.[64] Similarly, in north China *sankō* promoted peasant-Communist collaboration. By the spring of 1943, the Eighth Route Army was again moving into the plains of Hopei and operating throughout Shantung. The Army's strength and the size of the guerrilla areas very soon surpassed those of 1940.[65]

With this renewal of its strength, the Eighth Route Army once again resumed guerrilla warfare against the North China Area Army. There was a difference, however, in the style and objectives of guerrilla warfare after the Hundred Regiments Offensive. That effort had been too costly in terms of ammunition to be repeated, particularly since the Communists were now strictly blockaded by both the Japanese and the Kuomintang, and were not receiving supplies from other sources. Battlefield seizures and the disarming of puppets constituted the Communists' major sources of military supplies for the rest of the war. Also, after 1940–41, the purposes of guerrilla warfare were altered when the threat of a negotiated peace with Japan receded and the United States entered the war against Japan. Before 1940, guerrilla activities had been primarily of a military nature, but after that time much greater stress was placed upon "economic guerrilla warfare."[66] Economic guerrilla warfare meant denying food crops and other Chinese products to the Japanese, interfering with the Japanese manipulation of the currencies in north China, interrupting the Japanese lines of communication, and creating conditions of self-sufficiency in the guerrilla bases.

Economic guerrilla warfare was obviously not the exclusive concern of the Army and required the close cooperation of mass movement associations, Border Area governments, and the Communist Party. During the period from 1942 to the end of the war, Party leadership of the resistance forces was perfected, and closer civil-military integration was developed in the so-called "liberated areas" (*chieh-fang-ch'ü*). These reforms had two aims: to make the protracted war as costly to Japan as possible, and to expand and consolidate the Communist areas.

One example of the new, rationalized guerrilla warfare was the Eighth Route Army's activity in Hopei and Shansi from May to July, 1944, when the Army devoted its energies to protecting the crops from Japanese grain confiscation units while the population of the guerrilla bases, especially mobilized for this purpose, harvested them. In the course of this operation the Army attacked the numerous Japanese blockhouses built in the countryside, ambushed looting parties, and recaptured grain from Japanese storage centers. Similar activities were carried on in Shantung. On September 30, 1944, Yenan Radio broadcast an "emergency order" to the Army and to the people of Shantung warning them of a new mopping-up campaign and stating that the Japanese objective was seizure of the autumn harvest.[67] The Eighth Route Army made maximum efforts to save the crops in Shantung by intercepting marauders and by contributing its manpower to the harvest. During its counterattacks against the Japanese mopping-up forces in Shantung, the Army also "liberated" various areas that had previously been under puppet, Chungking, or Japanese control. The Communists' biggest victory in 1944 came in Chü hsien, a large county 80 miles southwest of Tsingtao, where the Eighth Route Army took some 700 villages (out of 3,600 in the hsien) with a population of 300,000 (out of a total of 900,000). It was during the battle of Chü hsien, according to Yenan, that a large number of puppet troops (4,000) came over and cooperated actively "for the first time."[68] Defections of puppet troops soon became a common occurrence in north China in the last months of the war.

MILITARY ACTION AGAINST THE COMMUNISTS: CENTRAL AND SOUTH CHINA

The Japanese mopping-up campaigns in central China were less severe than those in the north. This was due, in the first place, to the fact that the resistance forces spent more time fighting each other than they did fighting the Japanese; warfare between the New Fourth Army and the Chungking forces was a constant feature of the central China occupied areas. Since the anti-Japanese guerrillas were never sufficiently united to mount an attack on the scale of the Hundred Regiments Offensive, the Japanese did not generally resort to reprisals of the *sankō* type as they had in the north. Moreover, without the threat of wholesale destruction driving the population into the ranks of the resistance forces, the guerrillas and the populace were not so completely identified as they were in the north. Thus, an area of central China actually could be pacified without being depopulated. Most of the real guerrilla pressure on the Japanese in central China was in the form of economic guerrilla warfare, and therefore the Japanese tended to seek out the guerrilla forces alone during a mopping-up rather than attacking the entire population. In addition to these basic differences, there were other aspects of Japanese policy that made the central China area less fertile, although by no means barren, territory for Communist expansion.

Since the Japanese occupation was everywhere designed to produce the same result, a pacified and subservient China, the differences in occupation tactics between north and central China probably derived from the way the Japanese viewed the two regions: north China was seen as analogous to Manchukuo or Korea, whereas central China was hopefully regarded as a friendly but independent state. The north China area took priority in Japanese strategic thinking and received sufficient forces (on loan from the Kwantung Army in case of need) to carry out anti-guerrilla operations. On the other hand, the limited Japanese armies in central China were mainly preoccupied with Chungking forces, and they had to develop measures other than straightforward military pacification to control the rural areas.

This difference in approach is illustrated by the Central China Expeditionary Army's 1939 order concerning rural pacification. The order was issued in mid-January to implement the Imperial General Headquarters' directive that made rural pacification one of the main objectives for 1939. The Army's order stated in part: "The Japanese Army shall eliminate enemy activities by constant positive action, while continuing its strict garrisoning of the area. . . . It shall also strengthen the self-defense capacity of towns and villages by encouraging the Chinese authorities to popularize the *Mutual Guarantee System*."[69] The Mutual Guarantee System—more commonly known by its Chinese name of Pao Chia—was one of the measures adopted in the occupied and pacified areas of central China by the Japanese to control the population. The Pao Chia system itself dates back to the middle of the Sung dynasty and was also employed in the early 1930's by the National Government's Bandit Suppression Commission to assist the anti-Communist drives in south central China. The National Government utilized Pao Chia in Kiangsi to enforce group responsibility on villages, and to threaten an entire village with reprisals if it tolerated any one family's harboring Communists. After the Communist-suppression campaigns were ended, the Chungking government continued the Pao Chia system as an official part of the hsien administrative machinery in a law of September 1939, since it was an excellent means for carrying out the national conscription law and for maintaining wartime social control generally.[70]

The Japanese utilized the Pao Chia system—they called it *hokō*—for exactly the same purpose that the Kuomintang did in Kiangsi: to enforce collective responsibility for acts committed by "Communists." The system was not unfamiliar to them; they had encountered it as a form of village self-government when they acquired Taiwan in 1895. They gave it legal status in a decree issued by the Governor General of Taiwan in 1898, when the *hokō* system was set up as a subsidiary organ to assist police administration. In Taiwan, as in China, ten households formed a *chia* (*kō*), and ten *chia* formed a *pao* (*ho*), with federated *pao* under the hsien, or county, government. The head of each *pao* was elected by the members of the *chia*, but their choice had to be approved at the local Japanese police station. An agreement was drawn up bearing the signatures of all household heads, and this agreement, after being approved by the governor of the province or district, was registered with the police. The duties of the *pao* and *chia* were defined as follows: (1) maintaining peace and order in the district, (2) taking the local census, and (3) encouraging good morals and good conduct. Although the system was of Chinese origin, the Japanese utilized it to Japanize the population—for instance, by requiring that a *pao* chief have a knowledge of Japanese. During the war, the Japanese used the Pao Chia system to integrate the Formosans more closely into the Japanese empire by establishing the so-called Imperial People's Hokō Association (Kōmin Hokō Kai).[71]

Following the occupation of central China, the Japanese fell back upon their experiences in Taiwan to guide them in the military government of China. In addition to the collaborationist Peace Maintenance Committees, which were set up immediately after the arrival of the Japanese Army, the puppet Reformed Government enacted, on May 30, 1938, "The Temporary Regulations of the Reformed Government for the Formation and Inspection of the Pao Chia Household System in Each Hsien of the Peace Areas."[72] One official Japanese source cited four categories of results that this law aimed to produce: (1) peace preservation, including the organization of self-defense and youth corps, collective responsibility for disturbances, gathering of intelligence, collection of all weapons from the populace, repair of roads, and utilization of Pao Chia heads for liaison; (2) administrative improvements, including the taking of the census and the control of movements between villages; (3) economic benefits, including the creation of cooperatives and the control of production; and (4) propaganda work, including the supervision of schools, the use of regular Pao Chia meetings for propaganda, and the dissemination of health information.[73]

The Pao Chia system was not employed solely in the occupation of the central China area; it was also used in north China in the early part of the war.[74] In the northern rural areas, however, the system was comparatively ineffective, in large part because it was not accompanied by other guarantees of peace and stable government. In the north, Pao Chia was chiefly a census-taking and registration device; the population was held responsible collectively for supposed guerrilla activities with or without the Pao Chia system. In the rural areas of central China, however, the Pao Chia system was only one of several measures which, taken together, made up the so-called Rural Pacification Movement, an aspect of the Japanese occupation that was never extensively used in north China.

Beginning in July 1941, this Rural Pacification Movement (*ch'ing-hsiang yün-tung*) was implemented by the Japanese and Nanking forces in various strategic areas of the Yangtze Valley. Its objective was the establishment of "Model Peace Zones" (*mo-fan ti ho-p'ing ti-ch'ü*)—areas in which the guerrillas had been exterminated and which were then rehabilitated, policed, and systematically exploited by the Nanking government. In these zones Japanese forces were used only in the anti-guerrilla phase; all political and social affairs were handled by the Nanking government.[75] The scope of the Rural Pacification Movement and its differences from the north China mopping-up campaigns is revealed in the movement's official eight-point program:[76]

1. Thoroughgoing mopping-up and destruction of the enemy's fighting strength and political system, particularly the Communistic structure.

    2. Strengthening of local military functions.
    3. Completion of the rural Pao Chia neighborhood system.
    4. Consummation of the rural autonomous administrative system [i.e., establishment of a hsien administration loyal to Nanking].
    5. Completion of the rural self-defense system [setting up of pro-Nanking *pao an tui,* "peace preservation corps"].[77]
    6. Completion of the rural production system.
    7. Completion of the New Citizen Movement.
    8. Stabilization of the rural financial system and improvement in collection of taxes.

Clearly, this campaign was a more reasoned undertaking than the wholesale destruction carried out in north China; it also achieved a much greater measure of success.

The area in which the Rural Pacification Movement was first put into practice was the Triangular Zone (Shanghai-Nanking-Hangchow) of the Yangtze delta. This region had been the scene of continuous fighting between Communist, Chungking, and independent guerrilla forces since 1937; but in early 1941, the Kiangnan Anti-Japanese Patriotic Army (which was affiliated with the New Fourth Army)[78] emerged as the dominant force. Its bases in the Ch'angshu-Wuhsi-Chiangyin-Soochow sector lay astride the Nanking-Shanghai railroad (the Huning line), and its strength among the peasantry was growing rapidly. By October 1940, the Kiangnan Army had gained sufficient popular support in the Triangular Zone to establish a local government known as the Teng-Hsi-Yü Special Area Administrative Committee. This Communist-dominated government controlled a large area of south Kiangsu only 60 miles west of Shanghai.[79]

On July 1, 1941, the Japanese Thirteenth Army based at Shanghai launched military operations against the Kiangnan guerrillas, who were located in Wu hsien around Soochow.[80] The Japanese quickly forced the guerrilla units to withdraw from the hsien, and then the Japanese themselves withdrew, leaving only garrisons to prevent the Communists' return. The Nanking government took over local administration and proceeded to implement the program of the Rural Pacification Movement; the result was that Wu hsien became the first Model Peace Zone. It proved to be quite successful. By replacing Japanese military administrators with Chinese officials from Nanking, the Model Peace Zone won a measure of popular approval; within a short time there was an increase in production, and food products started to flow to Shanghai, Nanking, and Japan.

A second zone was set up exactly one year later, on July 1, 1942, in a sector southeast of Lake T'ai on the Chekiang-Kiangsu border. This was in an area that the Japanese Thirteenth Army had tried to mop up in the autumn of 1940 (October 5–November 1)—an operation that resulted only in having the Army's Fifteenth division almost wiped out by Chungking guerrillas and by the New Fourth Army (near Ching hsien, the New Fourth Army's headquarters, in eastern Anhwei).[81] The third Model Peace Zone was located in the suburban wards of Shanghai; the military phase of this rural pacification began on September 1, 1942. The new Shanghai peace zone was under the control of Ch'en Kung-po, the Mayor of Shanghai and later head of the Nanking government (following the death of Wang Ching-wei in Nagoya, November 10, 1944). During September 1942, the Japanese Ambassador to Nanking, Shigemitsu, made an inspection tour of the Model Peace Zones around Shanghai and Hangchow. The report of his inspection undoubtedly played an important part in the December 1942–January 1943 negotiations between Nanking and Tokyo that led to Japan's New China Policy, as a result of which the year 1943 saw the greatest expansion of the Rural Pacification Movement to that date.[82]

Seven new Model Peace Zones were set up between February 1 and October 1, 1943, in very rich areas of central China.[83] This action was followed by a corresponding withdrawal of Japanese forces from areas that they could not garrison adequately but that they had been forced to pacify and repacify in the past (e.g., the New Fourth Army bases in north Kiangsu).[84] The north China puppet government sent a mission to inspect the Model Peace Zones in central China in July 1943; it was, however, too late to implement such a program in the north. The Japanese attempted to set up "special administrative areas" in central and east Hopei during 1944, but they could never get through the military phase; fierce fighting between Japanese troops and guerrillas in the east Hopei region was still under way on the day that the war ended. In central China the Japanese carried the idea of the Model Peace Zones to its greatest extension when, on February 1, 1944, they set up the new "model province" of Huaihai. With its center in the rich agricultural district of northeastern Kiangsu, the province consisted of 21 hsien in Kiangsu, Anhwei, and Shantung; the provincial capital was Lienyünkang, the eastern terminus of the Lunghai railroad and a seaport that the Japanese claimed to have rendered the equal of Tsingtao.[85] Huaihai was not so successful as the earlier Model Peace Zones, since it was clear by 1944 that Japan was losing

the war and there was little to gain from cooperating with Nanking officials. Huaihai itself was infiltrated by New Fourth Army political workers,
and most of its rural areas were in Communist hands by 1945.

The Chinese Communists themselves never ceased agitating against the
Model Peace Zones and the Rural Pacification Movement. As early as August 19, 1941, the Japanese picked up a Communist pamphlet in Tanyang
hsien, south Kiangsu, entitled "A Reader on the Struggle Against Rural
Pacification." Written in catechismic style, it starts with the question
"What is the Rural Pacification Movement?" The answer: "It is a plan
of the Japanese devils and Wang Ching-wei traitors to pacify the countryside in six months. They have mobilized 10,000 puppet troops and 5,000
Japanese soldiers in order to destroy the Kiangnan Anti-Japanese Democratic Base, to eradicate the New Fourth Army, to damage the anti-Japanese governments and the mass movement, and to turn the people of the
Kiangnan area into nationless slaves."[86]

The main element in the New Fourth Army's response to the Model
Peace Zones was a renewed propaganda effort to arouse nationalist sentiments in the rural populace. Party workers introduced a new vocabulary
to deal with the Pacification Movement: persons who joined the peace
movement were labeled *Han-chien* (traitors to China) if they were civilians, and *wei-chün* (bogus soldiers) if they were troops; and *fan-cheng
kung-tso* (return-to-rectitude operations) were activities designed to bring
back *Han-chien* and *wei-chün* to the "resist-Japan camp." The new Fourth
Army publicized "Ten Do's and Ten Don't's" in connection with the pacification campaign, which included such points as: "Do join resist-Japan
organizations," "Do pay all land taxes to the resist-Japan governments,"
"Do act as a spy for the anti-Japanese troops," "Don't join the *wei-chün*,"
"Don't become a *Han-chien*," "Don't buy goods made in Japan," and
"Don't have friends in the *wei-chün*."[87]

The pacification movements served the long-range interests of the Communist Party very much the way the *sankō* raids did in north China,
though less dramatically. The Communists, in preparing an area to meet
a pacification army, vehemently insisted that the Party's leadership be
accepted unquestioningly in the time of peril ("only the CCP has the experience of twenty years of struggle and the spirit of perseverance in a
hard fight") and demanded that all "traitors and reactionaries" be purged
at once.[88] Although the Party was successful with this approach in certain
areas, it may be noted that in areas in which the peasants were offered

reasonable security by Nanking and the Japanese, propaganda alone was not sufficient to induce them to join the guerrillas. From 1943 on, the Party bothered little with the Model Peace Zones themselves, being content with the Japanese withdrawal from other areas, and being more interested in expanding its own bases at Chungking's expense.

Propaganda, of course, was not the only method used by the Communists to undermine the Model Peace Zones. One important Communist target was the Pao Chia registration system, which made it difficult for the guerrillas to travel through a pacified area; and here a different technique was employed. To interrupt the census system, the Communists occasionally destroyed all residence certificates in a village so as to force it into opposition to the Japanese.[89] Also, Loo Pin-fei reported that in the Soochow area, in 1941, all the peasants had "Good Citizen Certificates," which were "small pieces of white cloth, bearing name, age, occupation, and address, written in ink with a large red government seal," and which were sewn to the clothing. In this case, the guerrillas simply copied the emblem and all wore them.[90] But, in general, Model Peace Zones near large urban areas, like the one near Soochow, were immune to Communist penetration until Japan's defeat was certain, and even then their residents were much less advanced in terms of national awakening than their brothers in the north. In Yugoslavia a similar situation existed among the rich but politically unconscious peasants of the Voivodina.

The measure of success achieved by the Rural Pacification Movement in central China was due to the political arrangements that accompanied Japanese anti-guerrilla military operations. The wisdom of these policies, from the Japanese point of view, is revealed by looking at the Canton area, where no effort was made by the Japanese to woo the peasant by political means. Kwangtung province did not set up a rural pacification bureau in the puppet administration until December 1943, and first implemented the Pao Chia system in Canton and surrounding cities in September 1943. Pao Chia was not extended to the rest of the province until May 1944. Thus, the Japanese forces in Kwangtung relied solely upon military pacification to keep the rural areas in the puppet economic structure throughout most of the war.[91]

After the fall of Canton, October 20, 1938, local Chinese guerrillas continued to smuggle munitions from Hong Kong and to create, in the words of the Japanese, "disturbances and disorders in the Canton delta area."[92] These forces operated along the Macao-Canton road and were particularly active in Hsinhui hsien, on the right bank of the Hsi (West) River, and in Chungshan hsien—an appropriate locale for national resistance, since Chungshan was the birthplace of Sun Yat-sen. In February 1939, the Japanese Twenty-First Army, in command at Canton, sent a small force to conduct a punitive campaign in the Hsinhui-Chungshan sector. Much to the embarrassment of the Japanese, this unit was encircled by a guerrilla force of 6,000 to 7,000 men, and had to be rescued by reinforcements from the Twenty-First Army.[93]

In October 1939, the Twenty-First Army again was forced to send a detachment to mop up the West River area. They occupied the town of Chungshan on October 7, 1939, and on the next day searched the surrounding countryside for guerrillas. This time a small number of soldiers was left behind to garrison Chungshan. By February 1940, however, the Twenty-First Army (now the South China Area Army) reported that from 6,000 to 7,000 guerrillas had infiltrated the area; and it ordered a whole infantry division (the Thirty-Eighth) to proceed against them. Operations opened on February 5, 1940, and on February 8 Chungshan was again taken, the guerrilla force having withdrawn in the face of overwhelming numbers. After this operation one battalion was left to garrison Chungshan; one company occupied Hsiaolan, about 25 kilometers northwest of Chungshan; and two companies patrolled the mountains north of Macao. In addition to this force, some 3,000 Nanking puppet troops were assigned peace preservation duties in the Chungshan area.[94]

As the war expanded into other areas of the Far East, large numbers of Japanese troops could no longer be used to garrison one or two rural hsien in Kwangtung. But the moment Japanese pressure was relaxed, the guerrillas returned, usually in greater numbers. Thus once-pacified areas were withdrawn from Japan's productive substructure and had to be either written off or repacified (an operation that entailed diminishing returns). The situation that prevailed around Canton in the later stages of the war shows how fruitless the task of rural pacification actually had been. On February 20, 1944, a two-stage mopping-up campaign was launched in the Canton delta and Tung (East) River areas of Kwangtung, with the ultimate objective of setting up Model Peace Zones. This time the chief targets for pacification were Tungkuan and Paoan hsien along the Canton-Kowloon railway, Shunte and Nanhai hsien near Canton itself, and Hsinhui and, again, Chungshan.[95] Five years to the month after the first pacification drive in Chungshan, the hsien was still a center of resistance. Again, in September 1944, Tokyo Radio gave details of Japanese battles with "armies made up of peasants" along the West River of Kwangtung; and it admitted that the appearance of such armed units "in every village" was a discovery of the then-current campaign.[96] In February 1945, Tokyo spoke of some 5,000 Communist troops and 5,000 "armed civilians" fighting Chungking forces along the West River; and, in March, Yenan claimed that 10,000 residents of Tungkuan hsien joined Communist-led guerrillas in an attack on a train in the delta zone.[97] In short, peasant guerrillas had been operating in Kwangtung province from the day that Japan invaded; and the Japanese had never been able to eradicate them. If military pacification had accomplished anything in Kwangtung at all, it was to alert the peasantry to China's national peril—a concept that hitherto had had no currency in the rural areas of China.

It is easy, two decades after the fact, to blame the Japanese Army for the rise of Communism in China and for all China's wartime misfortunes. That is not the intention here: Japanese policies certainly do not bear sole responsibility for the KMT's loss of prestige or for the eventual Communist victory. It may be useful here to sum up just what it was that Japan contributed.

Japan's invasion and occupation of China decisively altered the political interests of the peasantry. Prior to 1937, the peasants were a passive element in politics; even the earlier Communist bid for power, based on an appeal to peasant economic interests, was a conspicuous failure. The prewar peasant was absorbed in local matters and had only the dimmest sense of "China." Japan's invasion changed this condition by heightening the peasant's interest in such concepts as national defense, citizenship, treason, legitimacy of government, and the long-range betterment of the Chinese state. This came about as a result of certain specific new pressures on Chinese rural society that were contributed by the Japanese Army.

First, and most important of all, was the hostile activity of easily identifiable foreign soldiers against Chinese soldiers and civilians in north and east China. Although the peasantry, on the eve of war, was no more opposed to the Japanese than it was to other authorities, it acquired anti-Japanese attitudes as a result of the behavior of Japanese troops and the failure of Japanese leaders to offer a better alternative than resistance or slavery. If anti-Japanese feelings were not created by the invasion itself, they were created by the "mop-ups"—which were aimed directly at the peasantry. Japanese military activity in the rural areas compelled the Chinese peasant to join with other activated peasants for the common defense.

In addition to brute force, there were several other important developments connected with the invasion. (1) The traditional rural elites evacuated in the face of the invader and left the peasants to fend for themselves during the eight years of occupation. (2) The Japanese failed to create a Chinese government that could obtain popular support and also maintain friendly relations with Japan. (3) Japanese propaganda weakened the Chinese United Front by continually stressing, on the one hand, the alleged ulterior motives of the Communists and, on the other, the opportunism of the Nationalists. (4) Japan made an overambitious estimate of the area it could safely occupy in China; the result was that the Imperial Army drove out the KMT and then, in effect, left the territory empty for the Communists to enter. All these elements taken together restructured the environment in which the contest for political power in China took place. The resulting new environment was immensely favorable to the Communists—indeed, the most favorable circumstances they had encountered since the Party's founding in 1921. The advantage that the Communists took of the new situation is our next subject of inquiry.

THREE

The Communist Army

In the next three chapters we turn to a consideration of the activities of the Chinese Communists in organizing resistance to the Japanese invaders. The present chapter deals with the original size and expansion of the Communist Army and with its internal machinery for effecting alliances with the mobilized peasantry. The later chapters take up, first, the extent and general nature of the Communist guerrilla bases in north China; and second, the anti-Japanese resistance in the Yangtze area, with a close examination of the north Kiangsu guerrilla base as a case study. As these three chapters show, the Chinese Communist Party was the elite group that successfully placed itself at the head of the war-mobilized peasantry and became the political beneficiary of peasant mobilization.

The Communists, having gained access to the peasant villages as a result of the Japanese invasion, contributed to the mobilization of the peasantry in a variety of ways. Communist Army political workers spread anti-Japanese propaganda, assisted in the organization of rear-area governments, gave instruction in public administration, introduced education in reading, and generally established channels through which the popular anti-Japanese sentiment could be expressed. Internally, the Communist Army itself did much to mobilize its great numbers of new recruits via political indoctrination, migration (troop movements), and military training. The pressures from Communist organizers thus deepened and institutionalized the social mobilization begun by the Japanese. When Communist organizational initiatives bore fruit and the Japanese retaliated with mopups, Communist propaganda was confirmed in the minds of the peasants and the mobilization spread still further. As a result, by the end of the war 19 Communist-governed "bases" had been established throughout the

heartland of China—particularly in north China, an area previously regarded as essentially apolitical.

Although we must acknowledge the Communist Party's extraordinary
Leninist talents for organization (the subject of the present chapter), these
talents would have remained inoperative in China but for the growth of a
demand for leadership among the rear-area peasants. "Organization," as a
political tool, was well developed among the Communists in Kiangsi, but
it was not until after the Japanese invasion that the Communist Party was
able to put it to effective use. Analyses of Communist methods that make
much of organizational technique at the expense of operational context
are erroneous. My aim is not in any way to minimize the positive mobilizing pressure exerted on the peasantry by Communist organizing activity,
but only to remind the reader that no Communist Party has yet achieved
or held power solely by organization. The success of Communist organizational efforts was conditioned by the new context of Chinese politics following the full-scale Japanese invasion.

THE COMMUNIST MILITARY NUCLEUS: SIZE AND ORGANIZATION

At the beginning of the war, the Communists had virtually no interests
in common with the peasants of north China. The Communists at this
time were predominantly a corps of veteran military adventurers who had
engaged in warfare against the National Government for a decade. In
the fall of 1937, the Communist forces, then based in the area around Yenan
in central Shensi, crossed the Yellow River and invaded Shansi province
from the west at the same time the Japanese entered from the north and
the northeast. The invading Communist Army, known as the Eighth
Route Army, was the old Red Army which had been driven out of south
China in 1934-35 and which was redesignated and reorganized in 1937
following the establishment of the Chinese United Front. In Shansi, in the
early months of the war, the Communists fought alongside the Nationalists against the Japanese Army. Soon, however, with the defeat of the
Nationalist armies and with the China Incident having become a protracted war, the Communists began to give greater attention to infiltrating
the Japanese-occupied areas and to waging guerrilla warfare. One important result of the subsequent Communist-peasant alliance was the
enormous expansion of the Communist Army—a fact that can best be
appreciated by studying its growth figures.

The Chinese Communist military force at the end of the Sino-Japanese War (1945) was ten times the size of the Communist Army mobilized immediately following the Japanese invasion. If we compare the Eighth Route Army of 1937 with the entire military component under Communist guidance in 1945 (including militia, who were not detached from their civilian occupations) the growth of the Communist forces is much greater. In postulating a tenfold increase in first-rank, full-time troops of the Communist Army, I have put the strength of the Army at 50,000 men in 1937 and 500,000 men in 1945. Although these figures—50,000 and 500,000— are not arbitrarily selected, they are not unanimously accepted either; there exists a great disparity between the troop estimates of the regular Communist forces, depending upon what intelligence estimates or publicity releases are employed.

To consider the Eighth Route Army first, official Communist statements place its size at the time it changed its name from Red Army to Eighth Route Army (August 1937) at 45,000 men.[1] Actually, it is possible that the Red Army based in Yenan and available for reorganization in August 1937 was closer to 90,000 men. Between 1934 and 1937, the Red Army base in Shensi received troops from three sources. These sources—different columns of the Long March—were: (*a*) 30,000 troops of the (Red) First Front Army, including Mao Tse-tung, P'eng Te-huai, and Lin Piao, combined with the forces of Hsü Hai-tung and Liu Tzu-tan, which gathered in Shensi independent of the Long March; (*b*) 20,000 troops of the Second Front Army led by Ho Lung, Hsiao K'o, Hsia Hsi, and Jen Pi-shih; and (*c*) 30,000 troops of the Fourth Front Army under Chu Teh, Chang Kuot'ao, Hsü Hsiang-ch'ien, Lo Ping-hui, Ch'en Chang-hao, and Tung Chentang. As a result of this concentration, the Red Army existing in the Shensi base at the close of 1936 was probably between 80,000 and 90,000 strong.[2]

Following the rapprochement between the KMT and the CCP and the outbreak of the war, the National Government ordered the reorganization of the Red Army. The government placed the upper limit of the new Eighth Route Army's manpower at 45,000 men and divided this force into three divisions: (*a*) the 115th division, commanded by Lin Piao and Nieh Jung-chen and drawn from what were formerly the First Front Army and the Fifteenth Army Corps (the latter was the force of Hsü Hai-tung and Liu Tzu-tan, who had welcomed the survivors of the Long March to Shensi); (*b*) the 120th division, commanded by Ho Lung and Hsiao K'o (the old Second Front Army); and (*c*) the 129th division, commanded by

Liu Po-ch'eng and Hsü Hsiang-ch'ien (the renamed Fourth Front Army). All three of these divisions crossed the Yellow River in September 1937 and saw action against the Japanese before the end of the month. Since we know that the Communists did not leave Yenan undefended, it is probable that the forces in excess of the official 45,000 limit remained in reserve in Shensi province.

If the figure of 50,000 for 1937 is too low, the figure of 500,000 for 1945 may well be an underestimation also. Mao Tse-tung actually claimed in his Seventh Party Congress address (April 24, 1945) that the Communist forces had expanded to 910,000 men and that the strength of the civilian militia corps was more than 2,200,000.[3] This estimate seems to be inflated, even though it is known that large numbers of puppet troops joined the Communists during the last few months of the war. Mao's high estimate is probably based upon anticipated Communist recruitment in Manchuria and upon the just completed incorporation of south China guerrillas into the Communist ranks.[4] The over-all total of 500,000, which we have used as the approximate size of the Communist forces at the end of the war, is based upon a United States War Department estimate made in October 1944. At that time United States military intelligence placed the total strength of the regular Communist forces at 475,000. The Eighth Route Army accounted for 318,000 of this total, the New Fourth Army for 149,000, and the south China forces for 8,000.[5]

The New Fourth Army did not exist at the time the war broke out in July 1937; it was mobilized during the first six months after the invasion, drawing from Communist remnants left behind in central China when the main Red Army evacuated in October 1934. At the start of the war with Japan these rear-guard troops were scattered throughout south central China and included units in Kiangsi, Hunan, Fukien, Kwangtung, Che-kiang, Anhwei, and Hupeh provinces. Their strength at the time the main body retreated has been estimated at 30,000 men, made up of 3,000 Red Army troops, 7,000 guerrillas, and 20,000 militia.[6] Leadership of the force in the period 1934–37 was in the hands of Hsiang Ying, Ch'en Yi, Teng Tzu-hui, and others. Another Red Army detachment—the troops known as the "Anti-Japanese Vanguard Unit" under the old-time peasant organizer, Fang Chih-min, and his chief-of-staff, Su Yü—also contributed to the over-all strength of the Red Army's rear guard. Fang's Anti-Japanese Vanguard had left the Kiangsi Soviet in July 1934 and proceeded north-ward toward the Yangtze River. Although it was announced that Fang's unit had been dispatched to open resistance against the Japanese in north China, its real purpose was surely to test the escape routes from the Kiangsi blockade. The Vanguard was surrounded by Government forces in early 1935 in northeastern Kiangsi, and Fang was captured. He was taken to Nanch'ang, where he was paraded in the streets, exhibited in a bamboo cage, and finally executed on July 6, 1935. The leadership of his remaining forces passed to Su Yü, who later distinguished himself as one of the out-standing Communist generals in the civil war. Su led the survivors of the Vanguard into the Chekiang-Kiangsi-Fukien border region, where they continued to carry out guerrilla warfare under the over-all command of Hsiang Ying.[7]

The Kuomintang launched attacks upon these remnant troops from 1934 until the Japanese invasion, thereby forcing Hsiang Ying to move his base many times and constantly to divide his forces. Even the Sian Incident did not provide respite from KMT pressure. In April 1937 the Government sent some 250,000 troops under General Hsiung Shih-hui, the governor of Kiangsi, against Hsiang's ragged band of approximately 5,000 soldiers, then isolated in the mountainous area of the Fukien-Chekiang border.[8] It was not until two months after the Marco Polo Bridge incident that negotiations between Hsiang Ying and the Central Government were opened in order to bring the central China contingents of the Red Army into the United Front against Japan.

On the basis of orders received from the Party's Central Committee, Hsiang met with Hsiung Shih-hui—the representative of War Minister Ho Ying-ch'in—at Nanch'ang, during September 1937. On September 29, as a result of these talks, Chiang Kai-shek appointed Yeh T'ing com-mander and Hsiang Ying vice-commander of the "National Revolutionary New Fourth Army" (*kuo-min ko-ming hsin-pien ti-ssu-chün*), commonly shortened to New Fourth Army (*hsin-ssu-chün*).[9] Yeh was a well-known Communist military figure in the 1920's (his Eleventh Army was one of three units that revolted at Nanch'ang, August 1, 1927), but at the time of the formation of the New Fourth Army his Party membership had actually lapsed. Thus, he was a choice acceptable to both the Central Government and the Communist Party.[10]

Yeh T'ing established his headquarters at Nanch'ang in early 1938 and began calling in the various Red Army units scattered all over south China. Estimates of the number of troops collected vary from 4,000 to 12,000, the latter being the most commonly cited figure.[11] The Army was divided into four detachments on the basis of the areas from which the old Red Army men were regrouped and reorganized. The First Detachment, for example, which was commanded by Ch'en Yi, drew on Communist troops holding out in south Kiangsi; the Second Detachment, under Chang Ting-ch'eng, called in the soldiers of Su Yü and others in the Fukien-Chekiang border area. The latter unit established its headquarters for mustering the Red Army veterans at the old Soviet base of Lungyen in west Fukien, the one-time capital of the West Fukien (Minhsi) Soviet.[12] By April 1938 the reorganization of the New Fourth Army had been completed, and in May it went into action with guerrilla raids on the Nanking-Shanghai, Wuhu-Nanking, and Nanking-Hangchow railroads.[13] Thus, the New Fourth Army belatedly began to duplicate in central China the exploits of its elder brother in the north.

If we can accept the approximate accuracy of Japanese estimates of Communist troop strength (that is, of classified military estimates not made for propaganda purposes), both arms of the Communist Army increased in size at a fantastic rate. By the end of 1939, the Japanese Army and the Kōain were acknowledging the existence of a Communist force of several hundred thousand. On December 27, 1939, for instance, the North China Area Army published the following breakdown of the Communist forces: (a) 24,000 men in the 115th division, 26,300 men in the 120th division, and 30,600 men in the 129th division (a total of 80,900), all of whom constituted regular forces; (b) 7,100 men in regular units controlled by the Eighth Route Army; (c) 31,700 men in the Chin-Ch'a-Chi guerrilla army; (d) 20,000 men in units of the Shensi base; (e) 110,000 full-time guerrillas in Hopei, Shantung, Shansi, and Mengchiang (the Japanese puppet state in Inner Mongolia); and (f) 500,000–600,000 villagers in the rural self-defense corps. The approximate total of all varieties of Communist-affiliated military forces in north China at the end of 1939, according to the Japanese Army estimate, was 800,000.[14] A Kōain study two years later recapitulated the growth of the Communist Army in these figures: (a) troops of the Communist forces within the Japanese-occupied areas of north China at the end of 1939, 120,000 regulars and 160,000 guerrillas; (b) in the same area at the end of 1940, 140,000 regulars and 160,000 guerrillas; and (c) in both north and central China at the end of September 1941, a combined total of regulars and guerrillas of not less than 350,000.[15] Unlike the North China Area Army study, the Kōain study was not an operational estimate made by the Army, and does not include village-based forces; nevertheless, both estimates reveal that a very rapid increase in

Communist troop strength had occurred. We shall next examine the internal machinery of the Communist Army that facilitated this rapid expansion.

ORGANIZATION FOR POLITICAL WORK WITHIN THE COMMUNIST ARMY

As we have seen, there were three main types of Communist-controlled troops: regulars, guerrillas, and militia. The differences among these types of forces were very important, although such differences sometimes became blurred in the actual context of a given guerrilla area. Ideally speaking, the regulars were the uniformed, fully mobile divisions built around the old Red Army cadres. Known as "field forces," these units were the best equipped and best officered of the Communist Army, and they were transferred from one area to another in response to military developments. The guerrillas, on the other hand, constituted full-time military units, but were restricted to the area in which they were mobilized (e.g., the Chin-Ch'a-Chi Army) and were not usually uniformed. Some guerrillas had military leaders sent from the Eighth Route Army, others did not. Often guerrilla corps were set up prior to the arrival of Communist forces; when they were subsequently incorporated into the Communist Army, their original leaders were sometimes retained if they were Communists already or were prepared to join the Party. In other cases, we shall see in Shangtung, the leadership was more often shared with, or replaced by, Eighth Route Army officers.

The militia consisted of local men and women who participated in military activities only when the need arose. Most of the time they engaged in their regular farming occupations. They also carried out military support operations, such as collecting intelligence, controlling movements between villages (by means of an elaborate passport system), and mining highways, on a part-time basis.[16] Service in the militia was only one of the wartime activities in which most people in the Communist-controlled areas participated. An individual peasant militiaman was also a member of one of the so-called "mass movement organizations," such as the Peasants' National Salvation Association, the Women's National Salvation Association, or the Youth National Salvation Association. Militia units were generally established in response to a resolution passed by the mass movement associations, and it was from these organizations that militiamen were recruited. The militia units should therefore be regarded as one of the series of organizations included under the general heading of mass movement associations, rather than as part of the Communist Army.

The guerrillas and the militia were the most important organizational media for nationalistic mobilization of the masses. It was as participants in the work of these groups that the peasants came into contact with the "national enemy" and participated in the work of the resistance. It was the regular forces, however, that provided the organizing leadership for the mass associations and that assisted in the reorganization of local guerrilla bands. The regular Communist armies contained specific units whose mission it was to encourage and to guide the local populations in the organization of resistance, and to indoctrinate the huge numbers of new recruits that joined the regular forces. Such training and propaganda activities were the special duties of the "political departments" attached to all Communist military units.

Although the size and form of organization of the regular Communist forces varied greatly, all units had some political personnel at every level of the military hierarchy. In order to understand the function of the political departments, we must first look at the hierarchy itself, which was at least as complex as that of any fully mechanized Western army. The highest operational unit was the brigade (*lü-t'uan*), which was made up of three regiments. (The counterpart of the brigade in the guerrilla forces was the "detachment," *chih-tui,* while the equivalent of the regular division was the guerrilla "column," *tsung-tui.* Otherwise, terminology used by the guerrillas was the same as that of the field forces.) The three oversized regular Eighth Route Army divisions were not operational units—they were much too large to be used effectively in the style of warfare employed by the Eighth Route Army. Each of these divisions contained from two to three brigades, which were the largest independent formations in the Communist Army.

Each detachment or brigade was divided into three regiments (*t'uan*), each regiment into three battalions (*ying*), each battalion into three companies (*lien*), each company into three platoons (*p'ai*), and each platoon into three squads (*pan*) of 13 to 16 men each (plus headquarters and staff personnel at each level). In 1945, United States intelligence officers classified Chinese Communist regiments into three types according to size, quality of equipment, and specific mission. Type A regiments numbered 1,763 officers and men, Type B regiments 1,163 officers and men, and Type C regiments 866 officers and men.[17]

Today we can supplement this information with specific details of one large Eighth Route Army unit—the Third Column (guerrilla) that operated in central Hopei. On the basis of records captured near Shulu hsien (Hsinchi), Hopei, on October 17, 1938, and other materials gathered by the Japanese Miiltary Police, the organization of the Third Column was reconstructed by the Japanese Army in 1938.[18] These records show that one detachment was made up of three regiments of 2,304 men each and 415 headquarters personnel. Although the over-all size of this detachment (7,327) appears to be excessive when compared with other Communist units, no other information on the Third Column in Hopei contradicts this figure. Moreover, with regard to detachments as such, we have the following comment by Evans Carlson, who traveled in the guerrilla areas in 1938: "In addition to the regiment here at Lintsing [Linch'ing, Shantung], the Eighth Route Army had two *chih tuis* (a *chih tui* is a flexible military unit which may number anywhere from a thousand to ten-thousand men, depending on the mission) operating in north-east Shantung. Another unit was in the Taian [T'aian] district."[19] Actually, all the units that Carlson mentions were part of the Shantung guerrilla column and not elements of the three regular Eighth Route Army divisions; but it does appear from his observations that guerrilla detachments were sometimes as large as 10,000 men. However, on the basis of both U.S. Army and Japanese estimates, we may place the approximate size of the *average* Chinese Communist regiment at 2,000 officers and men.

The political education of the 2,000 men of such a regiment was well provided for by a variety of political personnel, by soldiers' clubs, and by newspapers, training manuals, and the like. A Japanese study observed: "The most distinctive feature of the Communist Army . . . is the existence in each unit of propaganda agitators and organizers."[20] These political workers were not exactly analogous to the familiar political commissars of the Soviet Army; the Chinese Communist political officers had both a different origin and a different function. As will be recalled, the Russians utilized political commissars to oversee and to guarantee the loyalty of the large numbers of ex-Tsarist officers brought into the Red Army in 1919. The problem of the political loyalty of these officers was discussed at the Eighth Party Congress in March 1919, when Trotsky supported the need for technically competent personnel. By August 1920, as a result of Party decisions, some 48,409 ex-Tsarist officers were in command of the Red Army. Their loyalty was supervised by political commissars and by a ruthless system of hostages.[21]

Instead of being a Party watchdog over non-Communist officers, the

Chinese regimental political officer had an educative function. He was a descendant of the "Party representative" attached to units of the KMT National Revolutionary Army at the time of the Northern Expedition (1926). The inspiration for using political personnel in the Kuomintang armies was, of course, Russian, since the KMT's Whampoa Military Academy was under Russian guidance; but the activities and purposes of KMT political workers differed from those of the Soviet political commissars. As F. F. Liu points out with regard to the KMT political officers, "These commissars took up the task of organizing the soldiers into party cells, educating them politically, teaching them to read and write, and acting as guardians and spokesmen for the underprivileged soldiers. . . . Their duties were all part of their dual purpose of reforming the army through bettering its morale and of strengthening party loyalty. At the same time they won the reputation of keeping the soldiers' welfare at heart."[22] The Communists themselves claim that their political commissars date from this early KMT practice. Fifteen years after the Northern Expedition, the Eighth Route Army included the following information in one of its catechismic troop indoctrination manuals: "What is the political commissar system? The political commissar system is the successor to the Party representative system of the National Revolutionary Army at the time of the Great Revolution [1926–27]."[23]

In addition to his main task of troop education, the political officer was also the Communist Party's representative in the army. As such, he certainly exercised a supervisory function similar to that of the political commissar in present-day Soviet armed forces. The political officer's direct access to the highest Party organs was the essential feature of this aspect of his work. However, since most of the high-ranking military leaders in the Eighth Route Army were also members of the Communist Party and had at least as much seniority as the average political officer, it is unlikely that the political officer had to exercise his powers of supervision except on lower levels.[24]

The official Eighth Route Army explanation for the system of parallel military and political officers extending down as far as each company was that it was a prerequisite for guerrilla warfare. Communist spokesmen told the Yenan press party of July 1944 that "no guerrilla army can fight successfully, or even last long, without the support of the people of the areas in which they campaign. Eighteenth Group Army [the Chungking designation for the entire Communist Army] indoctrination is primarily aimed at training the troops to act in such a manner that they will gain this total support."[25] If the short-term object of political training was to gain popular acceptance, its long-term effect was to revolutionize the attitudes of Army recruits and Chinese civilians toward the Army. The old image of the Army as a mercenary corps serving the particular interests of an individual or a class was destroyed. It was replaced by a conception of the Army as the servant of national interests—an Army that was scrupulous about its relations with civilians. This was a new concept for China.

There were two categories of personnel who carried out political policy within the Army. The first were the political officers or commissars (*cheng-chih wei-yüan*); and the second were the members of the political department (*cheng-chih-pu*), a unit composed of a chief and several subordinates. The political officer or commissar was attached only to units of regimental size or larger; and, according to official Communist manuals, he was chiefly concerned with the formation of policy and the supervision of lesser political personnel. For example, the New Fourth Army's guidebook, *Cheng-chih kung-tso tsu-chih kang-yao ts'ao-an* (Draft Summary of the Organization of Political Work), lists the following powers and duties of the political officer:[26] (*a*) the power to issue political orders on his own initiative; (*b*) the chairmanship of the unit's political meetings with the power of final decision; (*c*) the responsibility for commanding, supervising, and inspecting the work of political organs at the same level; (*d*) the responsibility for investigating and correcting breaches of general morals and rules among the troops, and for correcting bad political tendencies; (*e*) the duty, as the highest representative of the Party, of leading and supervising Party work in the army; and (*f*) the responsibility, jointly with the head of the political department, for the appointment and dismissal of political work personnel.[27] The political officer had few contacts with the Army rank-and-file; his main concerns were with policy and strategy.

The personnel of the political departments, on the other hand, actually implemented the measures designed to indoctrinate the troops and the civilian population in the area in which an army unit was located. Political departments existed at the division (column), detachment (brigade), and regimental levels (at the regimental level they were known as "political offices," *cheng-chih ch'u*); and their officers supervised the lower-level "political instructors" (*cheng-chih chih-tao-yüan*) who were attached to battalions and companies.[28] Below the company, there were "political fighters" (*cheng-chih chan-shih*) in each platoon or squad, as well as a soldiers' club (*chü-le-pu*) at the company level, which had important ideological functions. The political fighters and the soldiers' club were both under the general supervision of the company political instructor.

A political department or political office at any level of the military hierarchy had four standard subdivisions: organization, propaganda and education, mass movement, and enemy work. The general types of duties and jurisdiction of each of these sections (*k'o*) may be summarized as follows:

(*a*) *The Organization Section*: Army organization, and the appointment and dismissal of personnel.

(*b*) *The Propaganda and Education Section*: ideological education of troops, practical education (i.e., reading instruction), and internal propaganda (i.e., news of the international situation, war news of China, KMT-CCP collaboration, etc.).

(*c*) *The Mass Movement Section*: military-civilian cooperation, propaganda for civilians, civil organization, and military and civilian discipline.

(*d*) *The Enemy Work Section*: propaganda for Japanese and puppet troops, and instruction in the Japanese language.[29]

To clarify further the functions of a large political department, here are excerpts from the list of official duties of a division's political department: (*a*) the setting up of a training plan for the entire division, including the preparation of teaching materials; (*b*) the compilation of propaganda outlines in accordance with higher-level propaganda policies; (*c*) leadership and management of newspaper publishing; and (*d*) "*leadership of the propaganda, organization, and war participation work among the neighboring people, including the armed self-defense units, and joint execution with regional government, Party, and military organizations . . . of the resistance movement.*"[30] In addition to the four standard operating sections, some large political departments had other subordinate units such as theatrical troupes ("War Area Service Units") and military courts.[31] In short, the political department was a large, diversified appendage to all military formations, charged with a variety of tasks that ranged from teaching reading to the troops to propagandizing the civilian population.

The troops themselves received their indoctrination at the company level. In a company the political officer was called a "political instructor." His duties included giving political instruction to the soldiers, maintaining a "high activist spirit" in the company, guaranteeing strict compliance with the policy of good treatment of prisoners of war, and raising the cultural level of the unit.[32] To assist him in carrying out these tasks, the political instructor had a propaganda unit (usually five men) under his direct control. This unit was subdivided into an "enemy forces work group" for propaganda directed to the Japanese and puppet armies, and a "mass movement work group" for propaganda directed to the local residents. Also under the political instructor's supervision were the "political fighters" attached to each platoon or squad. The political fighter had no administrative functions; he was an activist, or "progressive," selected from the ranks to set an example for his fellow soldiers. He also reported to the company political instructor on the political attitudes of the soldiers. The political fighter's duties were to communicate instructions from higher levels to the soldiers; to report the current news; to direct sports, singing, newspaper-reading, and self-criticism activities; to lead platoon political meetings; to interpret important speeches for the troops; and to investigate breaches of discipline in the surrounding area.[33]

Another company-level political organ was the Soldiers' Club, a troop-organized, troop-governed association for all members of the company. It was designed to promote political education in off-duty hours, and a special room was often reserved for it in the barracks. The idea of a club or recreation center for political activities by the troops dates from the time of the Red Army in south China. In that period, the company recreation hall was known as the Lenin Room.[34] The wartime Soldiers' Club was similar in function to the Lenin Room; the main change was that the photographs of Marx and Lenin, and the red flags, were replaced by nationalistic trappings. The club was operated by a committee of seven to nine men elected by the entire company to serve for three months. The range of activities undertaken by the club is illustrated by the types of subcommittees that were set up within a standard Club Management Committee:

(*a*) *Hygiene Subcommittee*: for carrying out sanitation duties in the company area.

(*b*) *Economic Subcommittee*: for supervising the preparation of food and the company's budgeting.

(*c*) *Wall Newspaper Subcommittee*: for compiling and posting wall newspapers.

(*d*) *Culture and Recreation Subcommittee*: for organizing reading instruction, evening assemblies, self-criticism ("study") meetings, etc.

(*e*) *Physical Training Subcommittee*: for leading off-duty sports.

The Club Management Committee was guided by the company political instructor, but according to all sources the committee itself was popularly elected.[35]

By having a political department in every company (130 men), the Communist Army guaranteed the good behavior of its troops among the general population and also ensured that the peasant recruit would gain a political understanding of the war that had forced him to take up arms. Merely having a newspaper read to him every day had an important effect upon the illiterate peasant; and the entire range of political pressures experienced in the Army transformed the socially mobilized peasant into a nationally-conscious resistance fighter. Army political operations had an analogous impact upon the lives of mobilized civilians in the war areas.

COMMUNIST ARMY POLITICAL WORK AMONG RURAL CIVILIANS

The Eighth Route Army invaded the Japanese-occupied territories of north China in 1937–38, and the New Fourth Army infiltrated the downstream banks of the Yangtze during 1938–39. As the Communists moved into a new area, they attempted to secure the support of the local population for guerrilla warfare. Where their initial attempts at gaining influence were successful, they proceeded to establish self-defense corps, to drive other guerrillas from the area, and to set up local "democratic governments"—in short, to incorporate the territory and its inhabitants into the Communist sphere of influence. The factor that determined whether or not the Communist efforts succeeded was the social mobilization of the peasantry. Peasant mobilization in response to the Japanese menace, combined with the Communist readiness to lead the nationalistic upsurge in the countryside, was the essential ingredient of the wartime Communist-peasant alliance.

As we have seen, the Communist Army's political departments contained special sections known as Mass Movement Work Sections, which were charged with carrying out the Party's efforts at organizing the peasantry. Training manuals were written for cadres who worked in these mass movement sections, and a copy of one of them from the New Fourth Army—*Teaching Guide for Mass Movement Work*—was captured and translated into Japanese by the Kōain in 1941.[36] It is a valuable source of information concerning the form of wartime collaboration between the Communists and the peasants.

According to this manual, mass movement work was divided into two general types, one type for "war areas" (*chan ch'ü*), the other for "guerrilla areas" (*yu-chi ch'ü*). The war areas were those regions not actually occupied by the Japanese Army, such as the Communist strongholds in Wut'ai, Shantung, and Shensi. The guerrilla areas were territories occupied by the Japanese or frequently mopped up by them, or territories in which there was a strong puppet authority, such as in central Hopei.[37] The objectives of mass movement work differed in these two types of areas (both of which were part of the total area behind the Japanese front lines). In the war areas, the mobilized masses were to engage in military support operations, such as road construction work, defense of communication lines, care and treatment of the wounded, and guide duties. In addition, and perhaps most important, peasants in these areas saw to the regular production of food. In the event of a Communist Army withdrawal from a war area, the mass organizations were responsible for carrying out salvage operations and for destroying roads, bridges, and crops to prevent their use by the Japanese. Both guerrilla corps and self-defense forces (militia) were organized in these bases, and they continued guerrilla warfare if the regular field troops were forced to withdraw.[38]

In the guerrilla areas the masses, having experienced Japanese brutality, usually had a heightened sense of opposition to the enemy. However, Japanese destruction could have mixed effects; and the manual gives this warning: "As a result of enemy pressure and deception, wavering attitudes of compromise grow easily among capitulationist elements."[39] A combination of two circumstances made the guerrilla areas favorable for mass organization: the existence of spontaneously created armed self-defense units and the fact that Japanese military garrisons were usually confined to towns and to lines of communication. On the other hand, since Japanese troop strength was weak, anarchic conditions, including banditry, were common; and the economic structure was frequently near collapse.

The main aims of the Communists in these areas were to wage resistance warfare and to institute anti-traitor measures. The duties performed by mobilized peasants in the guerrilla areas included cutting communications, burning bridges, countering Japanese and puppet propaganda, using booby traps and other terrorist devices against the enemy, and seizing and executing traitors. Also, whenever possible, direct guerrilla raids were mounted. In this connection, the cadres' manual notes: "When carrying out military actions, it is not absolutely necessary to employ modern weapons; old-fashioned firearms, spears, knives, poles, axes, hoes, and stones can all kill enemy soldiers."[40]

If conditions permitted, the Communists also encouraged the establishment of anti-Japanese political authorities and permanent bases of operation in the guerrilla areas. These bases not only served as sanctuaries for the Communists, but also deprived the Japanese of exploitable territory. As the training manual points out:

> The enemy has adopted a policy of living off the land in areas that he has occupied and, by means of traitor and puppet organizations, of utilizing our manpower, financial strength, and resources to satisfy his military needs. Therefore, by mobilizing the broad masses and strengthening our internal unity, we must break this link with the enemy, and blockade him. By exterminating spies and traitors and by destroying all puppet organizations, we must isolate the enemy politically and blockade him economically and militarily. The result will be that the enemy cannot exploit a single tree or blade of grass that belongs to us.[41]

Although there were differences of emphasis, the methods employed by the Army's mass movement sections were fundamentally the same for the war areas and the guerrilla areas. In the war areas, mass movement workers did not have to concern themselves with access to the population (for instance, with infiltration), and there were no puppet political organs to complicate their work. Also, since they were in a more stable military environment, political workers used more refined propaganda techniques, such as printed newspapers and magazines, dramatic performances, and lectures by pro-Communist prisoners of war. However, in both kinds of areas, the main constituent of the Communists' mass organization work was a propaganda appeal for joint action against the national enemy; resistance to Japan provided the common ground on which cooperation between Communists and peasants was based.[42] It is instructive to note that the word "communism" is virtually absent from the political workers' training manual; with regard to improving the peasants' lot, the manual states: "The basic rule is, 'The interests of the people are superior to anything else, but even they are subordinate to the interests of the Resistance War.' "[43] Peasant strikes or slowdowns, for example, were not permitted. The manual warns political workers against seeming to sanction the exploitation of the peasantry and thereby leaving the Communist Party open to attack from "Trotskyites and other destructive elements," but it reasserts that the greatest danger is the introduction of violent, left-wing material that might give rise to internal opposition and disunity.[44]

In opening up a guerrilla area, the Army would first receive a request from a local delegation for military assistance and then await a decision from Party organs to expand into a particular region. After that, the Army's military and political departments would determine the method of access to be employed. The most convenient method was to detach a propaganda unit from its regiment and to leave it behind while the main force retreated before the enemy's advance. Another method was to send a regular column deep into occupied territory, and still another was for army political cadres to infiltrate into their native regions, where they would attempt to mobilize the masses without military backing.[45]

A great deal of preparation was required before beginning operations, since the cadres were supposed to have detailed knowledge of local politics, economic conditions, and specific grievances. Above all, they had to be able to use regional dialects and to communicate with the majority of the people.[46] A New Fourth Army guide entitled "Problems of Working with Youth in Peasant Villages"[47] emphasizes that the decision to enter a village must be carefully considered. It was necessary to obtain full information on the political, economic, and cultural life of the village, as well as on the general strength of pro-Japanese sentiment in the village. Even after this preparation, only experienced and trained workers were supposed to take positive action in the initial stages.[48] This same manual also stresses that political workers were to dress and talk like peasants, and were to pay attention to the problem of local superstitions.[49]

After the Army entered an area, mass movement workers scrutinized the local social environment in order to find people who supported the resistance. The cadres' training manual points out that "the broad peasant class is the chief object of mass movement work, but the peasantry has two distinctive characteristics: (a) a conservative or nativistic viewpoint, and (b) limited organization with no clear perception of the future."[50] To get around this difficulty, the manual advises cadres to direct their initial efforts to the handicraft workers, middle-school students, small businessmen, and "self-respecting" bureaucrats and landlords who sense the existence of a "national crisis." The support of such people would facilitate work with the peasants in general.[51]

In addition to wooing such high-status groups, the political worker also had to pay attention to vagrants and bandits. Vagrants, including deserters, lacked "national consciousness" but could be easily convinced by money. It was considered important to attempt to show them the reasons for serving the resistance, but it was of equal importance to prevent them from serving the enemy.[52] In one way or another they were to be brought into the mass associations. Bandits presented a different problem. As the manual points out, banditry usually arose because enemy political control and the masses' self-defense capacity were weak. The general policy of the New Fourth Army was that "all bandits can join in resisting Japan." If the bandits were aiding the enemy, they had to be crushed quickly; but if they wanted to participate in the resistance, they were to be incorporated into guerrilla columns and reorganized. Since discipline was the greatest problem, bandits were to be sent to fighting areas for combat. In Communist bases, where anti-Japanese political authority was strong, bandits were not tolerated; but they were encouraged in guerrilla or enemy-dominated territories.[53]

One of the most difficult problems faced by political organizers was the existence of local armed units or secret societies who were in control of an area prior to the arrival of the Communist Army. In general, Communist policy toward local guerrilla units was to absorb them and to secure their cooperation in the establishment of a base.[54] Of course, once the Communists were in an area, a local unit usually had to decide whether to join them or the puppets; if they attempted to remain independent, they invited destruction at the hands of a Japanese mop-up while the Communists stood idly by.[55] The Communists took a different attitude toward the secret societies. Although there were fairly large numbers of Red Spears in Honan, and many armed members of the Green Gang (Ch'ing Pang) in central and south China, as well as a few representatives of virtually every known secret society in Shantung,[56] the Army advised cadres to adopt a hands-off policy toward them. The cadres' manual contains the following information:

> The Red Spears, Big Swords, Lien-chuang-hui [United Village Associations], etc., are all simple, armed, self-defense organizations of the peasants, and they have a very long history in peasant villages. Since the Incident, they have undergone rapid development and commonly exist in all parts of the guerrilla areas. Their main objectives are the forcible collection of taxes and opposition to disturbances caused by troops or bandits. Therefore, they are opposed to Japanese imperialist aggression, but if they are not encroached upon by the enemy, they offer no resistance and fight only if attacked. Politically, they are neu-

tral, and they are led, for the most part, by rich peasants . . . The strongest force in these groups is a kind of superstition, and as a result their conservatism is particularly intense.[57]

The New Fourth Army's orders to its own political workers concerning secret societies included these instructions: maintain Army discipline; do not try to execute mass organization too hastily; "do not insult their religious beliefs and superstitions, but respect their creeds and leaders"; if they are attacked by the Japanese or by traitor enemies, help them to resist; heighten their national consciousness and lead them gradually to resist the Japanese.[58] This was, of course, only wartime policy; on January 4, 1949, the North China People's Government banned all "feudalistic" secret societies.[59]

The end product of a successful organization campaign was the creation of so-called mass movement associations. The most common mass organizations were "National Salvation Associations," based on occupation, sex, or age group—i.e., associations for peasants, women, young people, workers, teachers, merchants, and cultural workers.[60] These were large, hierarchically structured organizations with little internal democracy; their chief function was to educate their members both politically and by giving them training in reading and other skills relevant to their work. From these associations supplemental units such as self-defense corps, stretcher units, and transportation corps were recruited. The mass associations contributed to guerrilla base "government" by electing representatives to assemblies, although it was not actually intended that either the mass associations or the assemblies should exercise real political power. The purpose of the elections and assemblies was to afford the population a sense of direct participation in the resistance movement and thereby to ensure continued popular support for the Communist Army. Michael Lindsay, who was in the guerrilla areas from 1942 to 1944, describes the nature and function of the mass associations as follows:

> The mass movement organisations are the means by which the [Communist] government carries out its work of popular organisation and political education. . . . The total number [of people] in these organisations is very large. According to figures published in July 1942 there were over ten and a half million in the civil organisations and eight million in the military organisations. (The two figures overlap as a man who was in the self-defense corps or militia would also be in the farmers' or workers' union.) . . . Membership in the self-defense corps

is practically compulsory for able-bodied men in the Shansi-Chahar-Hopei [Chin-Ch'a-Chi] area and the corps is responsible for the observer service which reports Japanese movements and for the passport control system which is designed to restrict the movement of Japanese agents.[61]

Mass associations were first developed in Chin-Ch'a-Chi and were subsequently organized in every area through which the Communist Army passed. During the war the real nature of mass organizations was unclear to Western observers, who often equated these activities with the growth of democracy.[62] In actual fact, the government of an area such as the Chin-Ch'a-Chi Border Region was scarcely more democratic than the Chungking Government, although there was much greater contact between the leadership and the people in the Communist areas. Both the Nationalists and the border-region government possessed elected advisory congresses, but actual political and military power was in the hands of self-appointed elites. The mass associations' real contribution to Chinese political life was not democracy but, as the Communists themselves have stated, the structuring of mass mobilization.

Despite the size that some mass associations achieved, organization actually began on a very small scale. According to a contemporary Japanese analysis of the situation in central China, "When the New Fourth Army first reaches a certain village, the political workers distribute anti-Japanese and anti-Wang leaflets. Then they reduce taxes by 20 to 30 per cent and distribute food and other necessities to refugees and the poor."[63] Following that, they would call a mass assembly at which they delivered anti-Japanese propaganda speeches and taught villagers anti-Japanese and national-salvation songs. The next stage was to gather weapons from public and private sources and to arm the young men of the village. These youths were organized into self-defense and guerrilla units, and at the same time "Resistance Leagues" of peasants, merchants, workers, and women were set up. Organizers then spread out into the area surrounding the village, where they gathered new recruits for the mass societies. People who did not obey or who interfered with this work were labeled "Chinese traitors" (*Han-chien*), and were subject to harassment.[64] In their analysis of this procedure, the Japanese do not consider the attitudes of villagers prior to the New Fourth Army's arrival, but we know that in central China (except in the Shanghai triangle) the masses were less mobilized than in the north. Also, the New Fourth Army had many more Nationalist competitors than the Eighth Route Army, and as a consequence it had greater trouble projecting itself as a purely nationalistic, anti-Japanese force.

Occasionally, the New Fourth Army failed in its mass movement efforts. According to a presumably authentic proclamation captured by the Japanese and published in *Jōhō* in 1941, the citizens of an Anhwei village withdrew their support from the New Fourth Army out of disgust with its practices. The Japanese Army acquired the notice—entitled "Declaration of Withdrawal from the Party by Cadres of the Communist Party's Shou Hsien District Committee"—in Chuchiachi village, Shou hsien, on August 18, 1941. It was signed by one Sung Lung-t'ing and 300 others. According to this declaration, the residents of Shou hsien affiliated with the New Fourth Army in 1938, following the Japanese withdrawal from the area. The Japanese had burned many houses in the hsien and anti-Japanese sentiment was high. According to the declaration, the Communists sent political workers from "north Shensi," who organized anti-Japanese units in the hsien and rounded up wavering elements. Sung Lung-t'ing and others were "deceived" by these Party organizers and joined the Party, while others in the hsien joined workers' and peasants' leagues. By 1941, however, local residents had reacted violently against the Communist Party. The villagers specifically charged the Party and the Army with plotting an organizational expansion under the guise of supporting the resistance; and they accused the Communists of killing local administrative personnel, commandeering the people's weapons, and attacking friendly armies.[65]

It is possible, of course, that this particular document is a Japanese forgery (although *Jōhō* was a confidential publication), but it is not unreasonable to assume that Communist organizing efforts occasionally failed. In view of the Communists' great reliance upon the individual political worker's talent and incorruptibility, it is perhaps surprising that they were able to spread over such a vast territory without encountering more defections than they did.

FOUR

The Growth of Communist-Controlled Territory in North China

Between 1937 and 1945, north China was witness to a confrontation between two expanding political domains: that of the Chinese Communists and that of the Japanese. The Communists and the Japanese, having squeezed out the Kuomintang as a third participant early in the war, fought between themselves on the basis of winner-take-all. When the Japanese finally were defeated in the Pacific War, the Chinese Communists did take all of north China (except for certain major cities that the KMT managed to reoccupy and to hold for a few years). North China thus became the chief Communist stronghold in the civil war of 1947–49. The present chapter is a general survey of the initial Communist expansion in north China, with particular emphasis upon the political institutions created by the Communists. Our object is to trace the tremendous growth of Communist power and influence during the war, and at the same time to relate this development to the social mobilization of the Chinese peasants.

The first sign that social mobilization is occurring or has occurred, in whatever geographical setting, is that the mobilized population begins to participate to a much greater degree than in the past in the political life of the society. As Deutsch has remarked, "In whatever country it occurs, social mobilization brings with it an expansion of the politically relevant strata of the population. These politically relevant strata are a broader group than the elite: they include all those persons who must be taken into account in politics."[1] The peasants of China, who did not participate actively in Chinese politics prior to the war, became the primary political population during the war and remain so in the postwar Chinese Communist state.

Unfortunately, in studying the process of Chinese peasant mobilization, we are unable to examine directly the changes in political vision that the peasants underwent. This is not always the case. Researchers sometimes have statistical indications of the spread of literacy, of changes in the standard of living, of the development of communications, and of the causes and extent of migration; they usually have access to reasonably objective studies by native and foreign historians of major social cataclysms that have influenced the population. For wartime China this type of material is not available, and the Communists themselves are content with their own theory of their origins and of the contribution of the peasantry to the revolution. Thus, it is necessary to infer, where we can, what the nature of the peasant transformation was. In this undertaking we are greatly aided by the availability of quantities of raw data compiled by the Japanese Army as part of its war effort against the Chinese. During the crucial period 1937–41, the Japanese Army was the one important agency (except for the Chinese political actors themselves) seriously interested in day-to-day developments in the villages of north China.

The Japanese Army Archives reveal that the Chinese Communist Army carried out successful guerrilla operations against the Japanese Army, and that the Communist forces created numerous large, popularly supported anti-Japanese enclaves in each of the provinces of north China. This information, the details of which are presented below, allows us to make certain general inferences about the role of the peasantry in these activities. In the first place, we know from both Mao's works and a comparative study of guerrilla warfare that successful guerrilla operations require the closest cooperation between the active guerrillas and the local inhabitants. Since the Chinese Communists did conduct successful guerrilla operations, we may conclude that widespread Communist-peasant collaboration existed. In the second place, we have the fact of some 19 guerrilla bases established behind the Japanese lines, particularly in north China. Japanese reports indicate that these bases were usually expansions of areas already held by local non-Communist guerrillas, and that the Communist base governments were overwhelmingly supported by their large populations. Thus, a *prima facie* case exists that the Chinese peasantry played a greater role in the war than could have been anticipated in 1937; the peasantry was, as we have suggested, socially mobilized by the war. In studying the expansion of Communist territory in north China, we are thus seeking information that will elucidate the wartime activities of the CCP and that will also reveal the extent of peasant involvement in the war.

Another question of major importance, which is discussed more fully in

Chapter Five, is that of the incipient civil war between Kuomintang and
Communist forces. As we have seen, an analysis of the Chinese and Yugoslav Communist revolutions in terms of mass nationalism affords, among
other things, an insight into the processes whereby the prewar governments
were discredited on popular grounds during the war. When we compare
the strength of the CCP and KMT positions with regard to their defense
of mass nationalist goals, we are able to understand the "inexplicable ca-
pitulations" of KMT troops to the Communists that occurred during the
civil war. It is not possible to account for the Communist victory over the
Nationalists on grounds of military prowess alone; the fact was that the
Communists had won increasing recognition among the uncommitted as
the party that spoke for China. This was the contest that counted, and
when this contest was lost, the KMT (which never admitted that a contest
could exist on these grounds) was finished. In this chapter we review certain of the early armed clashes between KMT and CCP guerrillas that
promoted the rupture between Yenan and Chungking and that eventually
led to the New Fourth Army Incident. Although the early incidents considered here grew as much out of the anarchic conditions of the occupied
areas as they did from KMT-CCP rivalry, they contributed to the suspicions
that gave rise to the larger incidents. And in the large clashes, such as the
New Fourth Army Incident, the long-range victor was not the party that
sustained the fewest casualties, but the party that could project itself as the
true champion of Chinese nationalism.

THE CHIN-CH'A-CHI GUERRILLA BASE

When the Sino-Japanese war broke out in the summer of 1937, the
Communist forces were concentrated in central Shensi province, a back-
water of China in the loop of the Yellow River. Following the Japanese
invasion of Hopei, the CCP troops were integrated into the national military
force, to be employed against the invader in the same manner as were the
Nationalist and provincial armies. At this time they were made part of
the Second War Zone Army (in Shansi) and placed under the supreme
command of Yen Hsi-shan, Governor of Shansi province and Commander
of the Second War Zone. General Chu Teh, the Communist commander-
in-chief, was named Vice-Commander of the Second War Zone.

It was logical that the Eighth Route Army should be used in Shansi
province, which is just across the Yellow River from the Communist base
in Shensi; it was also a complicating element—but one that would soon

be turned to Communist advantage. In 1937, Shansi province was, in reality, not a part of the Republic of China, but a separate state under the domination of a single man, Yen Hsi-shan; and it had been in that status since the revolution of 1911.[2] Yen allied himself with the Nanking Government in 1928, only to revolt against it in 1930–31. Although this breach was smoothed over after the Japanese invasion of Manchuria, Yen never allowed the Kuomintang to develop Party strength in his province; relations between Nanking and T'aiyüan, Yen's capital, were more akin to those between sovereign states than between a national and a provincial seat of government. Yen's grip on the province in 1937 was weaker than it had been a decade earlier—for reasons that will be discussed later—but he was still in command.

The special political climate of Shansi was not the only thing about the province that made it ideal for the inauguration of guerrilla warfare by the Communists. The province was also one of the most swiftly overrun but sparsely occupied of all the areas invaded by the Japanese. By March 1938, both the north-south and east-west railroads in Shansi were in Japanese hands; and T'aiyüan was the headquarters of the Japanese First Army. However, in conquering Shansi, the Japanese did not actually defeat the Chinese Army; they simply caused a lot of Chinese soldiers to scatter into the mountains, where they remained while the Japanese occupied the raillines and the large cities. Yen Hsi-shan and most of his lieutenants fled to the relative safety of southwestern Shansi.

The Communists entered Shansi simultaneously with the Japanese occupation of the cities; the three divisions of the Eighth Route Army crossed the Yellow River and entered Shansi in the first few days of September 1937. The 115th division under Lin Piao advanced straight to Wut'aishan, the famous sacred mountain and Buddhist sanctuary in northeast Shansi; and it saw its first action against the Japanese at P'inghsingkuan, a few miles north of Wut'ai.[3] The other two Eighth Route Army divisions dispersed into different sectors of the province. Ho Lung's 120th division went to the northwestern part of Shansi, where it secured the communications routes between the main Communist base in Shensi and the Shansi battle areas. Liu Po-ch'eng's 129th division went toward the southeast, where, in October, it engaged the Japanese column (20th division) invading Shansi along the Chengt'ai railroad. Following the Japanese breakthrough on the Chengt'ai, the 129th division established its base in the T'aihang mountains north of Ch'angchih.

TABLE 3

THE EIGHTH ROUTE ARMY, SEPTEMBER 1937

Chinese Communist Party Central Committee, Military
Affairs Committee: Mao Tse-tung, Chairman

Eighth Route Army Headquarters

Commander: Chu Teh
Vice-Commander: P'eng Te-huai
Chief of Staff: Yeh Chien-ying
Chief, Political Department: Wang Chia-hsiang

115th Division

Commander: Lin Piao
Vice-Commander: Nieh Jung-chen
Political Commissar: Nieh Jung-chen
    Commander, 343d Brigade: Ch'en Kuang
    Commander, 344th Brigade: Hsü Hai-tung

120th Division

Commander: Ho Lung
Vice-Commander: Hsiao K'o
Political Commissar: Kuan Hsiang-ying
    Commander, 358th Brigade: Hsiao K'o
    Commander, 359th Brigade: Wang Chen

129th Division

Commander: Liu Po-ch'eng
Vice-Commander: Hsü Hsiang-ch'ien
Political Commissar: Teng Hsiao-p'ing
    Commander, 385th Brigade: Hsü Hsiang-ch'ien
    Commander, 386th Brigade: Ch'en Keng

After the battle of P'inghsingkuan, General Lin Piao of the 115th division detached a small force under his Deputy Commander, Nieh Jung-chen, and ordered it to infiltrate the Wut'ai area of Shansi and the Foup'ing area in the extreme west of Hopei. Lin then led the rest of the 115th division to the mountainous Shansi-Honan border area, where he temporarily left his 343d and 344th brigades (under Ch'en Kuang and Hsü Hai-tung, respectively) to operate independently. Lin himself returned to Yenan to head the Anti-Japanese Military-Political University (K'angta), and the two brigades remained, with the 129th division, in southeast Shansi, where they set up a major army base. The field headquarters of the Eighth Route Army, commanded by P'eng Te-huai, was organized at this time in the T'aihang mountain stronghold; and it was from this area that special Eighth Route Army task forces were later sent to Shantung to make contact with the guerrillas there.[4] Before considering these movements, however, it is necessary to investigate the extremely important operations undertaken by Nieh Jung-chen and his soldiers in northeast Shansi.

Estimates of the number of troops that remained with Nieh in Wut'ai vary considerably. One Japanese study says that Nieh's force was two battalions (ca. 800 men),[5] and another states specifically that he led 700–800 troops into the mountain region.[6] On the other hand, Harrison Forman reports (presumably from Communist sources) that Nieh took "a picked force of 2,000 guerrilla veterans" on his mission.[7] In any case, when Nieh arrived in the Wut'ai-Foup'ing area, he found that most of the local officials and Nationalist troops had fled, leaving the area in a state of confusion bordering on collapse.[8] Working with local people who responded sympathetically to the Communists' anti-Japanese propaganda, Nieh established "general mobilization committees" to fill the vacuum in government. The mobilization committees were given unlimited authority to collect weapons, organize militia, coordinate production, issue identity cards and passports, and bring some semblance of order back to the region. While these activities were being carried out by natives of the region, plans for a new regional government were being made by Nieh and a group of non-Communist politicians who had retreated to Wut'ai after the fall of T'ai-yüan.

The most influential of the non-Communist leaders who allied themselves with Nieh Jung-chen in the autumn of 1937 were several important figures in the Shansi Sacrifice League (Hsi Meng Hui). In order to understand the nature of the government created by the Communists in

NORTH CHINA

Wut'ai, it is necessary to review the origins and development of the Sacrifice League, since it was the nucleus upon which all mass mobilization in Shansi was based. Anti-Japanese, nationalistic agitation in Shansi began at the time of the establishment of the East Hopei Autonomous Government in November 1935, when students in T'aiyüan protested violently against the setting up of the puppets. Their demonstrations attracted the attention of the Red Army, which had recently arrived in neighboring Shensi, and in January and February of 1936, a large Red Army force under Liu Tzu-tan, Mao Tse-tung, and Hsü Hai-tung crossed the Yellow River into Shansi as part of a self-proclaimed "anti-Japanese expedition." The Communists had incredibly good fortune on this sortie; they occupied 18 hsien in Shansi in less than two months and totally discredited Yen Hsi-shan's warlord army. Yen was thrown into a state of panic and appealed to Nanking for arms and ammunition. Rather than sending weapons, Chiang Kai-shek chose this opportunity to "centralize" Shansi, i.e., to bring it under Nanking's control, and he sent the Central Army north to repel the Communists and to occupy the province. By May 1936, Liu Tzu-tan was dead of wounds received in battle and most of the Red Army units had been driven back into Shensi.[9]

During the summer of 1936, Yen Hsi-shan, now thoroughly aroused to the Communist danger across his western border, founded a mass association designed to absorb anti-Japanese elements in Shansi and to head off Communist underground activities. Apart from being anti-Communist, Yen's new "Just Way Association" (Kung Tao T'uan) had few clearly defined goals; as George Taylor has put it, the "Just Way Association" was intended to "dish the Whigs."[10] To Yen's everlasting chagrin, however, exactly the opposite happened. Hardly was the Kung Tao T'uan launched before most of the members of the left-tending Youth National Salvation Association of T'aiyüan joined it and infiltrated its leadership. On September 18, 1936, the fifth anniversary of the Manchurian Incident, the new leadership of the Kung Tao T'uan set up the Sacrifice League as a patriotic auxiliary to the Kung Tao T'uan. With the outbreak of the Suiyüan Incident in late 1936, and with the continuing anti-Japanese demonstrations in the Peiping area, the Sacrifice League drew upon the increasing anti-Japanese sentiment in Shansi and grew rapidly. Soon it overshadowed and absorbed the Kung Tao T'uan; and during the first months of 1937, it became the leading patriotic association in Shansi. Although Yen Hsi-shan was the League's titular head, he was not sufficiently farsighted to understand the virulent nationalism upon which it was based, or sufficiently respected (in the manner of Chiang Kai-shek) to control and lead it.

One of the leaders of the Sacrifice League in 1937 was Sung Shao-wen, a 34-year-old native of T'unliu, Shansi, and a recent graduate of Peking National University (1935, in economics). He had been active in the League in T'aiyüan from its founding—he was chief of the propaganda department—and he was known as one of the important so-called "new politicians" of Shansi.[11] As the Japanese armies approached T'aiyüan in the fall of 1937, Sung and others proposed to Yen Hsi-shan that armed forces be formed among the youth of the Sacrifice League. Yen agreed and turned over 30,000 rifles to the Sacrifice League, which then formed its own military units, called Dare-to-Die Corps (*chüeh ssu tui*), and sent them into the hsien of northern Shansi to wage guerrilla warfare against the Japanese. One of Yen's last official acts before abandoning the capital was to appoint several new, wartime hsien magistrates from the members of the Sacrifice League and the Dare-to-Die Corps.

In October 1937, Sung Shao-wen led a group of his associates and Dare-to-Die fighters to Wut'aishan, where he had been appointed magistrate of a "guerrilla hsien."[12] There he was joined by Hu Jen-k'uei, another Peking University graduate (in history), who was the magistrate of Tinghsiang hsien in the Wut'ai area.[13] Hu, who had no Party affiliation, was one of the few local bureaucrats who did not evacuate in the face of the invasion. Together, the two men established contacts with Nieh Jung-chen; and the three of them called the Foup'ing Conference of January 1938, which created the Chin-Ch'a-Chi Border Region Government. In the period January 9–15, 1938, some 148 delegates from 39 hsien of Shansi and Hopei met at Foup'ing and created the first Communist-sponsored rear-area government. The representatives to this conference included local magistrates and military leaders, but the majority were delegates from the mass organizations formed by the Communists upon their arrival in Wut'ai. Among the organizations represented were the peasants', workers', women's, and youths' National Salvation Associations, the mobilization committees, and the Sacrifice League, which by its own description was half political party and half mass organization.[14] There were also representatives of the Communist Party and of the Kuomintang. On January 30, 1938, the newly created government was approved by Chiang Kai-shek and the Chungking government (disapproval would have been futile, since the area was entirely surrounded by the Japanese Army).

The border-area government resembled a provincial administration. It was headed by a six-man Border Region Administrative Committee with Sung Shao-wen as Chairman and Hu Jen-k'uei as Vice-Chairman. The other four committeemen were Nieh Jung-chen, Communist Party representative and local military commander; Liu Tien-chi, representative of the Kuomintang; Chang Su, regional representative for Chahar; and Sun Chih-yüan, regional representative for Hopei.[15] These men also had collateral duties; for example, Sung was finance officer, Hu managed the Civil Affairs Office, and Liu was chief of education. The offices of the government itself were first established at Foup'ing, but in late March 1938 the Japanese Army carried out its first mop-up by marching up the Sha River and burning Foup'ing. Colonel Carlson, in his tour of the area in 1938, went down the same route that the Japanese had come up in March and reported that "hardly a house was standing."[16] As a result of the Japanese raid, the government moved to Machiach'uan on the Wut'ai hsien border and moved again in the winter of 1938 to the T'ailussu monastery. During 1939, the government moved three more times.[17]

The Wut'ai base was the most complex and highly developed of all the Communist rear-area strongholds set up during the war. It had under its control productive enterprises engaged in paper manufacturing, soap manufacturing, and mining, among other things. The government operated a bank and a state trading company to control the currency and "imports" of the area, and to ensure that the Japanese did not profit from enterprises set up in the border region. There were numerous newspapers published in the region, the one with the largest circulation being *K'ang-ti pao* ("Resistance News"), which came out every three days. The editor of *K'ang-ti pao* was Teng T'o, who later became editor of the *Jen-min jih-pao* ("People's Daily") after the establishment of the Communist government in 1949.[18] His Wut'ai paper had a circulation of 2,500 in 1938 and was printed on two presses smuggled into the border area from the coast across the Peiping-Hankow railroad.[19] Other border-area institutions included a second branch of K'angta, and a military hospital set up by the Canadian surgeon and Spanish civil war veteran Dr. Norman Bethune (Pai Chiu-en), who died of gangrene in Chin-Ch'a-Chi in November 1939.[20] There were border-region committees of both the Communist Party and the Sacrifice League. The CCP committee included among its members Lin Piao, Ho Lung, Nieh Jung-chen, P'eng Chen (supervisor of the mass movement in the region), Wang Ping (political commissar attached to Lü Cheng-ts'ao's central Hopei military command), and Teng T'o (editor of *K'ang-ti pao*).

The actual area of the Chin-Ch'a-Chi Border Region varied with the passage of time and with the fortunes of war. In 1940, a Communist writer claimed 70 hsien for the border region;[21] and in 1944 it was reported that the area contained 102 local hsien governments.[22] From the start, the border region consisted of two well-defined areas: the Wut'aishan base in the mountains of northeast Shansi and western Hopei; and the central Hopei guerrilla area, composed of approximately 29 hsien, in the great plain of Hopei. By the end of the war, there were two more large, disconnected subdivisions of the Chin-Ch'a-Chi Border Region—namely, the Kupeik'ou base northeast of Peiping, and the Yinshan base in the mountains north of Peiping. For the present, we shall consider only the two early bases, in Wut'ai and central Hopei.

In its broadest definition, the Wut'aishan base consisted of a rectangular area bounded by four railroads: on the north by the Pingsui (Peiping-Sui-yüan) railroad between Peiping, Kalgan, and Tat'ung; on the south by the Chengt'ai (Shihchiachuang-T'aiyüan) railroad; on the west by the narrow-gauge T'ungp'u railroad between Tat'ung and T'aiyüan; and on the east by the Peiping-Hankow railroad between Peiping and Shihchiachuang. These four railroads were the objects of guerrilla attack, and by the end of the war they could be cut at will by the Communists. Within this rectangle, there were four subareas which, like the larger bases, were entirely separate and often were surrounded by Japanese garrison forces: (*a*) Wut'ai hsien, Shansi; (*b*) Ihsien and Manch'eng hsien, western Hopei; (*c*) T'ang hsien, western Hopei; and (*d*) P'ingshan hsien, western Hopei.[23]

Wut'ai itself was the border region's main military stronghold; it was the location of Nieh Jung-chen's headquarters and the camp for his Eighth Route Army regulars. The Ihsien-Manch'eng base was under the command of Yang Ch'eng-wu, a veteran of the Long March, who entered the area in October 1937 as part of Nieh's forces and began recruiting among the peasantry. According to a Japanese study made in 1940, Yang's maximum strength in the area was about 7,000 troops.[24] Little is known of the T'ang hsien base except that it was located in the Chiuyangchien mountains and commanded by Ch'en Man-yüan. Ch'en achieved prominence later in the war as Lü Cheng-ts'ao's chief-of-staff in the Shansi-Suiyüan border area, but his early activities are obscure. Somewhat fuller information exists concerning the P'ingshan base, northwest of Shihchiachuang. The strategically located town of P'ingshan itself was held by the Japanese as a strongpoint in their control system for the Pinghan and Chengt'ai railroads. At one time the guerrillas retook the town, but a Japanese counterattack drove them off. According to Ke Han, the local guerrilla center was then located at the important commercial town of Hungtzutien (Chienp'ing) to the west. When the Japanese finally launched an attack against it, all doors and windows of the houses were sealed with brick and mud, so that attempts to burn the village would be less effective.[25]

Further information on the Communist-led guerrillas of P'ingshan comes from a Japanese military source. On July 2, 1940, a Japanese raiding party captured the "Party Members Registration Book" and other papers belonging to a company of the anti-Japanese guerrillas in the P'ingshan-Chinghsing area of western Hopei.[26] These papers describe 86 guerrilla residents of the region. Of the 86 members of the company, eight had military command duties; two had political duties; nine worked in the political mobilization section; 66 were soldiers; and one was a hygiene technician. In terms of class background, 70 were poor peasants and one was a middle peasant; there were no rich peasants. Of the remaining 15, 12 were workers, two were shopkeepers, and one was not reported (there were no "intellectuals").

There is some reason to believe that the leadership of the unit was not from the local area: of the 10 command personnel, six (five military and one political) came from Shansi or Shensi, while the other four came from Hopei or Shantung. On the other hand, 64 of the soldiers and the 10 specialists (the members of the political mobilization section and the hygiene technician) came from Hopei or Shantung; only two of the soldiers were from Shansi or Shensi. The P'ingshan-Chinghsing area is near the Shansi border, however, so these distinctions may only be coincidental.

With regard to education, only 11 (the leadership) had had any schooling and, of these, seven went no further than primary school. Seventy-three other members of the company were considered literate and only two were illiterate (one not reported). This high rate of literacy was credited by the Japanese to the Eighth Route Army's educational efforts. At the time the record book was captured, approximately one-third of the men in this guerrilla company were members of the Communist Party (29 regular members and one "candidate"). Of the 29 regulars, one had been a member for more than 10 years, three for between two and three years, 15 for between a year and two years, and 10 for less than a year. These figures illustrate what a windfall the Communist Party came into as a result of the Sino-Japanese war.

In addition to Wut'aishan and its four subdivisions, the second major base of the Chin-Ch'a-Chi Border Region was the central Hopei (Chichung) area, located in the plains east of the Pinghan railroad. Its origins are described in Chapter Two. According to Ke Han, Lü Cheng-ts'ao's forces were "voluntarily incorporated into the Eighth Route Army in December 1937," when Lü was contacted by a representative of Nieh Jungchen.[27] Following his affiliation with the Eighth Route Army, Lü continued as military commander in central Hopei; but he received political workers from Yenan to help him organize his area.

The military and administrative situation in central Hopei was very different from that in the mountainous strongholds on the Shansi-Hopei border. Central Hopei is flat terrain and was strongly occupied by the Japanese. At its greatest extent, the central Hopei area formed a rectangle defined—like Wut'aishan—by four railroads. The corners of the rectangle were Peiping in the northwest, Tientsin in the northeast, Techou (Shantung) in the southeast, and Shihchiachuang in the southwest. Unlike Wut'aishan, however, central Hopei was never a "base area" or a "war area" (*chan ch'ü*); it was always guerrilla territory. The region was subjected to continuous mopping-up campaigns by the Japanese and the puppets; and when Communist hsien governments were set up in May 1938, they were forced to move from village to village in the company of guerrilla units for protection. The situation became so serious that the guerrillas at one time changed all the names of the villages in order to confuse the Japanese.[28] The only communications with Wut'ai were by radio or by travel across the fortified Pinghan railroad. When the *sankō-seisaku* was in effect, Lü Cheng-ts'ao withdrew his forces to the west, and only as the war began to go against Japan did he reoccupy the plains.[29] An equally serious problem in the early years of the war was the bloody struggle between Lü Cheng-ts'ao and the KMT-affiliated guerrillas in Hopei. We shall return to the central Hopei area later when we consider the origins of CCP-KMT friction in north China.

OTHER NORTH CHINA GUERRILLA BASES

While Lin Piao's 115th division was establishing the Chin-Ch'a-Chi base in eastern Shansi and western Hopei, Ho Lung's 120th division was performing equally important tasks in northwestern Shansi. After the invasion of Shansi by the Eighth Route Army in September 1937, the 120th division occupied Kuohsien, Ningwu, Shench'ih, and Wuchai, in north-ern, Japanese-occupied Shansi. At the same time, various units of the Shansi Army under Yen Hsi-shan occupied the neighboring hsien of Chinglo, K'olan, and Lan.[30] The two military forces worked together to consolidate their control in the area and to carry out guerrilla attacks on Japanese rail transport. The region was relatively poor and therefore lightly occupied by the Japanese; its chief importance to the resistance forces lay in the fact that it constituted a vital corridor between Chin-Ch'a-Chi and Yenan. The T'ai-yüan area to the south was impassable owing to the presence of large num-bers of Japanese troops; therefore the northern region continued to be of strategic importance to Communist communications throughout the war. Although the 120th division made some attempt to set up mass organiza-tions in the area, no local governments were created until 1941.

The Shansi Army, which occupied northern Shansi along with the 120th division, was composed chiefly of Dare-to-Die Corps from the Sacrifice League and of "workers' brigades" from T'aiyüan. It was augmented with recruits from the peasantry and from local peace preservation units, who were mobilized when the Japanese armies passed through the area. These provincial units behind the Japanese lines were known as the Shansi "New Army" and were under the command of Hsü Fan-t'ing, a member of the KMT and a strong Chinese nationalist.[31] During the spring of 1939, Yen Hsi-shan reacted to the growing pro-Communism of the New Army and of the Sacrifice League by attempting to reassert his control over them. His efforts took the form of armed attacks by the regular Shansi Army on the offices of the Sacrifice League in the summer of 1939. The Sacrifice League suspected that Yen's moves were a prelude to collaboration with the Japa-nese in the manner of Wang Ching-wei—Yen, who was Japanese educated, was often spoken of as a potential puppet—and the League proclaimed, on October 10, 1939, their determination to continue the resistance even in op-position to Yen Hsi-shan. In November 1939, Chiang Kai-shek issued orders for Hu Tsung-nan, commander of the Central Government troops in the northwest, which were then blockading the Communists, to disarm the New Army; and Hu began to move his forces into position. A series of sharp clashes occurred between the new and old Shansi armies and Hu's troops in December and January. According to Taylor's Shansi informant, "Over a thousand military and political officials of the Sacrifice Union were killed or taken off for training [!]" in the autumn of 1939.[32] Before the New Army could be subjugated, however, it mutinied; and its 3,000 men, including Hsü Fan-t'ing, joined the 120th division of the Eighth Route Army.[33]

After admission to the Communist ranks, the New Army retained its name and regular leadership, but Eighth Route Army vice-commanders were added to its three brigades. The New Army attempted to smooth over the breach in the United Front by proclaiming its "continuing loyalty" to Yen Hsi-shan in the newspaper of the 115th division (March 10, 1940); but now that the old Shansi Army had retreated south of Fenyang (southwest of T'aiyüan), the northern part of Shansi was entirely in Communist hands.[34] With the addition of the territories formerly held by Yen's forces, the Communists and the New Army were now in a position to create a strong basis of popular support in the region. There were Japanese *sankō* campaigns in this region during 1941 and 1942, but the first assembly of the Shansi-Suiyüan Border Area was still able to meet in October 1941. Hsü Fan-t'ing was named both chairman of the new region and assistant military commander under Ho Lung. This arrangement continued until late in the war, when Ho Lung was named commander of the United Defense Headquarters (Lien-fang Ssu-ling-pu) at Yenan and was given over-all responsibility for the defense of the Shen-Kan-Ning and Shansi-Suiyüan Border Areas. Since he was concurrently in command of the 120th division and the Yenan Garrison Army, his place as local commander in northwest Shansi was taken by Lü Cheng-ts'ao.[35]

The third general area of Eighth Route Army operations in Shansi was in the strategically important southeastern part of the province. The southern Shansi area has been a battleground for centuries, because it guards the access to the vast plains of Honan across the Yellow River. It was in the T'aihang range, paralleling the Shansi-Honan border, that the Eighth Route Army established its field headquarters; and it was from this area that all Communist expansion southward and into Shantung was launched. Following the invasion of Shansi in 1937, the 129th division—under the one-eyed general Liu Po-ch'eng—penetrated the south central part of Shansi and centered its initial operations in the hsien of Hoshun, Liaohsien (Tso-ch'üan), and Yüshe, in the mountainous area north of Ch'angchih. Liu's troops were particularly active in creating local militia and guerrilla forces in this area.

The situation in Hoshun hsien was typical of Liu's achievements. A battalion of the 129th division entered the area shortly after the invasion of Shansi. It organized mass associations, distributed anti-Japanese propaganda, and enlisted members of the Sacrifice League into the Communist

Party. Then, as if to convince the local population of the wisdom of joining the Communists, the Japanese Army attacked Hoshun in April 1938. When the Japanese withdrew in May, the Communists returned at once and implemented their "full" program without delay. General mobilization committees were set up, the "reduce taxes, reduce interest" movement was instituted, and Army troops helped the local peasantry to carry out the harvest. According to a Japanese report, landlords in Hoshun in this period were either "robbed" as a result of the Communists' wartime rationalization-of-debts propaganda, or eliminated as traitors.[36] By November 1938, the economy had been placed on a military-support basis, local armed organizations had been set up, and a new Communist-sponsored hsien administration under one Teng Chao-hsiang was in operation. In early 1939, the first of the Japanese mopping-up campaigns directed specifically at the Communists came through Hoshun. This forced the Communists into a policy of dispersal, which in turn spread the anti-Japanese mobilization to every village of the region.

One of the Japanese studies of Communist control in Hoshun concerns the structure and function of the Peasants' National Salvation Association in Nanliyang, a village in Hoshun hsien. According to the "proclamation" and rules of this mass organization, "The Peasants' National Salvation Association has as its primary objective the armed defense of the homes of the peasants."[37] The organization in Nanliyang had a total of 77 members, with a chairman and four department heads, the departments being organization, the armed forces, propaganda, and the people's welfare. The membership of the Association, as revealed in statistics captured by the Japanese, was concentrated in the 42–56 age group, although many of the leadership positions were held by peasants in their late twenties or early thirties.[38] One of the main operations that the Hoshun hsien peasants' association had successfully carried out was the joint mobilization of hsien governments, mobilization committees, the army, and mass organizations to get in the autumn harvest of 1938. On September 19, 1938, the Hoshun peasants' association also issued a call to mass groups in four hsien to form *chu-keng-tui* (plowing-aid corps) to help the farmers.[39]

The first area to be colonized from the 129th division's base near Liaohsien, north of Ch'angchih, was southern Hopei. Political organizers were sent eastward across the Pinghan railroad into Nankung and Chülu hsien in early 1938, and were followed by units of the 129th division under Vice-Commander Hsü Hsiang-ch'ien in August 1938. The Southern Hopei Mili-

tary Area was set up in the summer of 1938, with Hsü as military commander. He incorporated a unit of guerrillas under the command of Yang
Hsiu-feng, a former head of the Hopei Provincial Education Agency and
a professor of history at the National Teachers' College in Peiping. When
the war broke out in 1937, Yang led a group of students from the Peiping-
Tientsin area into southern Hopei, where they organized the peasants into
guerrilla units. In July 1941, Yang was made head of the expanded Chin-
Chi-Lu-Yü (Shansi-Hopei-Shantung-Honan) Border Area Government,
which connected southern Shansi with western Shantung. The southern
Hopei area, like the Shansi-Suiyüan base set up by Ho Lung, had its greatest strategic significance as a communications route—in this case providing
access to Shantung. The boundaries of the original South Hopei (Chi-nan)
Military Area were the Pinghan railroad on the west, the Shihchiachuang-
Techou line on the north, the Grand Canal in Shantung on the west, and
the Chang River on the south.[40]

Communist expansion south of Ch'angchih and into southwest Shansi
was accomplished in a very different way from that in south Hopei. The
vast area of the Chungt'iao mountains and the western T'aihang range in
southern Shansi were held, in 1940 and 1941, by a large Kuomintang force
under General Wei Li-huang. These troops had been the object of fierce
Japanese attacks in the spring of 1940, but had managed to defend themselves and even to counterattack in some areas. In response to this resistance, the Japanese First Army launched one of the major operations of the
entire Sino-Japanese war in the spring of 1941: the campaign to eliminate
all Kuomintang forces north of the Yellow River. Known to the Chinese as the Battle of Chungt'iao and to the Japanese as the Chungyüan
Operation (Chungyüan was the code name given the operation by the Commander of the North China Area Army, Tada Hayao),[41] it took place during the period May 7–June 15, 1941, and was entirely successful from the
Japanese point of view. From 3,000 to 5,000 Kuomintang troops were "destroyed" in this operation, by Japanese estimate, and the way was cleared
for the Communists to enter the area as soon as the ability of the Japanese
Army to garrison such a region was reduced.[42] One source indicates that
by 1943 there were 59 pro-Communist local governments set up in the
Chungt'iao range, and the United States War Department's study concludes that the Communists were well entrenched in southern Shansi by
the end of the war.[43]

There were other examples of Communist expansion in the wake of the

Japanese Army and at the expense of the Kuomintang—notably, Ho Lung's breakthrough at T'ungkuan (Shensi) in December 1944 and his advance all the way to Hunan and Kiangsi in the confusion of the 1944 Japanese offensive.[44] But these cases were exceptional. The most common form of Communist territorial expansion was by alliance with local guerrillas on a mutually advantageous basis. Shantung province, which produced more locally organized guerrillas than any other province, offers several examples of Communist colonization by co-option.

THE SHANTUNG GUERRILLA AREA

Two major influences in Shantung promoted a spontaneous nationalist reaction to the Japanese invasion. One was scandal and treachery by the legal Shantung provincial government, which became a nationalistic *cause célèbre* throughout China; the other was a long tradition of rural military organization and of peasant rebellion. The treachery of the Shantung government—that is, the refusal of Governor Han Fu-ch'ü to give battle to the invaders—is revealing in the nationalistic pressures that it called forth. Han himself was no traitor, but neither was he a nationalist; the concepts of traitor and nationalist were both alien to his thinking. He was a warlord and a former subordinate of the militarist Feng Yü-hsiang; he became governor of Shantung in 1930, when he deserted Feng and allied himself with Chiang Kai-shek. His rule was similar to that of Yen Hsi-shan in Shansi: moderately efficient and wholly absolutist. Han, however, had one problem Yen did not have: Shantung was a Japanese sphere of economic influence and had been so since 1914. Han was scrupulously correct in his relations with the Japanese investors, who owned most of the enterprises in his province, and he was not an enthusiastic supporter of the demonstrations and propaganda carried out by the anti-Japanese National Salvation Associations.

When the Japanese invasion of north China began in September 1937, the Second Army (under Lieutenant General Nishio Juzō) was ordered to advance southward from Tientsin down the Tientsin-Pukow railroad toward Shantung. Although the Japanese met almost no resistance at this time, by September 24 the Second Army had only reached Tsanghsien, Hopei; and Tsinan, the capital of Shantung, was not occupied until December 24. During the same period the Japanese First Army had captured most of Hopei and Shansi provinces. The delay in Shantung was caused

by bargaining: the Japanese spent almost three months negotiating with
Han Fu-ch'ü for an unopposed Japanese entry into his province.[45] The
talks proved inconclusive, and after the Japanese cotton mills in Tsingtao
were destroyed by the Chinese on December 18, 1937, the Japanese Army
abandoned its interest in Governor Han and rolled into Shantung. Han
was ordered by the Central Government to use his Shantung Army to defend the capital, but instead he expropriated the provincial treasury and fled
with his army to the south. The Japanese advanced through Tsinan and
the important city of Tsining (Chining), and on to T'aierhchuang on the
southern border, without meeting any resistance.

Han's behavior in this case was neither surprising nor unprecedented;
he had acted almost exactly the way other northern warlords (Sung Che-
yüan, Liu Ju-ming, Fu Tso-yi, and Yen Hsi-shan) had acted on earlier occasions. But a new era had dawned. Han was apprehended by Chiang Kai-
shek's troops at K'aifeng and taken to Hankow for court martial. Li
Tsung-jen and Feng Yü-hsiang testified against him at the trial; and the
court, which was headed by Ho Ying-ch'in, sentenced Han to death. He
went before a firing squad at Hankow on January 24, 1938.[46] This demonstration of strong national determination bolstered the morale of the Chinese troops, who defeated General Nishio at T'aierhchuang in April, and
it created strong feelings against collaborators in Shantung generally. Many
students and nationally conscious elements in Shantung were brought into
the resistance as a result of denouncing Han and other *mai-kuo-tsei* ("coun-
try-selling thieves") who fled with him.

The most important aspect of the Han affair from the standpoint of local
guerrillas was that Han, in deciding not to contest the crossing of the Yellow
River by the Japanese, had issued a general retreat order to his army. This
order was respected, with certain outstanding exceptions, by the majority
of hsien magistrates, police, local leaders, landlords, and members of the
social establishment generally. The pre-invasion social fabric of rural Shantung was completely torn by this exodus, and the peasants were compelled
to provide for their own rule and protection.[47] There were several factors
in the geographic and social environment of Shantung that made the self-
organizing efforts of the peasants successful. The mountainous nature of
the province, for example, made guerrilla warfare possible with less extensive social organization than was required in more vulnerable areas. In
addition to the bases set up in T'aishan and on Mount Fenghuang (Phoe-
nix) in the Liaoch'eng area of northwest Shantung, there were also moors
and swamps in the Yellow River flood plain that served as excellent guer-

rilla bases.[48] Moreover, the peasants of Shantung had a strong tradition of local armed organization. There were numerous secret societies, village associations, and outright bandit groups among the peasantry; even a Communist study notes that the Mount Fenghuang area had been a bandit base since the establishment of the Republic. Attempts at subjugating it were a continuous source of grief to the local government.[49]

In many of the articles written by local guerrillas and captured by the Japanese there are laudatory references to the rebellious past of Shantung. One writer observes that the 42 hsien of the Yenchou and Ts'aochou regions (the area west of the Tientsin-Pukow railroad and east of the Hopei border) have witnessed the following famous peasant uprisings in Chinese history: the Huang Ch'ao rebellion of T'ang (which began in Shantung in A.D. 875 and spread all over China), the Sungchiang rebellion of Sung, the Wang Lun rebellion of Ch'ing (a secret society under Wang Lun that rebelled at Linch'ing, Shantung, in 1774), and the Boxer Rebellion at the turn of the century.[50]

Other forces favorable to the speedy opening of guerrilla warfare in Shantung were the large numbers of weapons possessed by peasant households owing to the presence of bandits in the area (still more arms and ammunition had been collected from the retreating troops of Han Fu-ch'ü and salvaged from the battlefield at T'aierhchuang); the extreme density of the population in western Shantung, which afforded concealment for guerrillas in villages and which provided large numbers of recruits; the relatively strong anti-Japanese spirit in Shantung, dating from the Manchurian Incident (most Chinese immigrants to Manchuria had come from Shantung prior to September 18, 1931); and the presence of many students from Peiping and Tientsin who had moved to Shantung after the occupation of those cities.[51]

Among the many pockets of guerrilla resistance that sprang up in every part of Shantung within the first year of the war, the most famous was that created by Fan Chu-hsien in western Shantung. Fan was the administrative inspector of the sixth district (roughly, west of the Tientsin-Pukow line) under Han Fu-ch'ü, but he did not respect Han's order to retreat in November 1937. Instead, Fan took a battalion of his own peace preservation corps into the moor surrounding Liangshan, where he organized an anti-Japanese guerrilla force. His nucleus of organizers grew very rapidly. A youth association, called the Chinese National Liberation Vanguard and built around some 1,600 Peiping-Tientsin students from Shantung and elsewhere, joined Fan and opened an office in Liaoch'eng. Fan's sons, Fan

Cheng-heng and Fan Shu-min, were important leaders of the Vanguard. Members of the Vanguard were dispatched to every village on both banks of the Yellow River to pay calls on local figures who might support the resistance, and to mobilize the masses for "national salvation" work. The Vanguard also published a newspaper, *Lao-hsiang jih-pao* ("Rural Daily News"), which was used to spread the news of the resistance and to teach the peasants guerrilla techniques.[52]

The greatest of Fan Chu-hsien's problems in the early period was the determined opposition he received from Ch'i T'i-yüan, magistrate of Shouchang hsien, which lay just across the river from Liangshan. Ch'i was a Japanese collaborator and the brother of the "big traitor" Ch'i Hsieh-yüan, a former warlord figure (commander of the Chihli armies in 1924) and a high-ranking official in the Peiping puppet government.[53] After Fan finally succeeded in driving Ch'i from Shantung in early 1938, Fan's guerrilla organization flourished. He built up a full-time force of 70,000 soldiers operating under his newly established Sixth District Guerrilla Command. The political department of this command alone consisted of some 500 workers. Even the local secret society, the Red Spears, was persuaded to lend its support. The new guerrilla command also sent officials and hsien chiefs to fill vacancies in areas from which former officials had fled.

This early phase of Shantung guerrilla resistance, known as the "Liangshan moor" period, came to an abrupt end in November 1938, when units of the Japanese Tenth Division (Lieutenant General Isogai Rensuke) attacked Liaoch'eng. Fan Chu-hsien was killed in battle and his guerrillas were scattered all over northwest Shantung. Puppet military and civil authorities were set up under Hou Tzu-liang and Ch'i Tzu-hsiu, and it appeared for a time as if armed resistance in this part of Shantung had been completely broken. However, in response to a request for aid from the Shantung guerrillas, the Sixth Plenum (November 1938) of the Chinese Communist Party's Central Committee had decided to send reinforcements to Fan's scattered column.[54] One of the two brigades that Lin Piao had left behind in southeastern Shansi in 1937—the 343d—was augmented with various specialists from the division (115th) and designated the Eastern Advance Detachment (Tung-chin Chih-tui). This force, under the overall command of Ch'en Kuang, departed from the Pinghan railroad area of southern Hopei in March 1939 and established contacts with guerrillas in Yünch'eng, a few miles southwest of Liaoch'eng, in the late spring of 1939.[55]

By this time, however, Ch'en's column was not the only Eighth Route Army force in Shantung. In August and September of 1938, portions of the 386th brigade, 129th division, which were then engaged in colonizing southern Hopei, had advanced into northern Shantung east of the Tientsin-Pukow line. There they joined with guerrillas in the Loling area, although there is no record of their making contact with Fan's forces across the railroad. The Loling unit was called the Eastern Advance Volunteer Column (Tung-chin T'ing-shen Tsung-tui) and was under the command of Hsiao Hua.[56] In the Liangshan moor area to the southwest, the arrival of Ch'en Kuang's forces in early 1939 revived the local guerrillas and brought the area under Communist control. Hou Tzu-liang's puppet forces were disarmed, and the puppet hsien administrators fled from the territory. The peasants and students who had been defeated by the Japanese in November were rearmed and reorganized; they took the name of the "Fan Chu-hsien Column," in honor of their former commander.[57]

Because residents of the area had already seen extensive anti-Japanese action, there was little work for the political mobilizers. The immediate task of the Eighth Route Army in Shantung was to coordinate their rapidly expanding military operations in every part of the province. (The first guerrilla attack on the important seaport of Chefoo, at the eastern end of the Shantung peninsula, took place on April 5, 1938; the Liangshan operations were only part of the extensive resistance organized all over Shantung in the first year of the war.) This coordination was achieved in April 1939, when Hsü Hsiang-ch'ien, until then vice-commander of the 129th division, was sent to Shantung to head a new guerrilla command. It was called the First Column, and all Eighth Route Army regulars and guerrillas in Shantung came under its jurisdiction. Hsü remained in command in Shantung until 1943, when he became Ho Lung's chief-of-staff at the United Defense Headquarters. At that time, over-all command in Shantung was transferred to the New Fourth Army's commander, Ch'en Yi, with headquarters in northern Kiangsu (see Chapter Five).

THE EAST HOPEI GUERRILLA AREA

Another example of Communist co-option of locally organized defense forces occurred in the east Hopei region, but with decidedly less success, from the Communist point of view, than in Shantung. The triangular area between Peiping, Tientsin, and Shanhaikwan was a traditional focus of Japanese interest, and it had been ruled by their puppets ever since the establishment of the East Hopei Autonomous Government in November 1935. A guerrilla base in this area would threaten the main routes to Manchuria as well as the ports of T'angku, Chinwangtao, and Shanhaikwan; it could also interfere with coal production at the important Kailan collieries at T'angshan. For all these reasons, the Japanese responded to Communist attempts at organization in this area with the greatest brutality. Mopping-up campaigns began in 1938 and were still under way in 1945; they resulted in a great loss of life among both the peasantry and the Eighth Route Army columns that invaded the area. Had it not been for the protection afforded by the mountains near Kupeik'ou, where the guerrillas made their base, and the fact that the Pacific War prevented the Japanese from giving their full attention to China, it is doubtful whether the Communist east Hopei base would have existed by the end of the war.

The initial Eighth Route Army penetration of east Hopei was carried out in the spring and summer of 1938. A unit, "several thousand" strong, under Sung Shih-lun and Teng Hua advanced from Shensi, through northern Shansi, along the inner Great Wall, and into east Hopei passing north of Peiping.[58] This force was first sighted by the Japanese at Nank'ou, north of the capital, on June 2, 1938. On June 4, the guerrillas passed through Ch'angp'ing, in the Peiping suburbs, and continued eastward, finally coming to a halt in the rural areas of Hsinglung, Ch'ienan, Paoti, Fengjun, Chi, Yüt'ien, and Tsunhua hsien.[59] By July 9, 1938, general rebellion existed throughout east Hopei as the peasants, under local leaders, united with the arriving Eighth Route Army units and carried out attacks on local Japanese garrisons. The results of the Communists' intrusion were immediate: rails were torn up and stations burned on the railroads to Manchuria, and raids were made into Jehol. The Japanese could not let such a provocation pass; as Taylor recalls, "On August 21, 1938, the 'Guerrilla Hunt' in East Hopei began."[60] By autumn, the main force of the Sung-Teng column had been "obliterated."[61]

In the winter of 1938–39, a second important Eighth Route Army unit reached east Hopei: the 358th brigade, 120th division, under the division's vice-commander, Hsiao K'o. Hsiao made contact with Sung Shih-lun and Teng Hua and began to rebuild Communist strength in the area. The Communist leaders decided that the greatest emphasis in the future should be placed on political work; in their judgment the peasants were insufficiently aware of the war in political terms, and were thus all too often simply terrified, rather than outraged, by the Japanese mopping-up campaigns, to the point where they were refusing support to the guerrillas. One of the main resolutions introduced at a meeting held in a village of Ningho hsien on August 29, 1939, over which Hsiao K'o presided, was that many more trained political workers be sent to the east Hopei area to assist in Communist operations.[62] During late 1939, National Salvation Associations and other propaganda organizations began to win strong support from the peasantry of east Hopei for the first time. In November, the North China Area Army was alarmed to find Eighth Route Army political workers in T'ung hsien and Tahsing hsien, both within 25 kilometers of Peiping itself.[63] A common organizational technique employed by the Communists in east Hopei was, according to Japanese intelligence, to gather all the residents of a village into a temple or public building and to deliver an anti-Japanese lecture lasting two or three hours.[64]

By work of this kind, the Communists were finally able to establish guerrilla bases in the area in the summer of 1941. These bases were known collectively as the "Chi-Ch'a-Je-Ning" (Hopei-Chahar-Jehol-Ninghsia) Military Area and were under the over-all guidance of the Communist authorities in Wut'aishan.[65] During most of the period between 1941 and 1944, however, the east Hopei guerrillas were quiescent and self-sustaining, since the moment that they took direct action against the Japanese, severe reprisals were carried out. The Kupeik'ou contingents interfered with Japanese troop withdrawals from China during 1944 and 1945, but they also had to fight special Japanese police units whose sole task was to mop up guerrillas in east Hopei.[66]

In the long run, the significance of the Communist operations in the east Hopei area proved to be not the damage that was inflicted upon the Japanese during the war, but the fact that it gave the Communists control of the area in the immediate postwar period. Even though the Communist bases were tiny and the actual membership of the anti-Japanese organizations small, the Communists symbolized resistance in these areas during eight years of occupation. When it became perfectly clear that Japan was losing the war, many undecided or cautious persons joined the Communists, and the size of the "liberated areas" increased greatly. The east Hopei base, like the other anti-Japanese guerrilla bases in north China, provided the Communists with the men and supplies necessary to defeat the better equipped and professionally trained Nationalist armies when the civil war broke out.

INCIPIENT KMT-CCP CIVIL WAR: NORTH CHINA

It is as difficult today as it was in the 1937–41 period to place blame on either the KMT or the CCP for breaking the United Front by making an armed attack on a Chinese military formation. On the one hand, there was a great cooling-off of anti-Japanese fervor among the Nationalists during the dark days of 1940, and this led them to cast a suspicious eye on the Communists' "anti-Japanese" activities in the occupied areas. On the other hand, the Communists were demonstrably expanding into certain rear areas already held by KMT guerrillas. Thus, there were many possible motives for civil war: the KMT might well have preferred Japan or Nanking to Yenan in the heyday of the Axis; and the Communists were certainly trying Chungking's patience and threatening the United Front by their continuous insubordination. Lacking inside information to the contrary, we may assume today that conflict between the KMT and the CCP in the occupied areas was a virtual certainty without presuming any ulterior motive or bad faith on the part of either party. The very situation that existed within the rear areas, and the fact that civilian resistance to the Japanese had developed, promoted the beginnings of civil war just as a similar situation did in Yugoslavia.

In its broadest perspective, the problem of civil war between the KMT and the CCP during the Sino-Japanese war was one of two mutually opposed resistance policies: "waiting in preparation" versus "fighting strengthens the resistance." Neither of these two points of view was ever enunciated by KMT or CCP spokesmen, but the two parties' actions can be summarized by the two terms. Both Chiang and Mao were agreed that the middle period of the war with Japan was to be a war of attrition (the three periods of the war, popularized by Mao in *On the Protracted War,* were retreat, stalemate, and counterattack; the last stage never actually occurred in China). They differed on how to carry out the war of attrition. From the Kuomintang's point of view, Japan's only real weaknesses were her violations of international law and her infringements upon the interests of other powers (for example, the Panay Incident, and the blockade of the Tientsin concession). Therefore, according to the Kuomintang, the greatest threat to Japan's war-making ability came simply from publicizing the nature of the Japanese war in China, with the ultimate aim of establishing a world-wide trade blockade against Japan. The chief weapons of the KMT's war of attrition were to be international propaganda and multilateral diplomacy. From the Communists' point of view, direct guerrilla action was preferable. In addition to inflicting physical damage and demoralizing elements of the Japanese rank-and-file, guerrilla raids had the salutary effect of prompting Japanese retaliation, which swept away the old order and unleashed the forces of mass mobilization—two by-products of the resistance that were highly desirable to the Communists.

The Kuomintang had to oppose the Communist policy. No government wishes to risk popular disfavor by supporting questionable military operations that invite known and certain reprisals. Moreover, the Kuomintang had no desire to see the resistance to Japan turn into a social revolution. An important segment of the Kuomintang's political support—the landowning classes—certainly did not wish to see all of the Japanese-controlled areas come under the influence of Communist political commissars. The right wing of the Kuomintang expressed its concern in this respect by frequently drawing attention to Communist expansion into "unauthorized" areas. The Communists, in responding to these charges, cited the requirements of the war against Japan and accused the Nationalists of being little better than puppets when they suggested that the Communists had ulterior motives for their rear-area activities. Thus, although the KMT's policy may have been realistic, it was based on a faulty appreciation of peasant mobilization in the rear areas; and it was extremely vulnerable to an attack on patriotic grounds.

A long series of military clashes between Communist and Nationalist forces took place in the period 1938–40, in both north and central China. These clashes were the first skirmishes of the 1947–49 civil war. They grew partly out of the nature of guerrilla warfare itself; for one of the greatest problems in such warfare is centralized supervision of essentially independent operations. Even when communications between the guerrillas on the one hand and Chungking or Yenan on the other were technically adequate, the chain of command was never clear. (For example, General Tai Li in Chungking supervised some KMT guerrillas, while the wartime pro-

---

THE MAPS *on the following pages show a Japanese Army estimate of Communist expansion between January 1938 (the first map) and August 1939 (the second). Each dot represents a Communist-affiliated hsien government. It should be noted that the concentration of dots in southwest Shansi probably overstates the case for mid-1939. In other areas—particularly Shantung—the second map does not record the full extent of Communist expansion. These maps have been redrawn for printing here on the basis of originals in Chief of Staff, Tada Corps (i.e., Headquarters, North China Area Army), CHŪGOKU KYŌSANTŌ UNDŌ NO KAISETSU ("Explanation of the Chinese Communist Party Movement") (n.p. [Peiping]: February 17, 1941; secret), pp. 16ff. The original maps were too faded for accurate reproduction. I would like to thank Mr. Hatano Ken'ichi, in whose library the Tada Corps document now rests, for allowing me to photograph these maps in 1962.*

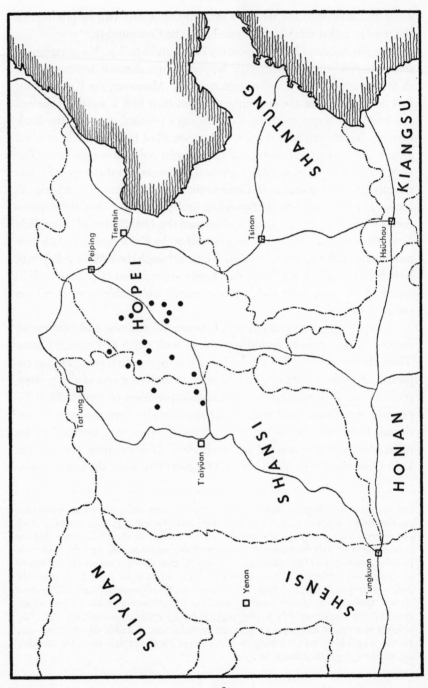

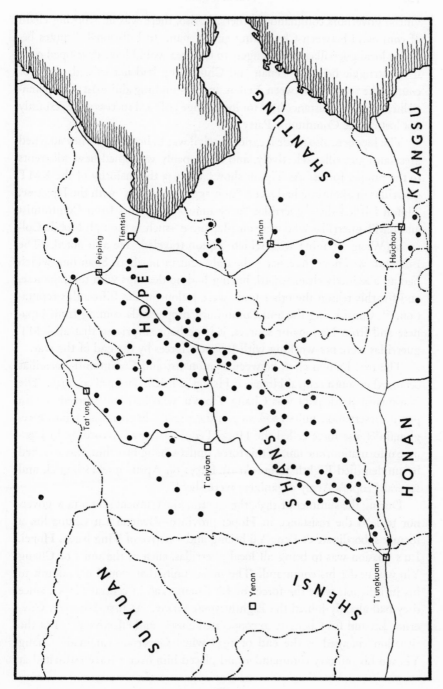

vincial governors commanded others.) Also, there was no working chain
of command between Chungking and Yenan. Jurisdictional disputes between local guerrillas and strangers to the area would have developed even
if the struggle between Yenan and Chungking had not existed. And, of
course, the struggle between Yenan and Chungking did exist; the potentialities that the resistance held for long-range political success were certainly
not lost on the Communist Party.

The Japanese also made it easier for civil war to break out. They attacked
areas and guerrillas selectively, and they openly welcomed new adherents
to the puppet forces. As Tipton shows, by 1943 the majority of the KMT
guerrillas in Shantung had secret "non-aggression pacts" with the Japanese.
Tipton labeled these guerrillas "grey units," as distinct from Communist
and KMT guerrillas who were anti-Japanese—such as the 15th Mobile Column (Wang Yu-min) with which Tipton traveled. He also noted, "The
Fifteenth was now [late 1943] the only unit in northern Shantung which
had an absolutely clean record, having had no dealings with the Japanese,
and for this reason the other units were jealous of the Fifteenth's reputation."[67] Considering the anti-Communist propaganda coming from Japanese and from Nationalist sources, it is perhaps surprising that all KMT
guerrillas were not working with Japanese forces by the end of the war.

The first known clash between Nationalist and Communist guerrillas
occurred in south central Hopei, at Hsingt'ai hsien, on April 29, 1938. The
Nationalist participant was Chang Yin-wu, who had reorganized certain
peace preservation units (*pao an tui,* the prewar hsien militia) into a regional defense force called the Hopei People's Army. According to Japanese information, one unit of this force, under Chang Hsi-chiu, was attacked
by unidentified Eighth Route Army forces on April 29 at Hsingt'ai, and
several People's Army organizers were shot.[68]

During the summer of 1938, the Central Government sent a new governor to lead the resistance in Hopei province—General Lu Chung-lin, a
former subordinate of Feng Yü-hsiang and a native of Ting hsien, Hopei.
Lu's mission was to bring all local guerrillas, such as the units of Chang
Yin-wu, under his command. The major units that would not submit to
his jurisdiction were the forces of Lü Cheng-ts'ao in central Hopei, since
they had already joined the Eighth Route Army. At first, however, Governor Lu and Lü Cheng-ts'ao cooperated closely and effectively.[69] But the
situation changed at the end of 1938 when Governor Lu made Chang
Yin-wu his military commander and placed him over a force estimated at

16,000 men. Chang was known for his violently anti-Communist attitude —possibly as a result of the April incident, but probably dating from an earlier period.[70] In either case, during December 1938, the KMT guerrillas under Lu Chung-lin and Chang Yin-wu made four separate attempts to eliminate Lü Cheng-ts'ao and Communist influence from central Hopei. On December 16, 1938, simultaneously with a Japanese advance from Paoting on the west and from Ts'ang hsien on the east, the army of Chang Yin-wu attacked Lü Cheng-ts'ao's headquarters. In other villages of central Hopei, Chang's chief of staff rounded up Communist organizers who had not escaped and had them shot. (According to the KMT version of this incident, Lu Chung-lin had ordered Chang Yin-wu to advance northward from Nankung, in the far south of Hopei, in order to intercept the advancing Japanese; while passing through open country in Ankuo hsien on the night of December 15, Chang and his forces were supposedly surrounded by a Communist army of 3,000 men under Lü Cheng-ts'ao, and had to fight their way out of the encirclement.)[71]

Although either version of this particular incident is plausible, several other anti-Communist attacks in the same month suggest that Chang's attack on Lü was part of a plan. In Hsinho hsien, south Hopei, units under Chao Yün-hsiang, a subordinate of Governor Lu Chung-lin, attacked local Communist troops, broke up newly formed National Salvation Associations, and executed political workers and Communist Party members. Similarly, in Shulu hsien, a small unit of the Eighth Route Army that was separated from its regular formation was arrested by troops of Lu Chung-lin and the political instructor and 21 others were killed.[72]

During 1939, the Communist Army retaliated against Chang Yin-wu's Hopei People's Army. In April, forces from the 129th division, which were colonizing the southern Hopei area, attacked a detachment of the People's Army in Jen hsien and killed 10 soldiers.[73] In the summer of 1939, the showdown came. On June 12–16, People's Army forces in the hsien of Shen, Shulu, Hengshui, and Chi, under the leadership of Lu Chung-lin and Chang Yin-wu, were engaged in a fierce battle with the Japanese Army, which ultimately cost the People's Army 150 casualties. Shortly after they had retired from this action to regroup, they were attacked by a huge Eighth Route Army force, north of Machuang, a small village about 14 kilometers southeast of Shulu. The battle took place on June 21–22, and resulted in several hundred casualties on both sides. According to Japanese accounts, the People's Army was liquidated and Chang

Yin-wu fled the province. Governor Lu's escape is not recorded, but escape
he did, since he turned up in 1944 as Minister of Conscription in Chungking and in 1949 he defected to the Communists. (He was a member of
the National Defense Committee in September 1954.) The Japanese noted
that in January 1940 the last survivors of the Hopei People's Army were
disarmed in Lingshou and Chin hsien by units of the 129th division, and
that its commanders were shot. Also, during the period September 1939–
January 1940, the Communist Army made vigorous efforts to disarm all
peace preservation units in Shantung.[74]

The chief problem in Hopei, an area in which the Communists were
authorized to operate, was one of jurisdiction. There was a plethora of
commanders, all of them with men to be fed and sheltered by the local
population, and none of them having a clear understanding of priorities or
a higher command to which disputes could be referred. Though we know
that the Communists advocated a "forward" policy of expansion during
the war, this does not, of itself, prove that Yenan or Wut'aishan gave the
orders for the pseudo-Communist Lü Cheng-ts'ao to attack the pseudo-
Nationalist Chang Yin-wu. Such attacks surely would have occurred without orders being issued, guerrilla warfare being what it is. These attacks
did, however, give rise to suspicions; and these suspicions, when translated
into policy, gave rise to major incidents, such as that in east Kansu (where
the forces of Governor Chu Shao-liang clashed with Eighth Route Army
regulars under Hsiao Ching-kuang in December 1939),[75] and to the New
Fourth Army Incident itself.

FIVE

The New Fourth Army
and the North Kiangsu Base

The New Fourth Army, whose origins were described in Chapter Three, is best known today as the Communist military formation that clashed with Kuomintang troops in January 1941 and thereby irreparably damaged the anti-Japanese United Front. The "New Fourth Army Incident" has been cited numerous times by both Communist and Nationalist spokesmen as an illustration of the treacherous motives of the opposite camp in fighting the war of resistance. In Nationalist eyes, the activities of the New Fourth Army typified the Communist policy of expansion under cover of fighting the Japanese; the KMT, therefore, viewed their attack on the New Fourth Army as a justified act by a sovereign government against a conspiracy during wartime. According to the Communists, the Government's attack on the New Fourth Army was final proof that the Kuomintang feared mobilized Chinese peasants more than it feared Japanese invaders, and that it was ready to negotiate peace with Japan. There is some truth to both views. Our concern here is not with weighing one view against the other, but with understanding how the dispute between the Communists and the Nationalists contributed to the national awakening of the illiterate masses in central China during the Japanese occupation.

As stated earlier, the New Fourth Army was created in September 1937 from Communist survivors of the 1927–37 civil war who were hidden out in central China. The establishment of this Army and its alliance with the KMT, coming as they did on the heels of an internecine war, might be compared to the Manchu-Boxer alliance of 1900. The difference is that whereas the Manchu-Boxer association was an opportunistic farce, the use of the former Red Army against Japan was a genuine expression of the desires of many nationally conscious Chinese. The Japanese were widely recognized as a threat to China's existence, and even Chinese Army officers who counseled caution in dealing with the Japanese Army did not desire a repetition of Manchukuo in the rest of China. Thus, the wartime union between the Communist and Nationalist armies was not clouded by distrust from the very beginning; it was, in fact, strongly welcomed by Chinese of many different political views. In re-examining the United Front tactic of the Communists in the late 1930's, we too often forget that the unification of domestic factions in the face of an external threat is a common political phenomenon frequently encountered in a non-Communist context. The Japanese threat of 1937 accomplished what the Japanese war of 1894 had not: the overcoming of internal disunity in order to meet the invasion from without. To be sure, the United Front was advanced in Moscow in 1935 and the Soviet Union was primarily concerned with the threat posed by Japan to its own borders; but the Japanese threat *to China* actually existed and actually materialized. It was the fact of Japanese aggression more than any other that gave the New Fourth Army Incident extraordinary political significance, and that gave to the New Fourth Army its victory over the KMT in north Kiangsu.

ORGANIZATION AND EXPANSION OF THE NEW FOURTH ARMY: 1938–1940

In January 1938, after the creation of the New Fourth Army, Yeh T'ing, the newly appointed commander, established his headquarters at Nanch'ang, the capital of Kiangsi, and began to organize his forces into a working military unit. By April he had gathered a total force of some 12,000 soldiers in various collection centers for the inspection of representatives of the Third War Area Commander, Ku Chu-t'ung, under whose over-all command they were to serve.[1] Yeh's army was subsequently subdivided into four detachments, three of which—the first, second, and third detachments—were concentrated at Yenssu, in She hsien, just north of the important Anhwei city of T'unch'i. In late April they dispersed to various positions, from which they launched guerrilla attacks on Japanese lines of communication. The area occupied by the three detachments lay south of the Yangtze River and extended from Tanyang, in southwestern Kiangsu, to Fanch'ang, which is located southwest of the Yangtze city of Wuhu, in

Anhwei province. Specific locations of the headquarters and operating zones of the three detachments were:

First Detachment
    Headquarters: Chutsech'iao village, Liyang hsien, in the Maoshan Range of south Kiangsu.
    Zone of Operations: the hsien of Tanyang, Chüjung, Lishui, Chint'an, Chenchiang, and Yangchung.

Second Detachment
    Headquarters: Chint'an
    Zone of Operations: Tanyang, Chüjung, and Chiangning hsien of Kiangsu, immediately south of the Yangtze; and Tangt'u hsien, south Anhwei.

Third Detachment
    Headquarters: Machiach'ung, in Fanch'ang hsien, Anhwei.
    Zone of Operations: Fanch'ang and Kuangte hsien, south Anhwei.[2]

The New Fourth Army itself moved its headquarters several times after the detachments dispersed to their operational positions. Headquarters were finally located, in 1940, at the New Fourth Army's permanent base at Ching hsien, about 75 kilometers south of Wuhu, Anhwei.

The Fourth Detachment had an entirely different history from the other three. Consisting of about 1,000 men, it was sent directly from Hankow, in March 1938, to occupy the area around Huangan, in northeastern Hupeh province. By local recruitment it raised its total strength to about 2,000 men and, in January 1939, moved eastward to Tungchiangch'ung, Shuch'eng hsien, in north Anhwei. There it continued its recruiting activities and reached a total size of about 3,000 men. It then transferred about 1,000 men to the vicinity of Luchiang, Anhwei, where these transferees formed the nucleus of the newly created Fifth Detachment. Continuing to act chiefly as a cadre army that trained other armies, the Fourth Detachment moved, in April 1939, to the region of Out'ang, in Tingyüan hsien, Anhwei, and sought more recruits. It established strong bases in this area and reached a troop size of about 4,000 men.

In early 1940, however, the Fourth Detachment had its first clashes with the Kwangsi Army, which had occupied the northern bank of the Yangtze in Anhwei province after withdrawing from the T'aierhchuang campaign. These Kuomintang troops—actually the semi-independent but highly skilled Kwangsi Army was allied with the Chiang Kai-shek government

CENTRAL CHINA

—constituted the Fifth War Area Army (north Kiangsu, north Anhwei, and south Shantung), commanded by the most famous Nationalist general, Li Tsung-jen. Under the Anhwei governorship of General Liao Lei (a Kwangsi general), relations between the New Fourth Army and the Kwangsi Army had been fairly good. However, following Liao's death in 1939, and the appointment of General Li P'in-hsien (also a Kwangsi general) as his successor, the situation worsened. This was partly due to Communist expansionist activities and partly due to General Li's strong anti-Communist sentiments. The first clashes between the two armies occurred in February 1940; by May fighting in north Anhwei was continuous. Pressure from the Kwangsi Army, and from Japanese mopping-up campaigns, caused the Fourth Detachment to be cut off from New Fourth Army headquarters south of the river; and it decided to retreat eastward. In mid-1940 it moved east of the Tientsin-Pukow railroad into north Kiangsu, where it occupied the area around Hsüi on the shores of Lake Hungtze.[3]

Meanwhile, in early 1939, the vice-commander of the Second Detachment, Lo Ping-hui, led a small group of cadres from the Second Detachment's headquarters at Chint'an, south Kiangsu, to the staging area for the new Fifth Detachment. Lo joined the 1,000 soldiers transferred from the Fourth Detachment at Luchiang, Anhwei, in May 1939, and formed the Fifth Detachment of the New Fourth Army with himself as commander. Building on the 1,000-man nucleus by local recruitment, the Fifth Detachment soon reached a size of 2,000 men and began a northeasterly march from Luchiang, In July 1939, it set up bases in the Laian-Liuho area, straddling the Anhwei-Kiangsu border opposite Nanking, and continued recruiting until it reached a size of approximately 5,000 soldiers. The detachment moved north to the area around Lake Kaoyu at the end of 1939 and clashed severely with KMT troops in Kiangsu (this battle is discussed later). It was scattered again by the Japanese mopping-up campaign of late summer 1940 (the "Three Rivers Operation"); but after the Japanese withdrew, the Fifth Detachment came back with renewed strength.[4] At the end of 1940, it was located in T'ienchang (Pinghui) hsien, Anhwei, on the western shore of Lake Kaoyu, where it was working to establish an anti-Japanese base.[5]

The last of the regular New Fourth Army units, the Sixth Detachment, was not formed on the basis of Red Army remnants in central China, but was made up of Eighth Route Army cadres from Shansi. At the end of September 1938, a small unit—about the size of a regiment—under the command of P'eng Hsüeh-feng, advanced into eastern Honan from Shansi. According to Japanese accounts, P'eng's unit settled in the area of T'aik'ang and Ch'enchou (Huaiyang) hsien, where it increased in strength by local recruitment and by reorganizing KMT troops who were defeated in the fighting around K'aifeng. In June 1939, this force was incorporated into the New Fourth Army as the Sixth Detachment. During 1940, the Sixth Detachment moved into northern Anhwei, establishing its headquarters at Koyang, where it expanded its strength to approximately 6,400 men. It became the most powerful New Fourth Army unit north of the Yangtze prior to Ch'en Yi's entrance into north Kiangsu (June 1940).[6]

With the establishment of the Fifth and Sixth Detachments and the considerable enlargement of Communist areas north of the Yangtze by 1939, the New Fourth Army reorganized its command structure. Two regional authorities—the South Yangtze Command (Chiang-nan Chih-hui-pu) under Ch'en Yi, and the North Yangtze Command (Chiang-pei Chih-hui-pu) under Chang Yün-i—were set up in November 1939 to provide regional supervision. The South Yangtze Command directed the operations of the First, Second, and Third Detachments; the North Yangtze Command directed the Fourth, Fifth, and Sixth.

TABLE 4

NEW FOURTH ARMY, JANUARY 1940[7]

Headquarters—Commander: Yeh T'ing
    Vice-Commander: Hsiang Ying (political commissar)
    Chief of Staff: Chang Yün-i
    Chief, Political Department: Yüan Kuo-p'ing
    Vice-Chief, Political Department: Teng Tzu-hui

  South Yangtze Command—Commander: Ch'en Yi
    First Detachment—Commander: Ch'en Yi
      Political Commissar: Liu Yen
    Second Detachment—Commander: Chang Ting-ch'eng
      Political Commissar: Su Yü
    Third Detachment—Commander: T'an Chen-lin
      Political Commissar: T'an Chen-lin

  North Yangtze Command—Commander: Chang Yün-i
    Fourth Detachment—Commander: Tai Chi-ying
      Political Commissar: unknown
    Fifth Detachment—Commander: Lo Ping-hui
      Political Commissar: Kuo Shu-hsün
    Sixth Detachment—Commander: P'eng Hsüeh-feng
      Political Commissar: Wu Chih-yüan

In addition to these regular forces, the New Fourth Army was allied with several regional guerrilla corps of great importance. One of these irregular units was the Honan-Hupeh Volunteer Column under the well-known Red Army officer Li Hsien-nien. Li's force held an extensive area on both sides of the Pinghan railroad between Hsinyang (Honan) and Yingshan (Hupeh), north of Hankow. This unit was incorporated into the regular New Fourth Army in the reorganization that followed the New Fourth Army Incident.[8]

Another of the New Fourth Army's guerrilla affiliates was the Hunan-Hupeh-Kiangsi Border Area Guerrilla Column led by Fang Pu-chou. This unit operated in the old Red Army base located in the mountainous region north of Chingkangshan—i.e., in the three border hsien of P'ingchiang, Hunan; Hsiushui, Kiangsi; and Yanghsin, Hupeh. P'ingchiang was the place where P'eng Te-huai had instigated the mutiny of July 1928 which led to the formation of the Fifth Red Army; it was also the scene, on June 12, 1939, of the earliest known clash between KMT and New Fourth Army forces, an attack by KMT troops on the recently established New Fourth Army Communications Office in which all members of the Communist staff were killed.[9] The guerrilla forces in the Hunan-Kiangsi-Hupeh border area were never formally integrated into the New Fourth Army as a detachment, but they held on to their base until 1945, when Ho Lung's raiding column met them in south China.

Still another major group of the New Fourth Army's guerrilla affiliates was concentrated in the Shanghai-Nanking-Hangchow triangle. The importance of Communist operations in this area, coupled with the fact that relatively little has been known about these forces in the past, requires that we examine the south Kiangsu guerrillas in some detail. In addition to the south Kiangsu guerrilla units mentioned in Chapter Two—namely, the Communist-affiliated Kiangnan Anti-Japanese Patriotic Army and the Chungking-affiliated Loyal National Salvation Army[10]—there was another Communist unit in the Shanghai triangle that played a major role in the Communist expansion into north Kiangsu. This was the Kiangnan Advance Column (Chiang-nan T'ing-chin Tsung-tui), under the command of Kuan Wen-wei. Kuan led the first important body of New Fourth Army troops into KMT-controlled north Kiangsu; subsequently he headed the North Kiangsu Administrative Committee, established in 1940. After 1949, he was made Vice-Chairman of the Kiangsu Provincial Government. In the following paragraphs we shall trace the fortunes of all three of these guerrilla units in the Shanghai vicinity.

The Japanese themselves admit that the cause of guerrilla activity in the Kiangsu triangle was the disruption produced by the fighting of 1937. According to the Kōain, after the battle of Shanghai "the entire area from the Yangtze south was thrown into confusion"; many KMT troops were left behind as the battle moved westward, large quantities of arms and ammunition were hidden in the area, and both regular and guerrilla soldiers were compelled to live off the land, thereby adding to the difficulties of the peasantry.[11] The chaotic situation gave rise to a large number of guerrilla bands, bandit gangs, troop remnants, and village self-defense corps—all of which fought among themselves for hegemony and all of which eventually established contacts with either the puppets, the Communists, or the Nationalists, in order to receive funds and supplies. The period 1937–41 can be roughly divided into four phases according to who was on top in this continuing struggle. The first phase was a period of survival-of-the-fittest; there was little political content to the fighting between various bands for spheres of influence. The second period was one of dominance by the Loyal National Salvation Army under the control of General Tai Li in Chungking.[12] The third phase saw the intrusion of Communist-controlled guerrilla units, which resulted in driving the former KMT-affiliated units into the ranks of the puppets. During the fourth phase the Japanese occupied the strong points and moved to establish Model Peace Zones.[13]

The Loyal National Salvation Army (KMT) was set up in 1937 by local KMT leaders on the basis of recruitment in the Chiangyin-Ch'angshu sector, roughly 100 kilometers northwest of Shanghai. Tai Li's original agent, Chou Tao-san, made contact with the Chiangyin guerrillas and offered them supplies from Chungking; these supplies were accepted, in return for which the guerrillas gave their political allegiance to Tai Li. Chou Tao-san was ousted in 1938 as a result of an intrigue promoted by one Yüan Ya-ch'eng, a former member of the KMT Blue Shirt Society (Lan-i She), who replaced Chou as Tai Li's representative in south Kiangsu. Subsequently, Yüan actually headed the Loyal National Salvation Army.[14] With regard to its guerrilla activities, this unit appears always to have been more anti-Communist than anti-Japanese. According to one Kōain study, its motto was "Not one Communist soldier allowed east of the Huning [Shanghai-Nanking] railroad";[15] and Ch'en Yi once complained that whenever the New Fourth Army attacked *puppet* forces in Kiangsu towns, Tai Li complained that the Communists had attacked his troops![16] With the revival of Communist strength in the area in 1940, the Loyal National Salvation Army formally joined the Nanking regime.[17]

The Kiangnan Anti-Japanese Patriotic Army—the Communist unit—
was also founded in the Chiangyin-Ch'angshu area in October 1937. However, owing to its leftist leanings, the Kiangnan Army was hardly a fraction
of the size of the Loyal National Salvation Army; it was also very poorly
equipped. Under pressure from the KMT-affiliated unit, the Kiangnan
Army withdrew west of the Huning line into Tanyang and Liyang hsien
in 1938; and, in the summer of 1939, this unit—then consisting of only a few
sick and wounded soldiers—placed itself under the control of Leng Hsin,
the Nationalist military commander in the Kiangsu-Anhwei border area.
In the autumn of 1939, as a result of extremely harsh treatment from Leng,
the survivors of the Kiangnan Army joined Kuan Wen-wei's unit on the
river coast area; and the first Kiangnan Anti-Japanese Patriotic Army
ceased to exist.[18]

However, in November 1939, the nucleus of a second Kiangnan Army
was formed in the village of Tungt'ang, Ch'angshu hsien. A small group
of men who remained behind in the Soochow-Ch'angshu sector when the
Kiangnan Army was first driven out organized a cadre platoon and began
a movement to recreate the Kiangnan Army. The unit grew by local recruitment, by incorporating old Kiangnan members, by alliances with
bandits, and by annexing a KMT peace preservation regiment that had
been mauled in a Japanese mopping-up campaign.[19] In April 1940, the
New Fourth Army sent an officer, Lin Tsun, to command the new unit, and
in October 1940 Lin organized three guerrilla columns, which together
totaled 1,500–2,000 men. Also in October, the Kiangnan Army set up the
Teng-Hsi-Yü Administrative Area—the local Communist-sponsored government—consisting of the rural areas of Chiangyin, Ch'angshu, and
Wuhsi. The Kiangnan Army remained the ruling authority in the area
west of Shanghai from the spring of 1940 until the first Model Peace Zone
was set up in July 1941. Even after that, the Kiangnan Army maintained
clandestine units in the Ch'angshu-Wuhsi-Wuchin area.[20]

The third important guerrilla unit in the south Kiangsu area between
1937 and 1941 was that of Kuan Wen-wei. The origins of his force were
similar to those of the other two guerrilla armies except that Kuan's area of
operations was further from Shanghai and he did not have any KMT competition in his area. In the midst of the battle of Shanghai and before the
fall of Chenchiang, Kuan—then a local commander at Chenchiang—went
to the village of Fanghsiench'iao, in Tanyang hsien, and established a guerrilla training unit. Working with his brother, Kuan Wen-tsao, Kuan recruited villagers for his guerrilla unit and organized village self-defense

corps. The Kuan brothers were aided in this work by the fact that they
were natives of Tanyang hsien and were of middle-peasant origin. They
also collected a sizable amount of money from the villagers with which to
support the band. In May 1938, when the New Fourth Army's First and
Second Detachments infiltrated the Tanyang area, they contacted Kuan
Wen-wei. From that time on, Kuan took orders from Ch'en Yi's headquarters at Maoshan.

During 1939, Kuan Wen-wei's unit was neutralized by an internal dispute. One of Kuan's commanders had taken a bribe from the Japanese, and
the forces under this officer had to be disarmed. By early 1940, however, the
whole unit was reorganized; and, with the help of the New Fourth Army,
it began to expand its territories. Kuan's forces had gained complete control of strategic Yangchung hsien, on the Yangtze, by late 1939. In January
1940, the Japanese carried out a mopping-up campaign in the Yangchung
area that had the effect of scattering Kuan Wen-wei's forces into the hsien
north of the river from Yangchung. Although various sorties had been
made into north Kiangsu before—including an important raid by Kuan
in December 1939—this was the first large-scale influx. In mid-1940, the
Japanese listed the following areas as held by Kuan Wen-wei: the rural
areas around Chenchiang, Ch'angchou (or Wuchin), and Tanyang on the
south bank; and points in Icheng, Chiangtu, and T'ai hsien on the north
shore. Thus, Kuan Wen-wei's unit was holding a valuable area straddling
the Yangtze just at the time when the Nationalists were pressuring the New
Fourth Army to evacuate the south Yangtze area.[21] Kuan's corridor also
provided a useful escape route for the Kiangnan Army whenever Japanese
pressure became too intense in the Shanghai area.

THE NEW FOURTH ARMY'S SEIZURE OF NORTH KIANGSU

In the past, the area to the north of the Shanghai triangle across the
Yangtze was regarded, in comparison with south Kiangsu, as a socially and
economically backward area. One prewar writer noted that "in the rural
districts of the north, there is a much thicker atmosphere of pre-capitalism";
and north Kiangsu was traditionally an area from which peasants emigrated
to become peddlers, factory laborers, or ricksha pullers in the south.[22] National consciousness was nonexistent, and even in the heyday of the Red
Army in Kiangsi and Fukien only the most moderate Communist organization developed in the area around Nant'ung. One Communist unit

reached its peak in April 1930, in Nant'ung, and then quickly declined.[23] In short, there was not even a prewar tradition of peasant rebelliousness in north Kiangsu (such as that found in Kiangsi), much less one of nationalism. Nonetheless, according to an American intelligence study made in 1945, "North Kiangsu has probably been a purely Communist area since 1942."[24] Obviously, important changes occurred in the pattern of life in north Kiangsu between 1937 and 1942.

During 1938 and 1939, north Kiangsu was under the complete control of the Kuomintang Army.[25] The highest Chungking official in the area was General Yü Hsueh-chung, commander of the Shantung-Kiangsu war zone; but he was preoccupied with developments in Shantung during most of this period. The KMT official whose troops were actually occupying north Kiangsu and with whom the New Fourth Army collided in 1940 was Lieutenant General Han Te-ch'in, Governor of Kiangsu province.[26] Han's own forces totaled 60,000 to 70,000 men, and he also controlled certain local units said by the Japanese to be of a bandit character. The most important of these local forces were the units of Li Ming-yang, who later joined the New Fourth Army, and of Li Ch'ang-chiang, who later went over to the Nanking puppets.[27] However, none of these forces saw much action in 1938 and 1939. Han Te-ch'in's philosophy of resistance was generally one of "waiting in preparation" and of securely maintaining his own position; he did not carry out guerrilla warfare against the Japanese.

The first Communist threat to Han Te-ch'in's sanctuary came not from the south but from the west. As we have described earlier, the Fourth, Fifth, and Sixth Detachments of the New Fourth Army were ranged up and down the Kiangsu-Anhwei border in the Hungtze and Kaoyu lake areas during 1940. The maneuvering of these forces and their recruiting activities from approximately mid-1939 onward greatly alarmed regional KMT commanders, and, as we have seen, fighting broke out between the Kwangsi troops of the National Government and the New Fourth Army's Fourth Detachment in central Anhwei in the winter of 1939. The unit that seemed most threatening to Han Te-ch'in was Lo Ping-hui's Fifth Detachment. In the autumn of 1939, Lo's force of approximately 5,000 soldiers moved northeast from the Laian-Liuho area to the region between Lake Hungtze and Lake Kaoyu; and in November 1939 a serious clash occurred between Lo Ping-hui and Han Te-ch'in in the vicinity of Hsüi on the Kiangsu border. It appears that Lo's forces were attacked by Han's units for making an unauthorized advance into Kiangsu and that Lo was halted temporarily by this attack. A few days later, however, Lo defeated individual units of Han's army and captured large amounts of equipment.[28] Following this, Lo Ping-hui withdrew to the shores of Lake Kaoyu, where he awaited assistance from both the New Fourth Army and the Eighth Route Army to help him in his struggle with Han. Two Communist units were dispatched with the mission of rescuing the Fifth Detachment immediately after the November clash. Kuan Wen-wei, the Communist guerrilla leader on the Yangtze coast, led the first of several important raids into north Kiangsu in December 1939 to assist Lo Ping-hui; and, at the same time, about 1,000 men from the Eighth Route Army—the vanguard of a much larger force— marched south from Shantung, in the north, and joined Lo in January 1940.[29]

Kuan's December-January sortie took him from Yangchung to Yang-chou, one of the more important cities of north Kiangsu; but he was forced to return to Yangchung in January 1940, as a result of the Japanese mop-ping-up campaign that forced many of his units south of the Yangtze to cross to the north. However, in the spring of 1940, Kuan's guerrilla column set out again from its north bank enclave and marched all over the south-eastern part of north Kiangsu. Kuan established guerrilla units at Tach'iao, near Yangchou, and at Liuho; and he also made contact with Lo Ping-hui at Kaoyu. He fought three decisive battles with the regional forces of Li Ch'ang-chiang and generally cleared the area immediately north of the Yangtze, around Yangchung, of KMT troops. Han Te-ch'in did not participate in these actions; he probably remained north of Kaoyu, guarding against further advances by Lo Ping-hui's detachment. However, Kuan's activities, in addition to being a part of the rescue of Lo's Fifth Detachment, also were intended to prepare the way for the main force of the New Fourth Army; and the intrusion of the latter compelled Han Te-ch'in to take direct action against the Communists.

In south Kiangsu in the spring of 1940, KMT pressure on the New Fourth Army detachments had grown intense. The forces of Leng Hsin, the KMT commander on the south Kiangsu-Anhwei border, and of Ku Chu-t'ung, the Third War Area commander, had so constricted the move-ments of the First and Second Detachments that Ch'en Yi decided to join Kuan Wen-wei north of the river. Ch'en led the South Yangtze Command from its main base at Maoshan to the vicinity of Wuhsi in the spring of 1940, and at the end of June sent several thousand men of the First and Second Detachments—as well as units of the Kiangnan Army and other local guerrillas—across the Yangtze in the vicinity of Chiangyin. Upon its arrival in north Kiangsu, the New Fourth Army occupied the region around T'aihsing hsien.

One Japanese study comments that Ch'en hoped to avoid armed clashes with KMT troops in north Kiangsu, since he had experienced so much friction in the south.[30] Nevertheless, conflict with Han Te-ch'in broke out almost at once; and the chronology of events indicates that it was the Communists who committed the first breach. At the end of July, Kuan Wen-wei fought his way into the small town of Huangch'iao, 25 kilometers northeast of T'aihsing, and destroyed the local peace preservation units under Ho K'o-ch'ien, a subordinate of Han Te-ch'in. This action, known as the first battle of Huangch'iao, brought an immediate response from Han, who advanced south from his bases around Hsinghua and Paoying. Han's forces and the New Fourth Army came into contact during the first week of September and fought continuously throughout most of September and October. Ch'en Yi's soldiers defeated the Nationalists first at Kuhsi, and then, in early October, decimated Han's forces in the second battle of Huangch'iao. Han's troops retreated in disorder to the northwest, and Ch'en Yi pursued them as far as Tungt'ai. Casualties were very high on both sides, but the New Fourth Army's losses were more than made up when the local forces of Li Ming-yang and the survivors of Ho K'o-ch'ien's unit all joined the Communist Army after Han's defeat. The New Fourth Army sent several telegrams of regret concerning this incident to Chungking, explaining it in terms of Han Te-ch'in's treachery to the cause of Chinese resistance and of Ho K'o-ch'ien's being an "unworthy bandit."[31] Needless to say, Nationalist commanders south of the Yangtze were not reassured; they had their revenge in January at Maolin.[32]

At the same time that Ch'en Yi was securing the area as far north as Tungt'ai, an important column of the Eighth Route Army—the vanguard of which had already joined Lo in January 1940—advanced into north Kiangsu from Anhwei. This unit—variously identified as the Fifth or the Eighth Column of the Eighth Route Army—was a force of some 15,000 men under Huang K'o-ch'eng, which had been sent from Shansi in early 1940 to help in the relief of Lo Ping-hui. Huang proceeded on his mission via Hopei and Shantung; he linked up with New Fourth Army forces (Sixth Detachment) at Koyang, northern Anhwei, in August 1940. In the following weeks Huang proceeded eastward until he reached Founing, where he established a camp and placed his unit under the general command of

Ch'en Yi.[33] Ch'en, in the meantime, had advanced from Tungt'ai to Yen-ch'eng, where he established the headquarters of the New Fourth Army forces in north Kiangsu. By this time Han Te-ch'in's forces had been reduced to as few as 10,000 troops, according to Communist claims, and were restricted to a small area around Paoying.[34] The Communists now held all of north Kiangsu east of the Grand Canal.

THE NEW FOURTH ARMY INCIDENT

Prior to the seizure of north Kiangsu, the New Fourth Army had carried out guerrilla operations against Japanese lines of supply and communications in accordance with its orders and had enlarged its strength by regular, public recruitment. It had not sought to establish rear-area governments or to set up mass associations on the model of those existing in Wu-t'aishan. As late as December 1939, the New Fourth Army had been commended by the Third War Area commander, Ku Chu-t'ung, for its splendid record in fighting the Japanese.[35] However, with the flight of Wang Ching-wei from Chungking and with the move to establish a new central government, the New Fourth Army began to devote more of its time to political operations and to the expansion of the territories under its control. The Communists in central China were also influenced by the successes of the Eighth Route Army in the north and by the already apparent strains in the United Front, but the chief motivating force was the threat that the new Nanking government posed to their position. The Communists felt that if the Japanese were successful in their plan to "end the war," the New Fourth Army would find itself back in the desperate position it had occupied in the spring of 1937. The New Fourth Army also feared, in the winter of 1939, that Chiang Kai-shek might succumb to the combined pressure of Wang and the Japanese and join an anti-Communist front; thus they felt that immediate steps were needed in order to consolidate their holdings.[36]

As soon as the New Fourth Army began to undertake extensive organizational activities in the south Yangtze area, the suspicions of the Kuomintang forces in that region were aroused. After witnessing the Communist expansion from Shensi to Shantung, clear across north China, Nationalist officers in central China could not believe that Communist political work with the peasantry was designed only to keep the peasants out of the puppet armies. Suspicions of each other's motives were already far advanced when the Communists began establishing local governments not subject to Chungking's jurisdiction. The Nationalist government could not approve this challenge to its authority in the area of its greatest strength, and it reacted to the New Fourth Army's activities with a plan to relocate all the Communist forces in an area north of the Yellow River. The first objective of the Nationalists was to get the Communist forces south of the Yangtze to evacuate to the north of the river; the movement from the Yangtze to the Yellow River could be considered after the first move had been accomplished. The KMT plan to push the Communists out of the south Yangtze area was implemented by means of direct orders to New Fourth Army headquarters and to Yenan, and by local pressure on the detachments themselves.

In June 1940, CCP and KMT officials undertook negotiations in Chungking to delineate borders for both the New Fourth Army and the Eighth Route Army. No written agreement was drawn up, but a general understanding was reached whereby the area north of the Yellow River would be recognized as Communist territory (except for southern Shansi, which was to remain in KMT hands), in return for which the New Fourth Army would vacate central China.[37] In early July, Chungking issued directives ordering all Communist forces to concentrate in the north China area. To all appearances, the South Yangtze Command obeyed these orders promptly. As we have already seen, Ch'en Yi had led the First Detachment and most of the Second into north Kiangsu in late June; and T'an Chenlin's Third Detachment crossed the river into Anhwei, where it occupied the southern bank of Lake Ch'ao, in Wuwei hsien, in September 1940.[38] The only regular Communist force left south of the Yangtze was the New Fourth Army Headquarters detachment, consisting of 4,000 troops, about 2,000 wounded officers and men, and approximately 3,000 political workers, cadets, medical service personnel, and families.[39] It was located at Ching hsien, Anhwei, and was commanded by Yeh T'ing and Hsiang Ying.

Between October 19 and December 9, 1940, Yeh T'ing exchanged an extensive series of telegrams with the Nationalist chief-of-staff, Ho Yingch'in, concerning the evacuation of the headquarters force to north China. From all appearances, these negotiations were carried out in good faith. Following the virtual elimination of KMT influence in north Kiangsu in October, however, Chungking's attitude had noticeably hardened. Although Chungking had ordered the New Fourth Army troops to move north of the Yangtze, it had not—of course—ordered them to eliminate all

KMT troops in that area, as Ch'en Yi had done. Therefore, on December 9, the Government set December 31, 1940, as the deadline by which all New Fourth Army troops had to move north of the Yangtze and all Eighth Route Army forces had to be north of the Yellow River (the New Fourth Army had until January 31, 1941, to reach the Yellow River). Shortly thereafter, Yeh T'ing called on Ku Chu-t'ung, the Third War Area commander, to discuss a route to the north. From this point on, materials concerning the course of events are contradictory. Some sources say that Yeh T'ing arranged with Ku to move first into south Kiangsu and then to cross into north Kiangsu following Ch'en Yi's route, and that Ku agreed to this course. Then, prior to Yeh's departure, the Yangtze crossing was allegedly changed by Ku Chu-t'ung to a transit at Fanch'ang and T'ungling (Anhwei). The Fanch'ang crossing would have placed Yeh T'ing in the hands of the Kwangsi general, Li P'in-hsien, who had already clashed bitterly with Communist forces; and Yeh, therefore, refused to take this route. Other sources explain Yeh's failure to leave by citing Japanese pressures in the area and the refusal of Ku Chu-t'ung to send adequate ammunition with which the headquarters unit could defend itself. In any case, the New Fourth Army headquarters was not north of the Yangtze on December 31, 1940, but was marching instead in a southwesterly (!) direction from its Ching hsien base, possibly heading for the old Red areas in south Kiangsi.[40]

On January 4, 1941, the headquarters force of approximately 9,000 men was surrounded by Nationalist troops at Maolin, a few miles southwest of Ching hsien. The KMT unit that carried out the encirclement was the 40th division under the joint command of Ku Chu-t'ung and General Shang-kuan Yün-hsiang, the Nationalist commander in south Anhwei. A battle ensued between the two armies that lasted for ten days and produced casualties on both sides running into the thousands. The over-all result was a crushing defeat for the New Fourth Army: Yeh T'ing was taken prisoner by General Shang-kuan; and both Hsiang Ying, the vice-commander, and Yüan Kuo-p'ing, chief of the political department, were killed.[41] Then, on January 17, 1941, the Central Government in Chungking announced the dissolution of the New Fourth Army because of its continuous breaches of military discipline. Following this date, the United Front existed only as a poorly observed truce. Virtually all traffic between Yenan and Chungking came to an end; Eighth Route Army offices in Nationalist-held cities were closed; many non-Communist liberals, such as Liang Sou-ming, fled to

Hong Kong; and the Communists openly attacked KMT troops in the rear areas.[42]

An understanding of the origins and consequences of the New Fourth Army Incident is central to an analysis of the Communists' acquisition of nationalist legitimacy during the war. Both the Communists and the Nationalists were guilty of breaches of the United Front prior to the New Fourth Army Incident. KMT softness in carrying out resistance operations during the post-Hankow period certainly reinforced the Communist view that the KMT was trying to work out some kind of *modus vivendi* with the Japanese. In addition, the KMT had set up an extensive blockade of the Shen-Kan-Ning Border Area in the north in early 1939, and in June of that same year it enacted the "Limitation of Foreign Parties' Activities Law," legalizing the suppression of Communist activities.[43] On the other hand, although the Communist Army was actually continuing the fight against the Japanese, its methods left no room for more than one Chinese victor over Japan, as Han Te-ch'in knew only too well. Communist operations were intended to thwart and to defeat the Japanese invaders, but they also aimed at the displacement of the Kuomintang.

The significance of these respective violations of the United Front is that whereas the Communists erred in going beyond Government orders in carrying out the resistance against Japan, the KMT committed the mistake of lagging behind the CCP in anti-Japanese fervor. The Government was *legally* within its rights in denouncing the activities of the Communists and in attacking their armies or their newspapers, but in so doing it jeopardized its own reputation with the masses, whose predominant political concern was "national salvation" and "resistance to Japan." The Communists could violate Nationalist military directives with impunity so long as they appeared more anti-Japanese than the Government, and they knew it. In actual fact, the Communists had flouted Government orders in central China throughout most of 1940; but since they had won the allegiance of a constituency—the mobilized peasants of the rear areas, who did not regard Chungking as the "Government"—it was useless for the Government to charge the Communists with acting illegally. Moreover, by violating Government orders, the Communists forced Chungking into the difficult position of disciplining an army of popular (albeit self-proclaimed) "heroes."

If it is politically valuable to be thought of as a national hero, it is even more valuable to be a national martyr; and this points to the political significance of the New Fourth Army Incident. No single event in the entire Sino-Japanese war did more to enhance the Communists' prestige vis-à-vis the Nationalists than the destruction of the New Fourth Army headquarters while it was "loyally following orders." This defeat made the Chinese Communists martyrs to the cause of Chinese nationalism. If we remove the nationalistic coloration from the New Fourth Army Incident, and regard it solely as a power struggle between two regional guerrilla forces (for example, as a battle in the 1927–37 civil war), then it appears merely as a case of KMT retaliation following upon an extraordinary Communist provocation (the north Kiangsu invasion). However, a defeat that might well have been regarded as "just deserts" in different circumstances was transformed into an ideological victory because of the Communists' successful identification with Chinese nationalism. This becomes apparent when we view the extent of Communist expansion at KMT expense after the New Fourth Army Incident.

THE MISSION OF LIU SHAO-CH'I

Although the New Fourth Army Incident dealt a serious blow to the Communist forces in central China, it by no means eliminated them. Strong Communist units remained north of the Yangtze and continued their efforts to establish permanent rear-area bases; to be effective, these units needed only a new Army high command, since the old commander, Yeh T'ing, was in prison, and the other key officers were dead. A new command was announced by telegram from Yenan on January 22, 1941. Ch'en Yi was named acting commander; Chang Yün-i became vice-commander; Lai Ch'uan-chu was appointed chief of staff; Teng Tzu-hui headed the new political department; and Liu Shao-ch'i, a member of the Central Committee, became the New Fourth Army's political commissar.[44]

The appointment of Liu Shao-ch'i shows that the Communists appreciated the importance of political forces in the central China military struggle. Indeed, the New Fourth Army's needs were peculiarly political rather than military: permanent bases had to be set up, and the closest possible relations between Army and peasantry had to be created if the New Fourth Army Incident was not to be repeated north of the Yangtze. Liu was both an expert in political propaganda and completely familiar with the lessons that had been learned from similar operations in north China. His task was to lay down the line that the "post-Incident" New Fourth Army was to adopt in mobilizing and organizing the masses under its jurisdiction. The essence of this line was to paint the Kuomintang forces as identical to the puppets and justify the New Fourth Army's opposition to the KMT on these grounds. (As we shall see, in Yugoslavia an identical policy was adopted by the Partisans toward the Chetniks following an armed clash between the two forces.)

Liu spelled out these and other parts of his policy in an article entitled "Present Conditions and Tasks in Central Kiangsu," which he published in the New Fourth Army journal, *Chiang-Huai jih-pao* ("Yangtze and Huai Daily"), at Yench'eng, March 22, 1941.[45] Before we can explore Liu's formula in detail, however, it is necessary to consider the situation north of the Yangtze at the time. The extent of control already achieved by Ch'en Yi in north Kiangsu, the reorganization of all New Fourth Army forces north of the Yangtze, and the Japanese and puppet mopping-up campaigns of 1941—all these factors influenced the policy advanced by Liu, as well as its eventual success.

Immediately after defeating Han Te-ch'in's Nationalists in the second battle of Huangch'iao (early October, 1940), Ch'en Yi began consolidating his position along the northern bank of the Yangtze. His first action was to reorganize the military units that he had led into north Kiangsu in June. These forces included the First Detachment, part of the Second Detachment (the rest of the Second Detachment was destroyed at Maolin), the Kiangnan Advance Column (under Kuan Wen-wei), elements of the Kiangnan Anti-Japanese Patriotic Army, and the South Yangtze Command headquarters. All of these organizations were combined into one new formation entitled the North Kiangsu Command; and this force was then subdivided into four subordinate units, called "columns," each of approximately brigade size. Ch'en Yi headed this new North Kiangsu Command, which was the highest Communist headquarters in central China until February 1941, when the whole New Fourth Army was reorganized under Liu Shao-ch'i's direction. From October to February, the Third, Fourth, Fifth, and Sixth Detachments also continued to operate in north Anhwei; but they were under heavy KMT and Japanese pressure. The north Anhwei forces were scattered and on the defensive until after the re-establishment of a supreme command at Yench'eng.

Ch'en Yi's troops were deployed in the Tungt'ai-Huangch'iao region of north Kiangsu at the time of Han Te-ch'in's retreat. In October 1940 the Communists advanced northward in pursuit of the fleeing Nationalists, their aim being to link up with Huang K'o-ch'eng's Eighth Route Army reinforcements. Ch'en's units reached Yench'eng at the end of the month, and in November the North Kiangsu Special Administrative Committee (Su-pei Lin-shih Hsing-cheng Wei-yüan-hui) was established, with Kuan Wen-wei as chairman. The establishment of this Committee, which was the highest civilian agency in the evolving guerrilla base, marked the first step in bringing the civilian population of north Kiangsu into the Communist war effort. The functions of the Committee were analogous to those of the Border Region Administrative Committee in Chin-Ch'a-Chi; and, as we shall see later, the establishment of the Committee was preceded by the usual local assemblies and mobilization committees, just as in Wut'aishan. The seat of the Committee was located at Yench'eng, but it was moved often to such places as Haian and Tungt'ai in order to avoid Japanese mopping-up columns.

In addition to capturing north Kiangsu as far north as Yench'eng, the New Fourth Army also seized the so-called Fourth Administrative Inspector's District of Kiangsu, an area made up of the hsien of Nant'ung, Ch'i-tung, Haimen, and Jukao. This area is part of the fertile peninsula that makes up the extreme eastern end of the Yangtze's north bank. The Fourth District was one of the Communists' first objectives in north Kiangsu, since it is a comparatively rich sector and is strategically located at the mouth of the Yangtze. The third Column of the North Kiangsu Command (i.e., one of the units formed after the battle of Huangch'iao) invaded the Fourth District during October 1940, at the same time that Ch'en Yi was moving to Yench'eng. This column, commanded by T'ao Yung, separated from Ch'en Yi's main force in mid-October and advanced eastward to claim the southeastern part of north Kiangsu for the Communists. Passing through Chingchiang and Nant'ung hsien, T'ao Yung entered Chüehchiang (Ju-tung), the capital of the district, in early November, and established his headquarters.[46]

The peasants of the Fourth District were not entirely without military organization when T'ao Yung's troops arrived. Already in existence was the "Fourth District Guerrilla Command" under the old-time Whampoa instructor Chi Fang, a native of Haimen and a participant in the short-lived Fukien People's Government of November 1933.[47] During 1940, Chi had organized some local peasants into a clandestine guerrilla force not subject to the Fourth District Administrative Inspector, who was loyal to Han. Chi's unit was the most important anti-Japanese guerrilla force created independently of Communist supervision in north Kiangsu. With the defeat of Han's forces and the approach of the New Fourth Army, Chi led his unit to the town of Mat'ang, 15 kilometers west of Chüehchiang, and placed it under T'ao Yung's command. The Mat'ang meeting of mid-November 1940 established the basis for the integration of the Fourth District into the New Fourth Army's war effort. The Communists retained the pre-existing governmental structure in the Fourth District, but placed some of their own men in office. Chi Fang was named local military commander (of the Fourth District Guerrilla Command), and a member of the Communist Party became the new administrative inspector. T'ao Yung became vice-commander of the Fourth District Guerrilla Command. These appointments were all ratified at the Fourth District's first mass meeting, held in Chüehchiang on January 23, 1941. At that time, the citizens of the district declared their allegiance to the North Kiangsu Special Administrative Committee under Kuan Wen-wei and to the New Fourth Army North Kiangsu Command under Ch'en Yi.[48]

According to contemporary accounts and Japanese analyses, the New Fourth Army's entrance into north Kiangsu was characterized by model behavior on the part of the troops. The Japanese observed that despite their inferiority in arms, the New Fourth Army far exceeded the KMT troops in training and discipline. This was important because "the peasants did not necessarily give the New Fourth Army a warm welcome or trust it. Since the peasants did not receive honest government from the KMT or Nanking regimes, they did not expect the New Fourth Army to be different."[49] The peasants were impressed by well-disciplined soldiers, however, and the Communists' propaganda emphasized the contrast between their Army and Han Te-ch'in's. Again, with regard to New Fourth Army conduct, a different Japanese study reprints a letter addressed to a "known person" from a resident of north Kiangsu. This letter, dated October 17, 1940, states: "The New Fourth Army advanced yesterday from Haian toward Fuan and Anfeng. Because of their strict observance of military discipline, the masses welcomed them fully. They did not requisition coolies and showed kindness to the masses."[50] Thus, Ch'en Yi had established a favorable basis for an entirely new Communist stronghold in north Kiangsu precisely at the time when Communist influence south of the Yangtze was being eradicated.

As we have seen, the Communist Party's Central Committee dispatched Liu Shao-ch'i to Yench'eng immediately after the New Fourth Army Incident to aid the forces north of the Yangtze in consolidating their position. Liu lost no time in reorganizing the regular Communist troops and in assigning definite areas of responsibility. The new order of battle was published on February 18, 1941; it is shown in Table 5.

TABLE 5

THE NEW FOURTH ARMY AFTER FEBRUARY 18, 1941[51]

Headquarters—Acting Commander: Ch'en Yi
Vice-Commander: Chang Yün-i
Political Commissar: Liu Shao-ch'i
Chief of Staff: Lai Ch'uan-chu
Chief, Political Department: Teng Tzu-hui

Division	Commander	Political Commissar	Previous Designation
First	Su Yü	Liu Yen	First Detachment
Second	Chang Yün-i (concurrently Army vice-commander)	Lo Ping-hui	Fourth and Fifth Detachments
Third	Huang K'o-ch'eng	Huang K'o-ch'eng	Part of Eighth Route Army
Fourth	P'eng Hsüeh-feng	P'eng Hsüeh-feng	Sixth Detachment
Fifth	Li Hsien-nien	Li Hsien-nien	Honan-Hupeh Volunteer Column
Sixth	T'an Chen-lin	T'an Chen-lin	Third Detachment
Seventh	Chang Ting-ch'eng	Tseng Hsi-wang	Second Detachment

The reorganized New Fourth Army showed several changes over Yeh T'ing's old "bandit remnant" (*ts'an fei*), changes which suggest that the guerrilla quality of the original New Fourth Army had been deliberately eliminated. The use of "divisions" instead of "detachments" reveals a more professional military orientation, and both of the units sent to central China from the Eighth Route Army—the forces of P'eng Hsüeh-feng and of Huang K'o-ch'eng—were given full division status. Moreover, Li Hsiennien's guerrillas north of Hankow were incorporated as regular forces. The combining of the old Fourth and Fifth Detachments into the Second Division under the former head of the North Yangtze Command, Chang Yün-i, may indicate that these forces had been considerably weakened in the 1940 battles against Li P'in-hsien, Han Te-ch'in, and the Japanese in north Anhwei. One further change should be noted. The North Kiangsu Command established by Ch'en Yi in October 1940 was abolished; it became the First Division. Each of the four "columns" of the former North Kiangsu Command (e.g., the Third Column under T'ao Yung) became "brigades" in the new division.[52]

In addition to reorganizing and redesignating the units of the New Fourth Army, Liu Shao-ch'i redefined the units' operating areas. Some of the forces were kept in their positions as of February 1941, to carry out the mass movement and to set up Communist-supervised administrative organs; others were sent into new areas on colonizing missions. Each of the following military areas, which were assigned in the spring of 1941, was a Communist guerrilla base—with a functioning local government in control of the civilian population—by the end of the war.[53]

Division	Operating Area
First	*Central Kiangsu Military Area:*[54] the region bounded by the Yangtze on the south, the Grand Canal on the west, a line between Huainan and the coast on the north, and the Pacific Ocean on the east.
Second	*South Huai Military Area:* the region bounded by the Yangtze and a line between Nanking and Hofei on the south, Hofei to Pengpu on the west, the Huai River on the north, and the Grand Canal on the east.
Third	*North Kiangsu Military Area:* the region north of Huainan and Founing, bounded on the west by the Grand Canal.
Fourth	*North Huai Military Area:* the region bounded by the Huai River on the south, the Tientsin-Pukow railroad on the west, a line between the Grand Canal and Hsüchou on the north, and the Grand Canal on the east.[55]
Fifth	*The Hupeh-Honan-Anhwei Military Area:* Li Hsien-nien's guerrilla area north of Hankow.
Sixth	*South Kiangsu Military Area:* the region around Lake T'ai. T'an Chen-lin's unit, which had evacuated north of the river in September 1940, re-entered the mountainous Kiangsu-Chekiang border area in 1941.
Seventh	*Central Anhwei Military Area:* both banks of the Yangtze westward to Susung, in Anhwei. This area contained the fewest regular forces (5,000) at the end of the war, owing undoubtedly to the presence of strong KMT forces and the area's strategic value to the Japanese.

These seven areas were pacified and mopped up by the Japanese during the four years between 1941 and 1945, but they remained securely in New Fourth Army hands until the outbreak of the civil war. During the civil war some of the most decisive struggles—notably, the battle of Huai-Hai—occurred in north Kiangsu and north Anhwei, where the Communists profited from their long familiarity with the region. At the end of the

Sino-Japanese war, according to one estimate, these seven areas held field forces of 114,000 men; and the militia was estimated to total 265,000 in only the four areas of north, central, and south Kiangsu and central Anhwei (no estimates exist for the militia in the two Huai regions and Honan-Hupeh).[56] These estimates do not, of course, include the populations of large cities and towns, which were occupied by the puppets and the Japanese until the closing months of the war.

Before we can deal with Liu Shao-ch'i's prescription for mobilizing this large area, one further ingredient must be considered—namely, the contribution of the Japanese Army. As we have seen, one of the major wartime influences on the Chinese peasantry—one that often induced the peasants to accept and support Communist leadership—was the menace of Japanese military reprisals. As a general rule, the Communists were not able to establish guerrilla bases in regions that had had no direct experience with the Japanese Army. After the Japanese operations of early 1938, north Kiangsu experienced no further Japanese intrusions for three years. Then, as if to confirm the nationalistic propaganda of New Fourth Army political workers, the Japanese carried out two mopping-up campaigns in north Kiangsu in 1941. The first campaign was in February 1941, and went as far north as Tungt'ai; the Japanese occupied both Nant'ung and Jukao at this time. Kōain sources are perfectly frank about the results of this campaign:

> The mopping-up campaign of February caused a complete change in the power position in north Kiangsu. The Han Te-ch'in Army suffered a crushing blow from the Imperial Army; it collapsed and is virtually nonexistent. The Li Ch'ang-chiang Army [a former Han affiliate] changed to the Japanese side and has been reorganized into a pacification army. After the campaign the Imperial Army remained to occupy some points, but soon retired to its main bases. Immediately after that, the New Fourth Army returned to its former areas.[57]

Whether Han Te-ch'in's already weakened forces attempted to resist the Japanese or were simply trapped is not known, but this was the end of their activities.[58]

More than the elimination of Han, however, the mopping-up brought the war to the villages of north Kiangsu. People were forced to decide whether they would collaborate, evacuate, or join the guerrillas; former Nationalist troops (Li Ch'ang-chiang's forces) were observed going over to the puppets; and houses and villages were burned by the Japanese. Anti-Japanese propaganda from Communist sources was most effective in these circumstances. Then, in July 1941, a second mopping-up campaign went as far north as Yench'eng. The Communists retreated to the ocean shore, into Shantung, and into Anhwei; but again they returned as soon as the Japanese had withdrawn. From that time until the end of the war, north Kiangsu was a stronghold of the New Fourth Army.[59]

It was between these two mopping-up campaigns that Liu Shao-ch'i published his analysis of the situation in the central Kiangsu area. He begins by pointing out to his fellow political workers that such incidents as the Japanese mopping-up, the defection of Li Ch'ang-chiang, the defeat of Han Te-ch'in, and the New Fourth Army Incident have all produced one of two kinds of "emotional change" among the people. Either their spirit of resistance and their desire to eliminate "traitors" have been strengthened, or else they have chosen the path of nonresistance, obedience, and "slavery." Liu, of course, feels that the cultivation of the attitude of resistance is precisely the purpose of political work by the Army. Political work, he argues, has as its specific task the answering of four main questions that confront the peasantry as a result of recent political and military developments. "In order to broaden and deepen national education [*min-tsu chiao-yü*] among the people, it is necessary to give detailed answers to the following questions. The reactionary governments of the past, such as that of Han Te-ch'in, never gave the people clear answers to such questions."[60]

The first question is: "Should we fight the Japanese or not?" Liu calls this the problem of resistance or nonresistance, of war or peace. He defends the policy of armed resistance on the grounds that the only possible way of preserving the lives and occupations of the Chinese is by defeating the Japanese. First, he attacks the arguments advanced by the Japanese, the Wang Ching-wei supporters, and the capitulationists. They argue that China should be reconciled with Japan, that "even if we fight Japan, we cannot achieve victory over Japan. . . . In fighting Japan we merely increase the opportunities for exploitation of China by Europeans and Americans. If we fight Japan, houses will be burned and people killed."[61] Liu answers these arguments by saying that if China does not resist, it will become a colony of Japan. The reason that people do not want to resist Japan, he says, is that they believe resistance is impossible; actually, they do not know their own strength. The duty of political workers, according to Liu, is to awaken the people to the inevitability of victory if the war is transformed into a mass war. He cites the plan outlined by Mao Tse-tung (*On the Protracted War*) as a blueprint for eventual victory, but the main point of his argument is that victory over Japan can be achieved by mass mobilization.

His second question follows from his answer to the first: "Who will fight

Japan?" Too many people erroneously believe that the fighting should be done by specialists; their attitude may be summed up as "Let the Eighth Route Army do it." This is wrong, says Liu. "The army must indeed fight the enemy, but the people—every single Chinese citizen—also ought to be armed and ought to fight the enemy. Fighting the enemy is an unavoidable responsibility of each and every Chinese."[62] One of the main tasks of the political worker is to raise the anti-Japanese determination of the people and to encourage nationalistic self-sacrifice. (The political worker's task was, of course, made easier when the people of an area had already been mobilized by Japanese excesses and had spontaneously decided on a policy of resistance.)

In his third question, Liu examines further the problem of victory: "Can China be victorious over Japan?" The people want to know, he observes, "how self-defense corps and guerrilla corps, which are so deficient in weapons and training, can obtain a victory over the Japanese Army." Here Liu underscores the great importance of technical education. "We must convey to the people in great detail our guerrilla strategy and the techniques of mass guerrilla warfare."[63] He refers by title to Mao's *On the Protracted War* and *On the New Stage* (*Hsin-chieh-tuan lun*)[64] and advocates making these works available in editions especially tailored to the educational level of the masses, particularly the peasantry.

Liu's last question raises the problem of KMT-CCP rivalry. "What is the best means for obtaining victory over Japan?" In Liu's view, victory is possible only by following the Communist policy and rejecting the policy of the "Kuomintang reactionaries." "Without democracy, without attention to the people's welfare, without mobilizing a positive anti-Japanese spirit on the part of all the people, and without strengthening the anti-Japanese national united front, victory in the resistance to Japan is not possible."[65] Each of these elements, Liu argues, is a prerequisite for the establishment and functioning of resistance bases; and such bases are required to frustrate the attacks of the Japanese and the puppets. Since the KMT policy is not a "victory-over-Japan policy," it is little better, according to Liu, than the policy of the puppets.

Having made it clear to the Kiangsu Party cadres and Army political workers that their task is to instill *national* consciousness in the populace, Liu concludes with a few specific hints on how to go about it. He regards the promotion of education as essential. He recommends using schools, night schools, winter schools, training squads, and the like, to raise the people's "anti-Japanese spirit, anti-Japanese resolution, national resolution, and national pride."[66] These schools are to be employed in addition to the usual mass organizations, newspapers, wall newspapers, speeches, etc., which are the stock-in-trade of all Army mass-movement sections. Liu stresses equally the need to carry out political work among the troops, particularly local troops and new recruits. Moreover, he advocates the use of certain instruments of indoctrination to heighten opposition to national enemies; thus, a "blacklist" naming all local traitors is to be published in wall newspapers.[67] In short, Liu recognized that although many forces were working to produce the national mobilization of the rear-area populations, Communist-sponsored mass education could greatly accelerate this process.

MASS MOBILIZATION IN NORTH KIANGSU

The "Central Kiangsu Military Area" (Su-chung Chün-ch'ü), located between Yench'eng and the Yangtze in north Kiangsu, contained the headquarters of the New Fourth Army as well as the central China branch of K'angta and Su Yü's First Division. It was the New Fourth Army's equivalent of Wut'aishan—that is, the most highly developed Communist guerrilla base in central China. In the following pages we shall explore the institutional structure of Communist-peasant collaboration in Suchung (central Kiangsu), and we shall also examine communications media, mass associations, and training units set up by the Communists to increase peasant participation in the resistance war. I have selected the Fourth District of the Suchung area—i.e., the hsien of Nant'ung, Jukao, Haimen, and Ch'itung—to illustrate national mobilization activities at the local level. Communist operations in this district are extensively documented by materials collected by the Japanese in the mopping-up campaigns of 1941.[68]

The structure of Communist-sponsored institutions in Suchung was very complex; it included Army, government, and mass organs, all of which exerted an influence upon the local population. The most influential were the mass-movement sections of the political departments attached to New Fourth Army units in the area. (The First Division, under Su Yü at Yench'eng, and the Fourth District Guerrilla Command, under Chi Fang and T'ao Yung at Chüehchiang, made up the New Fourth Army regular forces in Suchung.) Army mass-movement sections were originally responsible for setting up both civil governments and mass associations. During the early months of the guerrilla base, the local government and the mass associations accordingly looked to the Army political department for leadership. Later on, when the administration and mass bodies had gained more experience, Army control was relaxed, but the Army political department always retained a veto over the actions of both local governments and mass associations. The governmental organs set up in Suchung by Army political workers were the North Kiangsu Special Administrative Committee under Kuan Wen-wei (in Yench'eng) and the Fourth District Administrative Inspector's Office under Chi Ch'iang-ch'eng (in Chüehchiang). These were both set up in November 1940, and continued unchanged after the reorganization of the Army in February 1941.

Although ultimate political power was in Army hands, local Communist-sponsored governments performed numerous administrative functions, notably tax and grain collection, the operation of public schools, the maintenance of the anti-Japanese blockade, and the operation of the mobilization committees. Army personnel did not staff civil offices; on the contrary, civil government positions were held by local residents. The two highest administrative officials in Suchung, Kuan Wen-wei and Chi Ch'iang-ch'eng, as well as the Fourth District military commander, Chi Fang, were all Kiangsu men even though they were also Communists. This was standard Communist practice. Local leaders served in similar capacities in Chin-Ch'a-Chi, where Sung Shao-wen and Hu Jen-k'uei, both natives of Shansi, headed the Border Region Administrative Committee. The use of local leaders in Army-sponsored governments was one of the methods by which the Communists advanced local civil-military cooperation.

Another medium by which the Communists generated mass backing for New Fourth Army activities was the mass association. After establishing numerous resistance societies based on occupation in the Fourth District during November and December of 1940, the Fourth District Guerrilla Command's political department called a congress of federated mass associations to meet in Chüehchiang on January 23, 1941. This congress was composed of delegates from resistance societies of peasants, workers, merchants, young people, students, and women, and even from the "semi-public" Communist Party committee in Nant'ung.[69] The congress passed resolutions declaring its support for the new Communist government of north Kiangsu, calling for greater organizational activity among the peasantry, establishing military support units, and creating reading instruction squads.

Most of the mass-association activities in north Kiangsu were the same as those in other Communist bases—the forming of militia, the gathering of intelligence, and so forth. There were, however, a few exceptions. The north Kiangsu mass societies stressed one undertaking above all others: battlefield searching operations to help relieve the extreme shortage of equipment in the New Fourth Army. After a battle with the Japanese or the KMT, all the people of the surrounding area were sent to the scene to look for weapons and ammunition. In December 1940, the Fourth District Guerrilla Command offered the following rewards for weapons found by local residents: 50 *yüan* for a heavy machine gun, 30 *yüan* for a light machine gun, 10–20 *yüan* for a rifle, and 5 *yüan* for a pistol.[70]

An undertaking particularly stressed by the mass associations was reading instruction. In teaching the masses to read, the Communists introduced one of the most powerful forces of social mobilization commonly encountered in national movements: the sense of liberation given to previously illiterate adults by the mastery of even a few words. Reading instruction had a double value for the Communists; the materials used in the training contained nationalistic and anti-Kuomintang slogans, and after the masses achieved some reading ability, they could also read Communist newspapers. The Japanese captured a set of twenty graded reading cards in western Kiangsu during the Three Rivers Operation of 1940. Here are Cards 1 and 20, illustrating the easiest and the hardest of these particular reading exercises:

1. Men.	20. Reactionary elements.
Men and women.	Reactionary elements specialize in making trouble for anti-Japanese armed forces.
All are Chinese.	
All love China.	They kill young men and women who oppose Japan.
	They destroy anti-Japanese work.
	They secretly help the Japanese devils, and they secretly help Wang Ching-wei.[71]

Presumably, the impact of the nationalistic message included in these reading aids was increased by the student's normal respect for the "lesson" and by his desire to learn to read.

The Communists also experimented with romanized Chinese in north Kiangsu as an aid to reading instruction. One of the mass associations in the area was the "North Kiangsu Romanization Diffusion Unit" (Su-pei La-ting-hua Po-chung Tui), whose mission it was to popularize the "new writing movement." The "working guide" for the romanization unit was published in the March 18, 1941, issue of the *Chiang-Huai jih-pao,* along with the slogan of the association: "Although you study for ten years, you will have only an imperfect knowledge of the Han characters; the new writing may be learned in three months."[72]

The extensive use of newspapers has always characterized Communist mass-movement activities, and the Suchung area was no exception. The journal with the largest circulation published in north Kiangsu was the *Chiang-Huai jih-pao.* It was edited by the Army's political department, which brought out the first four-page edition in Yench'eng on December 2, 1940. This paper often printed the views of Liu Shao-ch'i, Ch'en Yi, and others; it reported a circulation of 5,000 for the introductory issue. As for other newspapers, the First Division's political department published a four-page journal, *K'ang-ti pao* ("Resistance News"), every three days, and also published a small internal organ, *Chan-shih pao* ("Soldier's News"), which was distributed only to enlisted men. *K'ang-ti pao* was the official New Fourth Army newspaper prior to the New Fourth Army Incident, when the First Division was the South Yangtze Command. Many other local papers were published in north Kiangsu, but only one of any importance: the *Tung-nan ch'en-pao* ("Southeast Morning News"), published in Chüehchiang. This paper, which existed prior to the New Fourth Army's entrance into north Kiangsu, became one of the most important propaganda organs for the New Fourth Army after November 1940. Many of the data used by the Japanese in their analyses of the Communist situation in north Kiangsu came from back issues of *Tung-nan ch'en-pao*; and after the February 1941 mopping-up campaign, the Kōain noted: "Although [the *Tung-nan ch'en-pao*] retreated along with the New Fourth Army [before the mopping-up began], it quickly returned to Chüehchiang after our Army withdrew and, on March 14, published a conspicuous proclamation of its return. It has continued in publication since that time."[73]

The most important of the north Kiangsu magazines was *Chiang Huai,* published by the Army's political department in Yench'eng for Army-wide circulation. Its first issue appeared on December 15, 1940. The table of contents for the second issue (December 25) reveals the type of magazine it was: "Required Readings for National Salvation," "The General Effect of the International Struggle in 1940 on the Resistance War," "A Brief Discussion of Political Work in Resistance Units" by Chung Ch'i-kuang, "The United Front and Class Struggle" by Hsieh Yün-hui, "On Sanmin-ism and Sanmin-ists" by Ch'en Tao, and "CC-CCP Instruction Relating to the Development of Popular Education in the Anti-Japanese Democratic Areas."[74]

There were several other specialized magazines published in north Kiangsu during this period. Although the exact impact of all of these new publications on the local population cannot be accurately determined, it is obvious that after the entrance of the New Fourth Army into north Kiangsu, the inhabitants had a much higher level of information about the war than before. Resistance newspapers thus contributed to the awakening of the people of Kiangsu to China's national war effort.

A more formal but equally important mobilizing influence was cadre education in Communist schools. According to several spokesmen, including Ch'en P'i-hsien, secretary of the Central Kiangsu Communist Party Committee, the most pressing need after the entry of the New Fourth Army into north Kiangsu was for cadres to staff the new regional and hsien governments and to lead the mass associations.[75] Between the end of 1940 and March 1, 1941, the New Fourth Army set up at least ten training units to help relieve this shortage. The most important of the schools was the Fifth Branch of K'angta, established in November 1940 at Yench'eng. Headed by Ch'en Yi and Army chief-of-staff Lai Ch'uan-chu, the school was an amalgamation of the staffs of two older New Fourth Army schools, plus a special training squad sent from the Eighth Route Army. The former North Yangtze Command's school at Hsüi and the cadres' school attached to Ch'en Yi's North Kiangsu Command were combined with a training unit belonging to Huang K'o-ch'eng's Fifth Column to form the Fifth Branch of K'angta.[76] (As will be recalled, Huang's unit was the force of Eighth Route Army reinforcements that was sent from central Shansi and that joined Ch'en Yi in the autumn of 1940.)

The entrance requirements for Yench'eng's K'angta were the same as those for a lower middle-school (junior high school), and the course lasted six months. According to *K'ang-ti pao* of November 7, 1940, the first enrollment for the school numbered some 2,000 men.[77] In addition to military subjects, the school taught politics ("San-min-chu-i, United Front, Chinese revolutionary history," etc.), public administration, education, dramatics, journalism, and other subjects relevant to mass operations. Among the military subjects taught were guerrilla tactics, infantry tactics, employment of artillery, and strategy. The school's curriculum was similar to that of the K'angta branch located in Shen-Kan-Ning.[78]

The second most important school in north Kiangsu was the Public Administration Institute, operated by the North Kiangsu Special Administrative Committee. This school was located at Tungt'ai until the Japanese mopping-up campaign of February 1941, when it moved to Yench'eng.

Kuan Wen-wei headed the institute, and one Chou P'ing, "a former instructor at K'angta in Yenan," was the "educational director." The school was founded in the autumn of 1940 specifically to train cadres to run the new local governments set up under New Fourth Army auspices. Each class of 400 men and women was trained for three months in basic public administration, economics, mass operations, and the like. Upon graduation they were sent to the various hsien governments throughout north Kiangsu.[79]

These were only two of the New Fourth Army's large number of schools in north Kiangsu. There were also (*a*) the "Lu Hsün Art Academy, Central China Branch," at Yench'eng (temporary director, Liu Shao-ch'i; educational director, Ch'iu Tung-p'ing); (*b*) several cadres' schools in Chüeh-chiang and Nant'ung; (*c*) the Nant'ung hsien Mobilization Committee's Mass Movement Workers' Training Squad at Peihsingch'iao, Nant'ung hsien; and others.[80] It goes without saying that these so-called educational institutions were not very elaborate; one training plan merely calls for someone to read the daily newspapers (*Chiang-Huai jih-pao* and *K'ang-ti pao*) to the assembled students.[81] Considering the nationalistic content of Communist propaganda, however, it is clear that the New Fourth Army's educational activities greatly accelerated the process of national mobilization. The number of students at first-rank schools in Yench'eng was large, but an even greater number of common people received a rudimentary nationalistic education in the local schools and mass societies.

The eventual fruits of Communist work with the masses in 1941 can be seen by looking at a few reports from north Kiangsu in 1944. With the passage of time, north Kiangsu had become as permanent a part of "New China" as Yenan. Among the new institutions in north Kiangsu was the "International Peace Hospital," a hospital of some 1,000 beds that served the Kiangsu and Shantung war areas. The Communists were also very active militarily in the last months of the war. According to Yenan Radio on January 6, 1945, the Third Division in the far north of Kiangsu "liberated" some 5,000 square miles of territory, containing 500,000 people, during 1944.[82] In November 1944, the New Fourth Army penetrated deep into Huaihai province at Tunghai hsien, where it recruited 2,700 soldiers in twenty days. By 1944, the Japanese garrisons in north Kiangsu (mostly composed of Formosans, Koreans, and Manchurians) were so demoralized that the Communists reported daily increases in desertion, suicide, and surrender; and some 1,500 Nanking puppets joined the New Fourth Army in north Kiangsu during the last two weeks of November 1944.[83] In short,

Communist forces occupied the region from Chekiang to Shantung by the end of the war, and these forces were locally recruited and locally supported. They were the same Communist soldiers that the future foreign minister of China, Ch'en Yi, led into Shanghai on May 25, 1949.

Before leaving the subject of Communist consolidation of the north Kiangsu guerrilla base, it may be useful to raise once again the question of the degree to which Communist interests coincided with those of the masses. One approach to this problem is to ask: Who *were* the Chinese Communists in Kiangsu? The Japanese archives suggest a partial answer. During the February 1941 mopping-up campaign, the Japanese Army captured in Tungt'ai a document entitled "Roster of Cadres of the Rank of Platoon Commander and Above of the Third Column [T'ao Yung], New Fourth Army North Kiangsu Command."[84] This roster gives information on place of origin, age, educational history, time of entering the unit, time of entering the Party, and other data on 210 New Fourth Army officers. Significantly, the data on place of origin indicate a strong Kiangsu affiliation: 140 cadres (two-thirds) were from Kiangsu. Fukien, the second most heavily represented province, accounted for only 23 cadres—probably Red Army remnants that originally formed the New Fourth Army. Sixteen cadres came from Anhwei, six from Chekiang, and from various other provinces five or fewer. Of the 140 Kiangsu cadres, 41 were from T'aihsing hsien, immediately across the Yangtze from Kuan Wen-wei's 1939 base, and 20 were from Chiangtu hsien, also on the north bank. Tanyang hsien, an area of early First Detachment operations, produced 19 Communist leaders. All three of these hsien experienced Japanese military operations or mopping-up campaigns from the earliest stages of the war. Consider this information in relation to the dates of entrance into the Army by these cadres: of the 210 officers, 25 belonged to the Communist Army in 1936 or earlier; 15 joined in 1937, 50 in 1938, 42 in 1939, and 65 in 1940 (dates of entrance of the remaining 13 are unknown).[85]

These data show that at least one important group of Communists in north Kiangsu were local men who joined the New Fourth Army after the outbreak of the Sino-Japanese war and came from areas that had felt the effects of the Japanese invasion and of the Communist response. This fact does not in itself make them any less Communist; but it does suggest that Communism in China has very little meaning apart from the trials China experienced during the war of resistance.

SIX

Peasant Mobilization in Wartime Yugoslavia

In the preceding chapters, we have studied the manner and extent of peasant participation in the Chinese resistance to Japanese aggression. We saw that approximately 100,000,000 Chinese peasants, concentrated for the most part north of the Yangtze River, reacted to the invasion of their territory in a manner unprecedented in recent Chinese history: they combined into new political and military associations in order to offer effective military defense against the invader. This peasant response was due, in the first instance, to the nature of the Japanese invasion. The objectives and manner of execution of the Japanese invasion made peasant accommodation with the Japanese impossible; the invasion even caused the destruction of the institutions that had fostered parochialism and political indifference among the peasants of China. The result was that after 1937, mobilized by an unavoidable military challenge and bereft of traditional loci of authority, the peasantry stood ready to resist the invaders but lacked effective leadership.

The Communist Party filled the need. Possessing a valuable cadre of battle-tested and militarily competent veterans, as well as a commitment to war as a mode of social change, the Communist Party was not only willing but eager to lead the Chinese *maquis*. The Party united with the peasantry in the occupied areas, and together the Communists and the peasants constructed various political and military instruments for battling the Japanese and for governing themselves. Prewar staples of the Communists' "Communist" program—such as alteration of the system of land tenure— were replaced by an ideology of patriotism, national liberation, and national self-sacrifice. One important concomitant of the union between Party and peasantry was the Japanese military reprisals against the peasantry, under the guise of exterminating Communism. Even more than the initial dislocations caused by the invasion, these reprisals and mopping-up campaigns awakened the peasantry to the personal danger posed by the "foreign invader." The peasant's participation in the war effort and his exposure to nationalistic propaganda at a time of great sensitivity caused him, for the first time, to equate personal danger with national danger. National consciousness entered the thinking of the war-mobilized peasants.

We have seen also that the growth of nationalism among the peasantry provides a basis for understanding how the Chinese Communists succeeded in discrediting the Kuomintang during the war when they had never managed to do so before the war. This was because the economic appeal of Communism was by itself insufficient to attract a mass following. In the prewar, and from the peasants' point of view pre-national, Chinese social setting, the peasant either was indifferent to the Communists, or, speaking generally, supported them only so long as the Red Army occupied his land and offered him comparative economic advantages. The Kuomintang was never challenged or its motives impugned if it attacked the Communists, and it was even welcomed by the peasantry when it combined enlightened social and economic policies with its anti-Communist measures. During the war, however, the struggle between the two Chinese elite groups was transformed into a contest for national leadership. The Kuomintang was ultimately discredited in the eyes of unsophisticated peasants by the fact that it opposed the Communists—who were fighting the Japanese.

Is this hypothesis of peasant nationalism, as outlined above, unique? Does it apply only to the special case of China, or does it have broader applicability? One other example of peasant mobilization exists in which virtually all of the same ingredients were present; that case is wartime Yugoslavia. (By using a more abstract definition of mass nationalism than the one used here, the hypothesis of social mobilization via a guerrilla resistance movement may be extended to include such cases as Cuba, Malaya, Greece, and Algeria. However, this level of abstraction obscures certain common elements in the Chinese and Yugoslav experiences that were of great importance—for example, the foreign origin of the initial military dislocation and the process by which the non-Communist nationalists were overturned—and is thus of limited use in testing our particular hypothesis about China.) The following conditions prevailed in both wartime China and Yugoslavia:

(*a*) The invasions of the two countries were of a "hyperbolic" quality, and the objectives of the invaders left little or no room for accommodation to the new order by noncombatants of the invaded country.

(*b*) Militarily trained Communist elites existed in both countries; they encouraged peasant mobilization and proposed a plan of resistance to the invaders that overcame initial peasant demoralization.

(*c*) The invaders and their puppets responded to the resistance movements in two ways: (1) they attempted to divide the resistance forces by harping on the Communist origins of a part of the resistance leadership, and (2) they intensified the scale and severity of their reprisals in an attempt to divide the guerrillas from the civilians. The first policy generally succeeded from the invader's point of view, but owing to the invader's eventual defeat, it had the long-term effect of advancing Communist claims to national legitimacy. The policy of military reprisals only broadened and deepened the mobilization of the peasantry.

(*d*) The joint Communist-peasant policy toward the invaders was one of guerrilla warfare and economic attrition. Because guerrilla warfare depends upon the closest military-civil cooperation, extensive political organization and education were carried on in every area through which the guerrillas passed. These organizational activities structured the peasants' response to the war in a nationalistic fashion.

(*e*) The guerrilla forces of the invaded countries were eventually able to accept the surrender of the invaders and to enter occupied areas as liberators—that is, foreign allied troops did not appear to be primarily responsible for victory (in the way that foreign troops were responsible for driving the Germans from France, for example). There are qualifications on this point in both China and Yugoslavia, but these do not erase the importance of victory as the cornerstone of postwar national authority in both countries.

These are the factors that mobilized the peasantries of China and Yugoslavia. To be sure, these influences were present in different degrees in each country, and as a result the two resistance movements are not identical. The Yugoslav case is actually more highly developed than that of China in the sense that the Yugoslav revolution was completed in a shorter period of time and gave a more clear-cut victory to the Partisans. There are three important reasons for this difference: German policies in Yugoslavia were even more destructive than Japanese policies in China; large quantities of arms and ammunition were available in Yugoslavia and thereby expanded the military possibilities of the guerrilla forces; and Allied policy in Yugoslavia strengthened the Partisan cause. Rather than detracting from the value of the comparison between China and Yugoslavia, however, these differences increase it; the particular features of each case underscore certain implications in the over-all process of peasant mobilization.

The early months of 1941 found Yugoslavia in a difficult international position. After the failure of Italy's ill-conceived invasion of Greece in October 1940, it was apparent that the Germans would have to come to the aid of their ally. To this end, Germany began to enlarge its Balkan sphere of influence beyond Rumania. Bulgaria signed the Axis Pact on March 1, 1941, and intense pressure was soon applied on Yugoslavia to join the New Order. Germany needed a Yugoslav alliance both to allow passage of German soldiers through Yugoslavia to Greece and to secure the Balkan flank during the coming invasion of Russia, plans for which were laid in December 1940.

Internally, Yugoslavia was beset by difficulties that seemed even more dangerous than her foreign relations. Bitter antagonism between Roman Catholic Croatia and Orthodox Serbia had only been slightly alleviated by the granting of a degree of Croatian independence in August 1939. Ethnic and religious animosity, combined with an impulse to follow the German lead in seeking radical solutions for endemic problems, characterized Yugoslav politics at the close of the interwar period. The government of Yugoslavia on the eve of war was under the virtual dictatorship of Prince Paul Karageorgević, the regent for 17-year-old King Peter, and of Paul's dutiful servant, Dragisha Cvetković, the Premier. The Prince was of White Russian background and had been educated in England; his susceptibility to the German offers of February and March 1941 derived from both his approval of the incipient German attack on the USSR and his recognition of Yugoslavia's military weakness.[1]

During February 1941, Cvetković and the Yugoslav foreign minister accepted Hitler's invitation to come to Berchtesgaden, where the Führer demanded Yugoslavia's adherence to the Tripartite Agreement. Prince Paul had little choice in the matter, but he kept the fact of Yugoslavia's joining the Axis secret until after the agreement had been consummated. Cvetković signed the pact at a meeting of Ribbentrop, Ciano, and Oshima in Vienna on March 25, 1941; and the general public, which was anti-German despite the close economic ties between Yugoslavia and Germany, heard of it first on March 26. The Serbs, in particular, were outraged; and Serbian air force officers led a *coup d'état* that overthrew the Cvetković government. They proclaimed young Peter king and made one of the conspirators, General Dushan Simović, the new Premier. Although the revolt was carried out by the officer corps, it was received with great enthusiasm by the Belgrade masses. Belgrade crowds attacked German shops and expressed strongly their disapproval of the Axis alliance; Prince Paul fled to England and was later interned in Kenya.

The inevitable was not long in coming; but there was another consideration, in addition to the Belgrade *coup d'état,* that made the German retaliation particularly brutal. March 27, 1941, happened also to be the date on which the Japanese Foreign Minister, Matsuoka, began his state visit to Berlin; and Hitler had made elaborate preparations for announcing German control over all of Europe to his ally. As Kris and Speier note, "The German radio had never been more anxious to present a festive appearance than it was on 27 March 1941. It tried to forget for the moment that a revolution was taking place in Yugoslavia."[2] The new Yugoslav leaders did not denounce the Axis Pact and also agreed to pay compensation for damaged German business establishments, but the Germans had been mortified by the Serbian show of defiance. On March 31, the German radio began to enunciate a new, pre-invasion propaganda line—viz., the Serbs were a Slavic people and therefore subhuman, etc.[3] The bombing of Belgrade, an open city, began on the morning of April 6, and shortly thereafter some 33 German, Hungarian, and Italian divisions invaded Yugoslavia. King Peter and the Simović government fled the country to Cairo and eventually to exile in London.

Just as the Japanese failed to establish a unified regime in occupied China, the Germans did not bring Yugoslavia under one strong pro-fascist leader. There were probably more new regimes and puppets established in occupied Yugoslavia than in any other occupied territory during World War II. Germany annexed most of Slovenia and garrisoned Croatia and Serbia; Italy annexed the Adriatic Coast and occupied most of Montenegro; Hungary annexed a small part of Slovenia and rich parts of the Voivodina north of Belgrade; Bulgaria seized all of Yugoslav Macedonia; and Italian-controlled Albania took sections of Montenegro and other border territories. In the two unannexed territories—Croatia and Serbia—puppet governments were set up. After this, Yugoslavia no longer existed.

There was no exact Chinese parallel to the Independent State of Croatia, which was headed by the fascist fanatic Ante Pavelić. In terms of its separatism and ideological inventiveness, Croatia corresponded to the north China puppet government; but no Chinese government ever went to the extremes of brutality practiced by Pavelić's elite guard, the Ustashe. Pavelić had been in fascist Italy since 1929, building his organization; he returned to Zagreb, his new capital, on April 10, 1941, and assumed the title of Poglavnik (Führer). During the next two years, the Ustashe and the regular Croatian Army (the Domobrantsvo) carried out a policy of systematic slaughter of the Serbs and Jews in Croatia, and in Bosnia and Herzegovina, which had been given to Croatia by the Germans. Pavelić's massacres of Serb peasants living in the villages of Croatia, Bosnia, and Herzegovina mobilized major sources of future Partisan manpower; virtually all the peasants who escaped the Ustashe became resistance fighters.[4]

In Serbia the situation was not so barbaric as in Croatia; and Serbia, generally, was the last area of Yugoslavia to experience the civil war. This is not to say that Serbia was peaceful; no part of Yugoslavia escaped a certain degree of destruction during World War II. Immediately after the German occupation, a caretaker government under Milan Aćimović, the former Yugoslav Minister of Police, was set up. Then, in August 1941, the Germans established a permanent Serbian puppet government under General Milan Nedić. General Nedić had been in charge of Royal Yugoslav troops in the southeastern regions of Yugoslavia at the time of the German attack, but he turned over his army to the Germans without combat (cf. Han Fu-ch'ü).

In addition to the Croatian and Serbian puppets, there existed in Yugoslavia a plethora of fascist and terrorist gangs, as well as many German, Hungarian, and Bulgarian agencies of exploitation and repression. Some of the better known of these units were the Serbian fascist party, Zbor, under Dimitrije Ljotić; White Russians of the former Imperial Russian Army who had been exiles in Yugoslavia after 1917 but who joined the Germans in 1941;[5] and the Chetniks of Kosta Pechanac, who were loyal to Nedić and the Germans, and who must be distinguished from Mihailović's Chetniks, discussed below.[6] There is a curious parallel here on a point of nomenclature: just as in China both the Chungking and Nanking governments—that is, the non-Communist nationalists and the leading puppets—claimed the same name ("Kuomintang"), so in Yugoslavia both the Serbian non-Communist nationalists (Mihailović's forces) and Pechanac's collaborators used the same name for their troops ("Chetniks"). "Chetnik" (from *cheta,* a guerrilla unit) is a good Serbian word, but this confusion of identities could well have contributed to a confusion about loyalties in the minds of some peasants.

YUGOSLAVIA

One other Axis group should be mentioned: the Yugoslav citizens of German descent (Volksdeutsche) living throughout Yugoslavia but concentrated particularly in the area of the Voivodina called Banat. Although nominally belonging to Nedić's Serbia, they actually constituted an independent German state in Yugoslavia during the war. The Yugoslav Germans also contributed their young men to make up a special SS division ("Prinz Eugen"), which was extensively used against the Partisans.[7]

The defense by the regular Yugoslav Army against the German invasion had been lacking in conviction at best; at worst, the defeat was abetted by Croatian treachery. However, the lack of battles left much of the Yugoslav Army intact and armed; and the first and most important locus of *irregular* armed resistance to the invaders was organized by Colonel Drazha Mihailović of the Royal Yugoslav Army's General Staff. Mihailović was an outstanding officer with progressive ideas (while a military attaché in Prague, he was known for cordial relations with the Soviet representative). His iconoclastic military proposals had even resulted, at an early date, in his arrest for thirty days by General Nedić, who was at that time Minister of War. At the time of the capitulation, Mihailović was chief of staff to the motorized units of the Fourth Army, then stationed in the medieval Bosnian village of Doboj. In order to avoid capture and to establish a base of resistance, he moved to Ravna Gora plateau, in the densely wooded Shumadija region of western Serbia. He and his associates set up camp on May 11, 1941, at Ravna Gora, where they were joined by other troops and Serb patriots who had responded spontaneously to the idea of continuing resistance.[8]

Taking the name of Chetniks, Mihailović's forces began sabotage operations against the Germans. Mihailović's movement was recognized by the exiled government in London as its legitimate agent in the occupied territories, and his Army was given the official title of "Royal Yugoslav Army in the Fatherland." Mihailović himself was named Minister of War. The composition of the Chetniks included Serbian peasants, Army officers, and Serbian intellectuals such as the writer Dragisha Vasić. The Chetniks carried out extensive operations during the summer and early autumn of 1941, and they liberated large sections of western Serbia. However, the Germans soon overcame their initial surprise and carried out a series of devastating reprisals. The most severe reprisal was the shooting of 6,000 people in one day at Kragujevać, south of Belgrade, on October 21, 1941.[9] These activities were accompanied by German military operations against the Serbian insurgents during the period from September 16 to the end of November, 1941.

The ferocity of the German retaliation led Mihailović to change his strategy. He decided against further direct military activities in favor of a policy of "waiting in preparation" for an Allied counterinvasion of Yugoslavia. This policy was supported by the firm belief that since World War I had been fought partly in the Balkans, this war would be fought there also—a standard principle of Yugoslav military academies, and what Major Rootham called the Chetniks' "Salonika front fixation."[10] Even though the policy of waiting involved the real danger that inactive guerrilla bands would degenerate into bandits, it was nevertheless in accordance with directives radioed to other European resistance units from London.

Taken alone, the policy of avoiding provocative acts would not have discredited Mihailović's Army, particularly if the Partisan competition had not developed. There was another aspect of Chetnik policy that seriously weakened Mihailović's ability to lead the majority of the Yugoslav masses: the Chetnik movement was suffused with the spirit of Serbian, rather than Yugoslav, nationalism. Playing precisely into German hands, Mihailović reacted to Ustashe murders of Serbs living in Croatia by carrying out similar violent acts of terrorism against Croat and Catholic populations wherever he found them.[11] The Partisan movement, on the other hand, carefully avoided identification with any ethnic minority and appealed only to the anti-fascist sentiments of the masses at large. Tito himself is a Croat. Of course, the pro-Serbian bias of the Chetniks was not the major cause of the movement's downfall; Chetnik Serbism was analogous to Chiang Kai-shek's favoring central China over north China. The major cause of the Chetnik defeat was the growth of the Partisans' reputation as anti-German fighters and Mihailović's developing community of interests with the Germans against the "Communists."

The history of the Yugoslav Communist Party before World War II, like that of the Chinese Communist Party, was a history of repeated failures. The first Congress of the YCP (officially named "The Yugoslav Socialist Workers Party") met in Belgrade, April 20–23, 1919, just a few weeks after the formation of the Comintern (March 2–6), which it immediately joined. The new Party's growth was very rapid in 1919 and 1920—just as in Hungary and Italy—but on December 31, 1920, the new Yugoslav Royal Government outlawed the Party by decree in order to stop Communist propaganda activities. Then, on July 21, 1921, a Bosnian Communist assassinated Milorad Drashković, the Minister of the Interior (i.e., the

JSKP

police), and this act resulted in the complete interdiction of the Party and the prohibition of Communist and anarchist propaganda (the "Law for the Protection of the State," August 1921). The Party went underground and soon all but disappeared; membership fell from 80,000 (1920) to 3,000 (1928) to 200 (1932). In the early 1930's the Yugoslav Communist movement was of interest only to the police of Belgrade and of a few other large cities. However, the Yugoslav Communist Party never went completely out of existence.[12]

Small though it was, the YCP on the eve of the war was in better condition than it had been at any time since 1920. There were three important developments in YCP history during the late 1930's that helped to strengthen the Party: the purge of all old leaders and the rise of Tito; the development of the University of Belgrade as a stronghold of Communism; and the participation of many Yugoslav Communists in the International Brigade in Spain. The purge of most of the YCP leaders occurred during the underground period of the 1930's, when many of them went to Moscow. While there, they quarreled with each other and divided into left and right factions. Dimitrov, the head of the Comintern, was on the verge of disbanding the Party when he decided to give it one last chance: all previous secretaries-general of the YCP were killed in the Moscow purges, and Josip Broz (Tito) alone was sent to Yugoslavia from the Soviet Union to rebuild the Party.[13]

Tito had a difficult problem, since there were only 3,000 Yugoslav Communists on the Party rolls in 1939. However, he did have one important recruiting center—the University of Belgrade, where large numbers of students were being indoctrinated into Communism by the fiery student leader Milovan Djilas. Success in gaining new members from the young intelligentsia helped to offset the Party's weakness, in those days, among unions and the proletariat. The Communist youth of Belgrade University constituted the main source of cadres for the Partisans after the invasion, and such famous Partisan officers as Kocha Popović and Ivo Lola Ribar were alumni of that institution. A few Communist Youth Corps members came from bourgeois backgrounds, but the majority were peasants. As Halperin observes, "During the war [Djilas's] work reaped a rich harvest. The Partisan army drew its officers from the ranks of young Communist students. They were familiar with every hide-out in their native hills, knew the feelings of the inhabitants intimately, and were able to report exactly in which cottage there were friends, in which potential traitors. Above all, these sons of mountain peasants obeyed the call to arms with a good and ready heart."[14] Djilas himself came from a provincial Monte-negrin background.

Certainly the most important contribution of the Chinese and Yugo-slav Communist parties to the resistance movements was the providing of leaders who were experienced in organizing and directing civilian-based irregular military operations. Such knowledge does not come naturally, nor did Communist manuals on this subject exist until after considerable experience in mass organizations had been gained (Mao's "theoretical" military works describe the *lessons* of Kiangsi). The Chinese and Yugo-slav parties both possessed cadres of veteran military revolutionaries: the survivors of the Long March in the first instance, and the "Espagnols"—the Yugoslav veterans of the Spanish Civil War—in the second instance. Some 1,200 Yugoslav Communists fought in Spain, where they formed two battalions of the International Brigade, the "Djura Djaković" and "Dimitrov" battalions, as well as two companies and an artillery battery.[15] At least 350 of these soldiers were interned in France at Gurs, St. Cyprien, and Vernet after the Republican defeat; and they succeeded in returning to Yugoslavia only in early 1941, by posing as German "workers."[16] Among the many high-ranking Partisan officials who fought in Spain were Ivan Goshnjak, former Deputy Commander of the International Brigade and today a colonel general in the Yugoslav Army, who was Partisan com-mander in Croatia; Peko Dapchević, later the Yugoslav Chief of Staff, who led the Partisans' First Corps into Belgrade on October 22, 1944; Kocha Popović, who was a Partisan general in Serbia; Kosta Nagy, who became commander in western Bosnia; Blagoje Neshković, who was a member of the Politburo until 1948; and Ales Bebler, who was Vice-Minister of For-eign Affairs and later Ambassador to Paris.[17] Without such capable cadres as these, it is doubtful whether the Communist Party would have been able to meet the challenge of leading Yugoslavia's mobilized but untrained and undisciplined peasantry.

The Communist Party did not play a part in the *coup d'état* and anti-German demonstrations of March 27, 1941; the credit for these actions goes entirely to the Serbs. In fact, the YCP was in a very ambiguous position between March 27 and June 22, 1941, because of the Molotov-Ribbentrop pact. Although Tito's politburo certainly undertook some initial planning for resistance in this three-month period, the official international position was alliance with Germany; and this position was not changed until after the invasion of Russia. Some writers have charged the YCP with defeatism during this period, and also with sabotage of defense industries.[18] The

Communists have never admitted to anything but the most patriotic motives, but postwar apologists have tried to conceal the Party's embarrassing tie with Moscow by playing down the March *coup d'état*. For instance, according to Kapetanović,

> The Simović group [the March 27 junta] carried out its putsch in response to pressure from the broad, anti-fascist masses. If this putsch had not been executed by Simović, it would have been by someone else. But what is characteristic of Simović's action is the attempt at salvaging the monarchy, which was already compromised by its policy of subordination to the Axis powers and suppression of the people's democratic rights. Simović's group hoped to be able to channel popular indignation against the monarchy by a change on the throne—that is to say, by placing on it the boy king.[19]

There is some truth to this; the Simović government itself did *not* denounce the Tripartite Pact. Nevertheless, during 1941 the Yugoslav Communist Party—although ultraleftist—was equally unimaginative. It was not until after its first defeat and its own "Long March"—the retreat from Uzhice to east Bosnia in the winter of 1941—that the Party began to act like a nationalist party and began to receive strong support from the peasant masses.

On June 22, 1941, the Communist International sent a telegram to all Communist Parties ordering them to reverse the pro-German policy. Tito met with his politburo in Belgrade, where he created his general staff; and he dispatched high-ranking politburo members to organize resistance in the various provinces. Edvard Kardelj, a Slovene and a theoretician, was sent to Slovenia,[20] Djilas went to Montenegro, Svetozar Vukmanović was given Bosnia-Herzegovina, and Tito remained in Serbia. Between May and August 1941 Tito lived in the Belgrade villa of Vladislav Ribnikar, publisher of the important Yugoslav daily *Politika*; but in mid-September he moved with his staff to the first "liberated" area cleared by Serbian Partisans. This Partisan base, popularly known as the "Uzhice Republic,"[21] was located in the Krupanj area of northwest Serbia, between Shabac and Uzhice. The town of Uzhice itself became the first important Partisan capital; the Communists set up a new government by "people's councils" (*odbors*), opened schools, published the newspaper *Borba* ("Struggle"), and, generally, created a soviet. Uzhice also contained an arsenal which the Partisans were operating at full capacity in the autumn of 1941, producing rifles.[22]

After Tito's arrival in the Uzhice Republic, he twice met with Mihailović in an attempt to coordinate the national resistance movement. The first meeting took place in mid-September at the village of Struganik, located at the foot of Ravna Gora. Tito proposed joint operations between Chetniks and Partisans; but this was rejected by Mihailović, who was understandably suspicious of Tito. (Mihailović is supposed to have taken Tito to be a Russian at their first meeting.) The second meeting took place on October 25, 1941, at the village of Brajici, at which time the stage was set for civil war. On October 21, just before the second meeting, the Kragujevać reprisal had taken place, and German plans for an attack on Uzhice were obviously in readiness. The reprisal had confirmed Mihailović in his policy of inaction, and he was in addition strongly opposed to the Partisans' habit of destroying existing local government institutions (even if they were collaborationist) and replacing them with "people's councils." No agreement was reached between Tito and Mihailović at the second meeting, and on November 2, 1941, the Chetniks followed up recent German attacks on the Partisans by themselves raiding Partisan headquarters at Uzhice. This incident marked the beginning of the Yugoslav civil war.[23]

In late November 1941, the Partisans began to retreat from Serbia, moving to the west into relatively primitive areas of Bosnia, where the population had been terrorized by the Ustashe. The ideology of the Yugoslav resistance at this time had striking similarities to that of the Chinese Communists while they were on the Long March.[24] The movement was still in a strongly "Communist" phase, although this was dimly recognized by some leaders to be a mistake. Dedijer, the official YCP historian, wrote in his diary at Uzhice in November 1941: "We have to pass from underground work to organization of the broadest masses of the people in this uprising against the Germans. Things had got rather stuck, but nobody knows better than partisans how to learn from mistakes."[25] As the Partisans marched through the Bosnian mountains, they discovered a source of potential resistance strength whose existence they had not previously suspected. The Partisans encountered leaderless Serbs in the mountains—refugees from the Ustashe—and young peasants with no political ideology at all, who wanted to defend their villages against the fascists. The Partisans, like the Eighth Route Army in Wut'aishan, organized and led these mobilized peasants and modified their own Communist program to emphasize a national, rather than a class, revolution. Dedijer described in his diary the situation that the Partisans discovered in these "backward" areas; here, for example, is his entry dated February 13, 1942, at Focha, Bosnia.

> Last night we had a party conference. Tito came to it. . . . In the vol-
> unteer units, former Chetnik units [many Chetniks joined the Partisans
> when they became disgusted with the policy of waiting], and in the
> Partisan units, 99% of the fighting men are peasants and, what is more,
> men who are politically very backward. . . . We are likely to have most
> success among youth, first because they have not been under fifth col-
> umn influence, and secondly because they most readily respond to the
> call to fight. The older Bosnian peasants are good partisans so long as
> they are defending their own villages. As soon as they get away from
> home they are weaker. At Goradzhe, ten-day courses of training in
> each company have begun, so as to educate them politically and mili-
> tarily.[26]

Change the place names and unit designations, and this description would become a model of the post-invasion situation in Wut'ai or in north Kiangsu—and of the Communist response to it.[27]

In 1943 a decisive shift in the fortunes of Mihailović and Tito occurred. In 1942 Mihailović was ascendant; he was regarded as the only legitimate anti-fascist leader in Yugoslavia and was the recipient of both lavish praise and military assistance from the Western powers. Tito was ignored or dismissed as a mere Communist. By the end of 1943, however, the positions of Tito and Mihailović were reversed, with the latter being regarded as a mere puppet, indistinguishable from Nedić except for the fact that he did not live in Belgrade. Many influences contributed to this shift: the recommendations of English liaison officers who were attached to both Partisan and Chetnik units, the establishment of strong Partisan bases in Bosnia-Herzegovina and Montenegro, open collaboration between the Chetniks and the Italians, the Italian surrender and disarmament of the Italians by the Partisans, large-scale fighting between Partisans and Germans during 1943, and, finally, the desertion of non-Ustashe Croatian soldiers to the Partisans rather than to the Chetniks because of the Chetniks' Serb chauvinism.

The reports by English officers accredited to Mihailović revealed to the Allies what was already known to the Yugoslav masses. One English officer attached to the Chetniks discovered the existence of close ties between Nedić's forces and the Chetniks, as well as a case in which Chetniks dressed themselves as Partisans to attack the Germans in order to avoid reprisals against the Serb population.[28] On September 1, 1943, all English representatives with Mihailović's forces were placed under one commander, Brigadier Armstrong, who then sought to "stimulate Mihailović to act more energetically against the Germans"[29] (compare General Stilwell's efforts to stimulate Chiang Kai-shek). He failed in this mission, and the result was the withdrawal of all aid to Mihailović. In addition, intelligence reached London of massacres by Chetniks of Muslims, Croats, and pro-Partisan populations in western Serbia, close cooperation against the Partisans between Italians and Chetniks (notably the Chetnik units of Dobrosav Jevdjević in Herzegovina), German messages concerning joint Axis-Chetnik operations, and other similar incidents.[30] The shift in Allied policy that followed receipt of this intelligence is best explained by Churchill himself:

> In May 1943, we took a new departure. It was decided to send small parties of British officers and non-commissioned officers to establish contact with the Yugoslav partisans, in spite of the fact that cruel strife was proceeding between them and the Chetniks, and that Tito was waging war as a Communist, not only against the German invaders, but against the Serbian Monarchy and Mihailović. At the end of that month, Captain Deakin, an Oxford don who had helped me for five years before the war in my literary work, was dropped by parachute from Cairo to set up a mission with Tito. Other British missions followed, and by June much evidence had accumulated. The Chiefs of Staff reported on June 6: "It is clear from information available to the War Office that the Chetniks are hopelessly compromised in their relations with the Axis in Herzegovina and Montenegro. During the recent fighting in the latter area, it has been the well-organized partisans rather than the Chetniks who have been holding down the Axis forces."[31]

The change in Allied support actually influenced the Yugoslav civil war only slightly; Mihailović was already discredited by 1944, when British aid began to flow to Tito. There is, however, this exception: the British knew in 1943 that Tito had strong nationalistic support and they did not complicate the Partisans' victory by denying their legitimacy and popular basis (compare Allied policy in China). As for Mihailović's decline, it was caused not by British policy but by the logic of the wartime situation itself. Mihailović's general policies, at least in early 1942, were "legal" and were in accordance with resistance practice in most of occupied Europe. As the legal representative of the King and as Minister of War, Mihailović fought the Communists, who were members of an illegal party in his country and who refused to follow his leadership. As a Serb, who feared for the extinction of the Serbs by the Germans if guerrilla warfare were undertaken, he decided to wait for a more opportune time to open armed attacks. Both of these decisions had merit, but they actually laid the foundation for his destruction. The force that tipped the scale in favor of the Partisans was the nationalistic mobilization of the population on a supra-ethnic—i.e., a truly Yugoslav—basis and the Partisans' accommodation to this mobilization.

The Partisans entered western Bosnia in early 1942 with 3,000 men, and by the end of the year their forces numbered 25,000.[32] During the same year Partisan uprisings were launched in Slovenia and Montenegro; and in the following year Partisan operations spread to Serbia and Croatia. Mihailović never accommodated himself to this peasant activity; instead, he continued to regard all Partisans as Communists and thus dangerous. At Mihailović's trial in June and July of 1946, the following revealing exchange took place:

> PROSECUTOR: Did you fight against the units of the National Liberation Army as a communist army, or did you fight for some other reason?
> . . .
> DEFENDANT [Mihailović]: . . . I think my answer on the whole is that it was a struggle against the communist units.
> PROSECUTOR: Did these units consist only of communists?
> DEFENDANT: (Thinks for a while and then answers) No, they did not.
> PROSECUTOR: Then, how could you fight against the other patriots in the National Liberation Army who were not communists?
> DEFENDANT: I shall be able to answer this question only after I have thought it over.
> PROSECUTOR: The defendant avoids answering. . . .
> PRESIDENT [Presiding Judge]: Did you fight against the National Liberation Army, which represented the struggle against the invader? Did you fight against the National Liberation Movement, which represented the struggle against the invader in Yugoslavia?
> DEFENDANT: Yes, I did.[33]

Thus Mihailović sealed his fate. The important point is that he was found guilty not of being a representative of a class "doomed by the laws of history," or of being a tool of finance capital, but of being a traitor. It was not Yugoslav Communism but Yugoslav nationalism that crushed Mihailović and his movement. Mihailović was shot at Topchider barracks outside Belgrade on July 17, 1946.

If, indeed, it was a nationalistic awakening that swelled the ranks of the Partisans with peasants, what were the forces that awakened the peasantry? The invasion itself, as in China, was the first major influence. But the invasion, again as in China, was not the only pressure. Counterguerrilla operations and reprisals by the Germans spread the movement, and Communist training activities and rear-area governments structured it in a nationalistic way. We shall consider the rear-area governments later; first, let us look at the quality of the German campaigns directed specifically against the Partisans.

The Partisans counted seven different German and Italian offensives against their strongholds in Bosnia-Herzegovina and Montenegro. These offensives were distinct from daily patrols by the occupiers in that they followed fixed phases, were carried out by large numbers of specially concentrated assault troops, and were verified by captured documents. Like the Japanese *sankō-seisaku* campaigns against the Eighth Route Army, the German offensives followed the tactic of encirclement and destruction. Moreover, again like the Japanese, the Germans did not grant the Communists recognition as a belligerent under international law, but regarded them only as "bandits"; no prisoners were taken by either side in Yugoslavia. Of the seven offensives, the first five were designed to eliminate the Partisans completely; and the fifth (May–June 1943) all but succeeded in doing precisely that. The objectives of the sixth (September 1943–January 1944) and the seventh (April–June 1944) were to contain the Partisan movement, and specifically to keep the Partisans from entering Serbia and Macedonia. Dedijer's diary gives us an idea of the scale of these operations: in January 1943, at the start of the fourth offensive, he noted that the Germans had mustered 65,000 troops and were making extensive use of aircraft and tanks against the liberated areas in Bosnia.[34]

If we can accept the official figures concerning civilian losses in Yugoslavia during the war, the extent of civilian persecution by the invader was staggering. According to Kapetanović, whereas in eighteen Allied countries during the war the average loss of life was one in 143, in Yugoslavia one in *nine* died. There were 3,741,000 persons interned in concentration camps—23 per cent of the population.[35] Under such pressures as these, it was inevitable that a political realignment should take place. Thus, the effect of the German offensives was to leave the Partisans temporarily weakened but potentially stronger. With each new offensive the lives of the people were disrupted, and they came to see that there was no alternative to resistance other than death, imprisonment, or starvation. The political meaning of this destructive challenge and subsequent resistance was the replacement of territorial, ethnic, and religious provincialism by an allegiance to the nationalistic goals of the Partisans. Clissold comments, for example, that the Partisan uprising in Slovenia broke the hold of the Catholic Church, which was collaborating closely with the Italians, for the first time since the Counter Reformation.[36] For the mountain peasant in areas other than Serbia, participation in the Partisan movement was his first introduction to Yugoslav nationalism. The legitimacy of Partisan-sponsored nationalism was then demonstrated to him by the Partisan victory that he had helped to achieve.

The Partisans, like the Chinese Communists, also organized many local and regional governments, which were democratic in style if not in spirit. These included people's committees (*odbors*) at the village level as well as the large general assemblies held in 1942 and 1943, which represented all parts of the country and which constituted the basis for the postwar Yugoslav government. The *odbor* was the Yugoslav equivalent of the hsien government, and the regional assemblies roughly corresponded to the assemblies called by the various Chinese border-region administrative committees. Before considering the Yugoslav governmental bodies themselves, however, let us briefly examine the size and nature of their constituent organizations—namely, the Army and the civilian mass-mobilization associations.

Considering the size of Yugoslavia's population and the original Communist nucleus, the Partisan Army at its largest—i.e., immediately after the liberation of the country—was huge. In February 1945, Tito's Army consisted of 54 divisions with a total of 800,000 soldiers, almost as many as the Chinese Communist Army numbered at the end of the war, despite the tremendous difference in the manpower of the two countries.[37] This figure includes many Chetniks and Italians who joined the Partisans under various amnesties proclaimed just before the end of the war, but the overwhelming majority of the Partisans were young men and women peasants from western Yugoslavia. (Montenegro provided the greatest number of Partisans, although all provinces and districts were represented.)[38] The relative size of the Partisan Army emphasizes the advanced state of the Yugoslav revolution in 1945. The Chinese Communist Army did not achieve truly phenomenal proportions until 1949, when the KMT troops were incorporated and when the entire country was conquered.

Mass associations were less extensively used in Yugoslavia than in China, but such associations did exist. The Party itself was something of a mass association, since Party membership was offered to virtually all who had distinguished themselves in battle.[39] The political education received by new members of the YCP constituted one important channel for the diffusion of nationalist sentiment to the peasantry. Other channels were the Youth Organization, which had nearly 100,000 members at the close of 1942, and a mass indoctrination unit for children, called the *Pioniri,* comparable to the "Young Pioneers" in China (Chung-kuo Shao-nien Hsien-feng Tui).[40]

The great expansion of Partisan and Party ranks by recruitment among the politically neutral peasantry helps to explain certain of the dislocations that occurred when the Partisans achieved power. For instance, Halperin raises the question of why the Partisan regime resorted to terrorist measures on taking office, despite its almost universal support. He replies: "It was not a mistake, an excess committed in the sudden intoxication with power. . . . The objective was simply to make room for the new masters— for several hundreds of thousands of partisans from the mountains. It was necessary for this purpose to remove the people who hitherto had directed the economic life of the country and occupied posts as public servants. It was as much a demographic revolution as a social one, if not more so: one of those periodical rapes of the fat lush plains by the people from the lean hills."[41] Of course, such purges were executed in the name of punishment of collaborators, a convincing enough charge since most city dwellers were in fact collaborators.

These new governors from the countryside were not wholly inexperienced in government. They had established and put into operation in the liberated areas parliamentary assemblies that had been ratifying Partisan policies for a large part of Yugoslavia since 1942. On November 5, 1942, the Partisans captured the ancient town of Bihać in the western part of Bosnia, and on the evening of November 26, 1942, they convened the first meeting of the new Partisan Congress there. This body, known as the Anti-Fascist Council of the National Liberation of Yugoslavia (AVNOJ), was made up of delegates from people's committees, political parties (including the Communist Party and other Serbian and Croatian peasant parties), and Army representatives. The most important action taken by the Bihać Congress, other than constituting itself as a functioning association, was to stipulate that people's committees (*odbors*) were to replace all other local authorities as the legal government in the liberated areas.

A second and more important congress of AVNOJ was held at Jajce in central Bosnia, November 29 and 30, 1943. This meeting reached several decisions that vitally affected Yugoslavia's postwar political life. In the first place, AVNOJ proclaimed itself the new government of Yugoslavia and named Tito Marshal of Yugoslavia. The King was forbidden to return to the country, and Mihailović was publicly denounced for collaborating with the Germans. These resolutions announced to the world the autonomy and legitimacy of the Partisan movement and of the government sponsored by it. In addition, the Jajce Congress resolved that the future Yugoslav state was to be created on a federal, rather than a central, principle. Thus, the Partisans went on record as opposing the fratricidal aspects of the civil war and condemning the Chetniks' Serb nationalism.[42]

The immediate effect of the Jajce decisions was to embarrass the British leadership, which had decided to give all-out aid to Tito but which also recognized the authority of the government-in-exile. During 1944, the British urged the King to drop the Serb chauvinists from his cabinet and to appoint a Premier who could negotiate with Tito. On June 1, 1944, the King selected Ivan Shubashić, a moderate and the first Croat ever to be named Yugoslav Premier. Shubashić and Tito recognized each other on June 16 and thereby paved the way for Allied recognition of Tito. The acceptance of the Partisans into the anti-fascist alliance symbolized the recognition by the Allies that most of the Yugoslav people were united behind Tito, and that Tito was more than a puppet of Moscow. What had begun as a peasant-based self-defense uprising ended as the legal government in a reconstituted Yugoslavia.

By contrast, the Chinese Communist movement did not succeed in totally discrediting its nationalist competitor and entering the Grand Alliance before the war ended. However, the mantle of Chinese nationalism had already passed to the Communists; and, as the Yugoslav case suggests, it was the achievement of nationalist supremacy that constituted the basis of success for both the Yugoslav and Chinese Communist parties. The relative insignificance of Allied wartime policy to internal developments in these circumstances is seen in the fact that both Communist China and Communist Yugoslavia became viable nation-states in the postwar world.

SEVEN

Communism in the Service of the Nation-State

In the previous pages, we have seen how World War II accelerated the social mobilization of the Chinese and Yugoslav peoples and how this mass awakening became the foundation for the postwar governments. It remains for us to inquire into the consequences that this particular mode of political success held for the foreign policies and ideologies of the resultant states. After coming to power, both the Chinese and the Yugoslav Communists concluded alliances with the Soviet Union, which for nearly thirty years the world's Communists had looked to as the fountainhead and exemplar of Communism in power. The masses of China and Yugoslavia also welcomed an alliance with the first Communist state as the natural concomitant of their acceptance of domestic Communism. However, neither China nor Yugoslavia became constituent republics or satellites of the USSR; and, as time passed, it became clear that the Marxist ideal of "proletarian internationalism" could not transcend three different conceptions of national—albeit Communist—interest, or reconcile three conflicting ideas of what foreign policy might best be pursued by the Communist bloc.

Yugoslavia clashed with the Soviet Union over the activities of Soviet intelligence organs and the conduct of Soviet troops on Yugoslav territory; it also began to pursue foreign policies designed to secure its economic and political interests in the Balkans, despite the fact that the Soviet Union had different plans for this area. This led to the rupture of 1948 and to the adoption, since that time, of an independent Communist policy by the Yugoslav government.

China's relations with the USSR preserved a semblance of equality from the start; but even in that context China had to defend its national interests—for example, in obtaining Russian aid and trade; in securing the renunciation of Soviet claims to Port Arthur and railroad interests in Manchuria; in ousting the pro-Russian leader in Manchuria, Kao Kang, who sought to establish his independence from Peking;[1] and in negotiating the abolition of the Sino-Russian Joint Stock Companies. At the same time, the Chinese Communist government actively upheld China's pre-eminent interest in the Far East by intervening in the Korean War. In more recent years, Chinese independence of the Soviet Union has been made fully manifest by open criticism of de-Stalinization, of Soviet policy toward the United States, of Soviet aid policy toward "bourgeois nationalist" leaders such as Nasser and Nehru, and of the Soviet attitude toward the developing revolution in former colonial territories. In turn, Chinese independence has provoked Soviet criticism of the Chinese communes and has led to Russian neutrality in the Sino-Indian border dispute.

This divergence in policies among the three independent Communist states—or, as it is called, national Communism—is a natural outgrowth of the politicization of the masses in China and Yugoslavia during the war. The spread of nationalism among the Chinese and Yugoslav peoples placed limitations on the extent to which the Chinese and Yugoslav leaders could follow the dictates of Moscow, or for that matter of any other external authority. Nowhere was this influence of mass participation in Communist politics more clearly felt than in the Soviet-Yugoslav dispute of 1948. As Fred W. Neal has observed,

> As a result of the wartime coalition on which it rode to victory, the Tito regime, minority dictatorship though it was, had a wider popular following than did the regimes in the satellites-proper, and this in itself was a factor in Tito's power position. To comply with all Soviet wishes in the realm of either political or economic policies would have adversely affected that position. . . . It was certainly the refusal—or, better said, inability—of the Yugoslavs to follow Soviet dictates generally that led to their excommunication.[2]

Thus, the crucial element in the emergence of Yugoslav national Communism in 1948 was the earlier mobilization of the popular will behind Tito, a mobilization that took place independently of Soviet initiatives.

However, as the Soviet-Yugoslav dispute also reveals, Soviet demands on Yugoslavia were the catalyst that brought Yugoslav national Communism into the open. This fact tells us much about the relationship between Communism and nationalism in the contemporary world. For national Communism already existed in the Soviet Union when the revolutionary governments of China and Yugoslavia came to power. As is well known, the international Communist movement was conscripted into the service of the Soviet Union before World War II; but Soviet propaganda in that period effectively camouflaged the degree to which Communist ideology had been subordinated to Russian nationalism. It required the creation of truly "fraternal" Communist governments in China and Yugoslavia after the war to point up just how national the national Communism of the Soviet Union was. Today we are able to recognize that Communism in all Communist states other than the East European and Asian satellites rests basically upon an indigenous national awakening. Indeed, one of the main lessons to be derived from this study is the extent to which nationalism and Communism have become synonymous.

We may illustrate this conclusion by comparing the popular weakness of the non-Russian Communist parties in the Comintern period with the popular support enjoyed by the Chinese and Yugoslav Communist parties at the time of their founding. With regard to the impact of Russian national Communism upon other Communist parties before the war, Hammond has noted that the USSR emasculated the local parties' effectiveness by forcing them to serve Soviet national interests: "For Stalin thereby brought Communism into conflict with nationalism. Being a Communist implied being an agent of a foreign power, which to most people seemed abhorrent. It is probably no exaggeration to say that the greatest deterrent to people becoming Communists has been the feeling that Communism implied disloyalty to one's own country."[3] But in China and Yugoslavia just the opposite is true: there, being a Communist is synonymous with advancing the interests of one's own country; and it is precisely this advancement of nationalism under Communist auspices that explains the great strength of Chinese and Yugoslav Communism. Moreover, if in the near future the Communist government of China or of Yugoslavia should be repudiated by the masses, it would probably be for nationalist reasons: for example, a conspicuous failure in the government's program of national construction (particularly in China), or a foreign policy seen by the masses as counter to the national interest.

A second illustration of the importance of the national component in national Communism is to be found by considering the nature of Communist authority in the East European satellites. These puppet governments were created by Soviet military power after World War II, and the agents of Moscow who rule in these territories do so by virtue of the Soviet military forces based in or near their areas. National Communism—the expression of nationalist impulses through Communist institutions—does not exist, save in a cautious and attenuated form in such a leader as Gomulka. Instead, in these areas nationalism is opposed to Communism, since Communism has meant only the furthering of Russian interests; and nationalist revolt against Russian Communism has long been endemic (it has, of course, actually broken out in Hungary, East Germany, and Poland, on different occasions). After the death of Stalin, the Soviet Union sought to soften the impact of the identification between Communism and Russian nationalism by the policy of de-Stalinization, which introduced the tolerance of what Hammond calls a "housebroken Titoism" (particularly in Poland). This policy, combined with a recognition of geopolitical realities by the satellites, has produced acquiescence in the status quo. Precisely because nationalism and Communism do not coincide, Communist government in the satellites must inevitably suffer from the instabilities of colonial regimes—a situation very different from that in China, Yugoslavia, and the USSR. For *popular* Communism without a basis in nationalism does not exist.

In recognizing the nationalistic basis of Communism in the independent Communist states (and, conversely, its purely military nature in the satellites), we are explicitly asserting that Communism itself is not either the focal point or the prime mover of these states, and that the reality underlying the creation of the independent Communist states is the social mobilization of their masses. In this study of the Chinese and Yugoslav resistance movements, we have touched upon only one aspect of the social mobilization of these peoples. In a sense, the conditions created by World War II in China and Yugoslavia served only to catalyze and channel the slowly developing forces of social change that had been undermining the traditional societies for decades. These long-range forces are essential to social mobilization, but it would be a mistake to overrate them—for example, to overrate the influence of imperialism and modern technology in rendering China's traditional social institutions obsolete. The short-range cataclysmic effects of direct physical assault upon populations can be just as important. In recent times, the two world wars have had as great a role in social mobilization as the spread of modern scientific culture.

Even when we expand the idea of social mobilization to include the effects of war and civilian resistance, we are still dealing with only one half of the over-all process. As much as social mobilization is concerned with the *destruction* of pre-modern social fabrics—detribalization, the evolution out of feudalism, the collapse of agrarian bureaucracy—it also deals with the subsequent reintegration of the affected populations into new, typically modern, political communities. Deutsch, the leading commentator on the concept of social mobilization, finds "two distinct stages to the process: (1) the stage of uprooting or breaking away from old settings, habits, commitments; and (2) the induction of the mobilized persons into some relatively stable new patterns of group membership, organizational commitment."[4] In narrowing down this general understanding to historical cases, we have attempted to specify more directly what is involved in the second stage of mobilization; our interpretation of the role played by "national myth" in reintegrating mobilized peoples corresponds generally to Deutsch's second stage. The acceptance by the mobilized people of a specific ideological construct that rationalizes and sanctifies their endeavors is one sure sign that reintegration is taking place. Such integrative ideologies are as varied as the number of national communities; they include a self-righteous anti-colonialism, philosophies of individualism, and religious or racial extrapolations reworked to fit given circumstances.[5] Communism is only one—if a very important one—of the various unifying and self-dignifying ideologies that serve mobilized communities.

Our characterization of Communist ideology in the independent Communist states as "national myth" is not primarily intended as a philosophical critique of Marxism; rather, it is an attempt to explain in functional terms the presence of a Marxist-derived ideological structure in mobilized national communities in which Marxism itself has no prescriptive role. What evidence do we have that Communism serves as a nationalist ideology? In addition to our study of the resistance movements, which indicates that the demands of national crisis rather than the logic of Communism brought the Chinese and Yugoslav Communist parties to power, there is a second form of evidence. This is the extensive revision and manipulation of Communist theory undertaken by the Chinese and Yugoslav Communists in order to bring it into line with various policies of a nationalist character: for example, the enlargement of the industrial and agricultural capacity of their nations, a single-party dictatorship, totalitarian control of society, the creation of buffer states surrounding the national territory, and the glorification of the activities of the national population and its leaders. Most significantly, this reinterpretation of Communist ideology for nationalist purposes has its roots in social mobilization—a subject to which we shall return presently.

It is rather a misnomer to describe the adaptation of Communism to national circumstances as "revisionism," since the orthodox Communism that is allegedly being revised is actually Soviet national Communist ideology. From the time of the Bolshevik Revolution to World War II, Communism was the ideological property of the Soviet Union, and during that period the Russians interpreted it in such a way as to legitimatize Stalin's development program and foreign policies. It was only with the occurrence of social mobilization under Communist Party leadership in two other areas that the Russian monopoly was broken. Chinese and Yugoslav leaders also began to adapt the Communist ideological heritage to their own political environments; and as substantive differences between the three independent Communist states emerged, these differences began to be reflected in intrabloc ideological conflict. However, it can only be a matter of personal choice to determine which version of Communism, or which side of a given dispute (the USSR's, China's, or Yugoslavia's) is orthodox, particularly when most of the subjects that give rise to ideological controversy have no connection with nineteenth-century Marxism. Much of the current "revisionism" naturally originates with the Chinese or Yugoslavs, since it is they who seek to challenge—on the basis of their national needs—the long-unchallenged tenets of Leninism and Stalinism. The Chinese and the Yugoslavs have had not only to adapt Communism to their own environments, but also to do this in the face of earlier Russian-oriented pronouncements on ideology.

The manipulation of ideology in China actually began during the war, simultaneously with the awareness of the Chinese leaders that they had finally achieved leadership of a mass movement. In Yenan in 1942, the Chinese Communist Party began the first of a continuing series of movements for internal Party education. These so-called *cheng feng,* or rectification, movements are peculiar to the Chinese Party in that they are not purges but, rather, intensive indoctrination sessions. *Cheng feng* movements are designed to ensure that the rank-and-file not only follow the directives of the Party's Central Committee in accordance with the principle of "democratic centralism," but also grasp and accept positively the rationale advanced by the Party to support its policies. The *cheng feng* of 1942 exhibited the first concrete manifestation of the CCP's well-known indoctrination technique: *ssu-hsiang kai-tsao* (thought reform)—a method sensationalized in the West as "brainwashing." Although it is doubtful that *cheng feng* possesses the Orwellian attributes claimed for it by some Western commentators,[6] it is unquestionably a powerful method for eliciting enthusiastic support from Party members and for isolating people who disagree with Party policy.

The Yenan *cheng feng* of 1942 concentrated upon the related problems of elevating the Chinese Communist Party at the expense of other Chinese political groups and elevating Chinese Communism at the expense of Soviet Communism. In concrete terms, it was aimed at two main targets: (1) the vast numbers of new members who had joined the Party primarily for patriotic reasons and who confused the CCP with other anti-Japanese organizations; and (2) "Russian formalists"—those Party members who were well drilled in Marxist, Leninist, and Stalinist maxims, but who failed to grasp the fact that the Chinese revolution required a new interpretation and application of the basic canon. The former were required to learn the Maoist version of Communism and to prepare themselves for a life of service in a Leninist organization. The latter, particularly the Moscow-trained group around Wang Ming (Ch'en Shao-yü), were told, in effect, that the CCP no longer required Russian translators; and they were demoted to minor positions in the Party hierarchy.

These activities by the Chinese Party were not so much anti-Russian as they were pro-Chinese—they represented the "Sinification" of Communism at the time when the CCP had graduated from Comintern agency to mass revolutionary vehicle. This conclusion is supported by other investigations into the 1942 *cheng feng*. Boyd Compton, who has translated the Party Reform Documents that were used in the Yenan *cheng feng*, observes that "[the movement's] principal importance to the entire Party was intensive indoctrination and education in the principles of Mao Tse-tung's communism. *Reform Documents* presented the Chinese Communist Party with an ideology. Since the war this ideology has come to be generally known as the thought of Mao Tse-tung."[7] The authors of the *Documentary History* reach a related conclusion: statements by Party leaders in the *cheng feng* movement "seem clearly to reflect the far-reaching influence of a sentiment of nationalism which affected the CCP during the Sino-Japanese War."[8] Precisely at the time when Chinese Communism had obtained a mass following, Mao was calling for "a theory which is our own and of a specific nature."[9] Mao himself soon supplied a theory that was conveniently both Communist ("scientific and universal") and Chinese ("nationalistic"); it satisfied the need for an integrative ideology during the last years of the war, and it continues to serve today as the state ideology of the new Chinese nation.[10]

Postwar Yugoslavia reveals more clearly than Communist China both the existence of ideological divergence from the other independent Communist states and the roots of this divergence in indigenous social mobilization. There is no question at all about the prewar political and ideological position of the YCP: it was the instrument of the Communist International, and its ideology was Stalinism. From the time of the dispute with Moscow in 1948, however, the Yugoslav Communist Party began reinterpreting Communist doctrine *ex post facto* in order to bring it into line with the new policies forced upon it by nationalist differences with the Soviet Union. If Yugoslavia was to maintain the unity and stability created by the Partisan resistance movement, it could neither become a Soviet satellite nor denounce Communism altogether. Stalin failed in his attempt to force the YCP's rank-and-file to unseat Tito and his politburo precisely because this rank-and-file owed an allegiance to Tito that canceled the Party's prewar loyalty to Stalin. At the same time, the YCP refused to admit that it was taking the national Communist path in order not to forfeit the real value of Marxism as national myth and legitimator of the regime.

Although "revisionism" in Yugoslavia did not come into the open until after 1948, its roots lay in the resistance movement. The expulsion from the Cominform only brought matters to a head. Tito had in fact made it clear as early as 1943 that he envisioned postwar Yugoslavia as anything but a Soviet colony; at the Jajce Congress of AVNOJ, he stated:

> I may boldly claim that the creation of a national army under such conditions as ours is unique in history. From barehanded partisan detachments, without factories, arms or ammunition, without store houses, military supplies or provisions, without assistance from any side, an army of about a quarter of a million has been created, not in a peaceful period of time but in the course of the most terrible and bloodiest struggle waged by the nations of Yugoslavia. This is a gain of which the nations of Yugoslavia may be proud and of which their future generations will boast.[11]

Indeed, the Yugoslav Partisans had earned the right to boast, but we must recognize that their claims derive less from Marxism than from more ancient and emotional sources of unity:

> . . . gentlemen in England now a-bed
> Shall think themselves accurs'd they were not here,
> And hold their manhoods cheap while any speaks
> That fought with us upon Saint Crispin's day.

After the war, the Yugoslav Party and people, still proud of their wartime accomplishments and confident of the acclaim that they felt would come from Moscow, closely allied themselves with the new Soviet empire.

But instead of celebrating the accomplishments of its most leftist ally, the Soviet Union persisted in regarding Yugoslavia as another of its satellites and, most irksome of all to the Partisans, as one that had been created by the Soviet Army just like all the others.[12] The ostracism imposed on Yugoslavia by the Cominform after 1948 forced the Yugoslavs to reappraise their own Communism vis-à-vis that of the Soviet Union and the satellites. In so doing, they created a new version of Marxist ideology that underwrote their independent road to Communism and retroactively ascribed a socialist character to the anti-fascist resistance. As evolved in recent years, the new ideology of Yugoslav Communism is one of the clearest examples of Communism in its role as national myth. On the one hand, it identifies the Yugoslav government's actions with "science" and "general human progress";[13] on the other hand, it conveniently ignores all aspects of the state's origins or subsequent policies that contradict Marxism-Leninism. While this development would assuredly have appalled Marx himself, he might at least have taken heart from the fact that his theory explaining ideology as the reflection of an "underlying reality" was being borne out. Of course, he had a very different sort of underlying reality in mind.

Given that the present Chinese and Yugoslav governments are the offspring of indigenous nationalism and that Communist ideology serves as the theoretical expression of these nationalisms, there remains the difficult problem of the extent to which Communist ideology *prescribes* policy for the Chinese and Yugoslav nations. In Chapter One, we stated that national myth is generally found not to possess a prescriptive function insofar as it relates to social mobilization; and this observation is borne out by the Chinese and Yugoslav cases. Communism did not mobilize the Chinese or Yugoslav masses; rather, Communism was legitimatized by the nationalistic credentials established by Communist parties in the period of mobilization. However, in the period after the Communist parties were installed in power and their national Communist ideologies—Maoism and Titoism —were accepted by the masses, ideology did begin to play a part in the over-all process of decision-making.

Today, Communist ideology makes itself felt primarily as a conditioning and limiting factor. It may, for example, restrict knowledge of unknown quantities—such as the internal politics of foreign countries, or the potentialities of literature and the arts—by burdening the leadership with ideological stereotypes. And it may exacerbate mistaken or unsuitable policies, even to the point of national disaster, by prescribing the form of institutions or by freezing information about the performance of the economy into an ideological gestalt. In all this there is very little Marxism, and what little there is in no way represents a source of authority independent of nationalism in policy formulation. The national Communist states are no more immune to the dangers of blindly pursuing nationalist impulses than non-Communist nationalist regimes. Nationalist ideology may influence any nationalist movement, and the extent to which national Communist ideology affects the independent Communist states should be a subject of continuing investigation. With regard to the Chinese and Yugoslav revolutions, however, we may reassert that ideology did not become operative until after mobilization was well advanced.

CONCLUSION

The social mobilization of large populations and the emergence of mass political communities must be ranked along with the host of other forces—scientific, medical, and technological—which have transformed the globe in less than a century. The acceptance by large groups of human beings of new or initial political identities has created unprecedented social needs, both rational and emotional, and has produced a type of nation-state not imagined at the time that political configuration first appeared. The current social mobilization of China's huge population dwarfs the now almost forgotten antagonisms that led to Japan's continental intrusion. For the sake of focus, I have consciously underemphasized some of the long-range factors that contributed to the mobilization of the Chinese people: imperialism, the deficiencies of indigenous political institutions and elites, the pathological condition of the former land tenure system and the like. Other studies have dealt at length with these problems. What this study seeks to emphasize is that the boiling point in China was reached during the period of the Japanese invasion.

The fact that this "boiling point" took the form of a war between the Chinese peasants and the Japanese Army is important. The war was not merely the final aggregate of foreign pressure on China; it ruptured the old order in a particular way. The invasion and the resistance movement gave definition to the Chinese mobilization: it placed the leadership of the awakened people in the hands of the Communist Party, and it determined the means by which the new Chinese nation was to emerge—namely, the military unification of China by its armed and militarized population. It discredited the Kuomintang government and, by extension, the KMT's foreign allies, not merely as political rivals of the Communists but as traitors and enemies to the cause of Chinese independence and sovereignty.

The experiences of the Party and its followers during the resistance are reflected in innumerable ways in the post-1949 government: the use of "thought reform" and "self-criticism" to do for the whole society what they did for the Party in Yenan in its darker hours; the more than passing similarity between the rural communes and the guerrilla bases; and the emphasis upon the organization of the popular will, rather than upon capital equipment and technical competence, as a means to accomplish difficult tasks. A full evaluation of the significance of the resistance for the postwar political order cannot yet be made; but it is not accidental that the leader of the Communist Party is also China's first thinker on military affairs, that the present head of state served as the political commissar of the New Fourth Army, and that the present foreign minister was the victorious commander of Communist forces in central China. In short, China's social mobilization was accomplished under fire, and this experience has exerted a greater influence upon the temper and policies of the post-mobilization government than is commonly appreciated among China's former allies.

In noting the military quality of the Communist rise to power, one should not be led into the mistake (or apologia) that the Chinese Communists succeeded solely through military prowess. Guerrilla warfare is not so much a military technique as it is a political condition.[14] It does not depend primarily on favorable geography, or mobility at the expense of supply trains, or the adroit employment of commando tactics; rather, guerrilla warfare is civilian warfare—that is, conflict between a professional army, possessing the advantages of superior training and equipment, and an irregular force, less well trained, less well equipped, but actively supported by the population of the area occupied by the army. It is precisely this mass backing for the full-time guerrillas that gives rise to the characteristic tactics employed by guerrillas: surprise attack or ambush, extreme mobility, and fighting only at times and places of their own choosing. The population aids the guerrillas by freeing them from logistic anchors, providing them with near-perfect intelligence concerning enemy movements, and hiding fugitives when the need arises.

This presence of an overtly neutral but covertly engaged population is made a prerequisite for the employment of guerrilla tactics by virtually all major guerrilla leaders. Mao Tse-tung states unequivocally, "Because guerrilla warfare basically derives from the masses and is supported by them, it can neither exist nor flourish if it separates itself from their sympathies and cooperation."[15] Thus, Communist military successes during the resistance must be understood, fundamentally, as a concomitant of peasant mobilization and of the Communist-peasant alliance. Otherwise, the successes of the Communist armies could only be explained by the incompetence of the Japanese and puppet troops—for which there is no objective evidence.

By way of conclusion, we may observe that the Communists' overwhelming victory in the civil war of 1947-49 clearly followed from their achievement of general rural support in occupied China during the war. The celebrated "military tactic" of "surround the cities" employed by the People's Liberation Army (the name of the Communist Army after March 5, 1947) reflected the Kuomintang's weakness more than the Communists' military ingenuity. The Kuomintang troops had to stay in the cities—there to be surrounded—because they were unwelcome in the countryside; most of the rural areas of occupied China had been in Communist hands since 1939. The political basis of the Communists' eventual military triumph was summarized by Mao Tse-tung himself as early as December 25, 1947. He wrote then:

> The Chiang Kai-shek bandit gang and the U.S. imperialist military personnel in China are very well acquainted with these military methods of ours. Seeking ways to counter them, Chiang Kai-shek has often assembled his generals and field officers for training and distributed for their study our military literature and the documents captured in the war. The U.S. military personnel have recommended to Chiang Kai-shek one kind of strategy and tactics after another for destroying the People's Liberation Army; they have trained Chiang Kai-shek's troops and supplied them with military equipment. But none of these efforts can save the Chiang Kai-shek bandit gang from defeat. The reason is that our strategy and tactics are based on a people's war; no army opposed to the people can use our strategy and tactics.[16]

Whatever Chiang's advisers may have thought at the time, it seems clear now that Mao was being candid, and clear also that he was correct. The truly significant element in both the resistance war and the civil war was the fact that the Chinese people were awakened and united behind the banner of Chinese Communism.

Appendix

The following is an alphabetical list of hsien named in this study. They are identified by name (Wade-Giles romanization) and, in order that they may be located precisely, by the number given in United States Central Intelligence Agency, *China, Provisional Atlas of Communist Administrative Units* (1959). Alternative names are given in parentheses when relevant to this study.

Ankuo HH-A-12

Antz'u (Langfang) HH-F-75

Ch'angchih SA-04

Ch'angchou KU-05

Ch'angshu KU-H-61

Chenchiang KU-07

Chenyüan KA-C-22

Chi HH-D-60

Chi HH-H-106

Chiangtu KU-B-11

Chiangyin KU-H-68

Chiaoho HH-F-87

Chiehhsiu SA-C-41

Ch'ienan HH-D-55

Chienp'ing
 (Hungtzutien) HH-H-115

Chin HH-H-100

Ching AN-D-48

Ch'ingho HH-K-126

Chinghsing HH-H-112

Chinglo SA-A-8

Ch'ingyang KA-C-25

Ch'ingyüan HH-A-1

Ch'itung KU-F-49

Ch'iungshan KT-Z-89

Chü SH-E-59

Chülu HH-J-130

Chungshan KT-A-5

Fanch'ang AN-D-50

Fanchih SA-A-4

Fengjun HH-D-51

Fenyang SA-C-44

Foup'ing HH-A-16

Haimen KU-F-51

Hengshui HH-H-104

Hochien HH-F-90

Notes

1. The maximum populations of the various districts under the direct control of the Soviet Central Government in 1934 were estimated by Mao Tse-tung for Edgar Snow in 1936 as follows:

Kiangsi Soviet	3,000,000
Hupeh-Anhwei-Honan	2,000,000
Hunan-Kiangsi-Hupeh	1,000,000
Kiangsi-Hunan	1,000,000
Chekiang-Fukien	1,000,000
Hunan-Hupeh	1,000,000
Total	9,000,000

Snow recalled that "Mao laughed when I quoted him the figure of '80,000,000' people living under the Chinese Soviets, and said that when they had that big an area the revolution would be practically won." *Red Star Over China* (New York: Modern Library ed., 1938), p. 73. By April 24, 1945, at the Seventh Chinese Communist Party Congress, Mao Tse-tung could announce that "China's liberated areas under the leadership of the Chinese Communist Party have now a population of 95,500,000." "On Coalition Government," *Selected Works of Mao Tse-tung* (London: Lawrence and Wishart, 1956), IV, 259. On August 13, 1945, Mao claimed 200,000,000 inhabitants for the Communist-controlled Great Rear Area (*Ta-hou-fang*). *Mao Tse-tung hsüan-chi,* IV (Peking, 1960), 1124. This last figure reflects the great expansion of Communist territories that accompanied the Japanese collapse; actually only about 100,000,000 had been securely organized in Communist bases.

2. Chiang Kai-shek's first speech calling for a movement to achieve a "new life" was made in Nanch'ang, Kiangsi, February 19, 1934. Chiang launched the New Life Movement (Hsin Sheng-huo Yün-tung) in conjunction with the final annihilation drive against the Communists. As Samuel Chu notes, "The Movement was an outgrowth of the immediate problem of reconstructing and rehabilitating those areas of Kiangsi taken from the Communists, but soon became a movement on a national scale." "The New Life Movement, 1934–1937," in John E. Lane, ed., *Researches in the Social Sciences on China* (New

York: Columbia University East Asian Institute Studies, No. 3, 1957), p. 2. It is of no immediate concern whether the New Life Movement actually helped the peasantry of Kiangsi or not (it certainly did not aid the peasants of other provinces); the point is that it competed economically with the Communists' program, offered peace, and was vigorously presented to the peasantry.

The assertion that the basis of peasant-Communist collaboration in the Kiangsi period was economic is, of course, an abstraction. In the actual village context, influences such as the peasants' lack of physical mobility, personal feuds, the history of banditry in the area, and the strength of secret societies would all enter into decisions for or against the Red Army. But, as one contemporary account puts it, "To unravel these criss-cross relationships [the sources of popular support for the Communists in the Soviet Republic] is almost impossible. The fact remains that economic inequities and iniquities have much to do with them. People who are economically secure or contented rarely respond to the enticements of Reds or any other revolutionary movement. In the territory held by the 'China Soviet State' the government is promoting a campaign to relieve these economic stresses—to improve upon the aims of the 'Soviet State.'" "The Red Hegira to Szechuan Province and the Future of the Movement," *China Weekly Review* (Shanghai, February 16, 1935), p. 382.

3. U.S. War Department, Military Intelligence Division, "The Chinese Communist Movement" (July 5, 1945) (declassified August 23, 1949). This useful report is published in U.S. Senate, 82d Congress, 2d Session, Committee on the Judiciary, *Institute of Pacific Relations* (Washington: Government Printing Office, 1952), as Part 7A, Appendix II. The quotation is from p. 2332.

4. According to Niijima Sunayoshi, the following numbers of "democratic political authorities" had been set up in the guerrilla areas by the end of the war: 22 Administrative Offices (*hsing-cheng hsing-shu*); 90 Inspectorates (*chuan-yüan kung-shu*); and 635 hsien governments. See his article "Kaihō-ku" (Liberated Areas), in Chūgoku Kenkyū-sho, *Gendai Chūgoku jiten* (Dictionary of Modern China) (Tokyo, 1959), pp. 46–49. The first two types of administrative agencies were located at the subprefectural level; their functions varied according to locality. According to Ch'ien Tuan-sheng, there were a total of 1,949 hsien in 28 provinces at the start of the war. "Wartime Local Government in China," *Pacific Affairs*, XVI (1943), 441–60.

The rates of growth in hsien governments established by the Communist forces were compiled in a Japanese study of 1942 as follows:

(a) Numbers of hsien in north China with magistracies set up under the sponsorship of the Chinese Communist forces.

January 1938 18
August 1939 130
July 1941 355
(plus 23 estimated to be in Shen-Kan-Ning)

(b) Central China (New Fourth Army)
October 1941 104

See "Chūgoku kyōsantō no genkyō, dōkō narabi ni taisaku" (The Present Condition of the Chinese Communist Party: Trends and Countermeasures) in Kōain (Asia Development Board), *Jōhō* (Intelligence), No. 57 (January 1, 1942), p. 5. (*Jōhō,* an invaluable source for the study of modern China, was a classified, bimonthly publication of the Political Affairs Bureau of the Asia Development Board (Kōain Seimubu) in Tokyo (first published September 1, 1939). The Kōain was founded December 16, 1938, in accordance with Imperial Ordinance No. 758; it became a part of the Greater East Asia Ministry when that agency was established on November 1, 1942. The Kōain's head office was in Tokyo with branch offices in Shanghai, Peiping, Amoy, and Kalgan; and with subbranch offices in Canton and Tsingtao. There were four divisions in Tokyo: political, economic, cultural, and technical. The Premier was President of the Kōain. Since its affairs dealt exclusively with China, it was commonly known in English as the China Affairs Board, but this is a mistranslation. See affidavit of Oikawa Genshichi, International Military Tribunal for the Far East (IMTFE), *Proceedings,* pp. 4761–62.)

5. "The New Nationalism," *Virginia Quarterly Review,* XXVI (1950), 436–37.

6. To facilitate the accurate location of places named in this study, an appendix has been provided in which hsien are identified both by name and by the number given in U.S. Central Intelligence Agency, *China, Provisional Atlas of Communist Administrative Units* (Washington: Department of Commerce, 1959). Although this atlas is not contemporary with the period in question, it has several advantages which outweigh this disadvantage: the maps are in Chinese characters, a uniform Wade-Giles system of romanization is used throughout, the index is superior to any other in present use, and the atlas is readily available in libraries.

7. Printed in Chief of Staff, Terauchi Corps, *Kyōsangun no seijibu ni tsuite* (Concerning the Political Department of the Communist Army), November 8, 1938, *Rikushi mitsu dai nikki* (Army, China, Secret Diary) [Rikugunshō (War Ministry) Archives], Vol. 64 (of 73 vols.), 1938, No. 3. The Japanese Army archives have been catalogued by John Young in his *Checklist of Microfilm Reproductions of Selected Archives of the Japanese Army, Navy, and Other Government Agencies, 1868–1945* (Washington: Georgetown University Press, 1959). Young's "T" (title) numbers are given in this study for works from this particular collection (original films located in the Library of Congress) as an aid to identification. In future citations the Rikugunshō series title and volume numbers will be omitted; full citations can be found in the Bibliography. The Terauchi Corps work, a collection of captured Chinese materials, is T912. The Japanese Army archives were returned to Japan by the U.S. government in 1957 and are at present housed at the Bōeichō Senshishitsu (Defense Agency, War History Office), Tokyo.

8. See the article "Sankō-seisaku" (The "Three-All" Policy) by Fujita Masatsune in *Gendai Chūgoku jiten,* pp. 209–10. The three components of this policy were "kill all, burn all, loot all." The Japanese began serious "mopping-up" campaigns following the so-called "Hundred Regiments Offensive" (August

20–December 5, 1940) of the Eighth Route Army. The first known mop-up was carried out in central Shansi and in the Foup'ing area of Hopei by the 108th division (Maj. Gen. Tomabechi Shiro), First Army, between March 10 and the end of April, 1938. One Japanese report reads: "Although the enemy suffered heavy losses during these operations the desired result was not achieved. Communist troops, particularly in the vicinity of Wut'ai and the area north of Ch'angchih, were not completely wiped out and powerful forces continued to roam the countryside harassing the Japanese rear. It was evident that the need existed for more aggressive campaigns and mopping-up operations in order to establish peace and order in the area. This was especially true as, with the withdrawal of various First Army units during the latter part of April for the T'ungshan Operation [Battle of Hsüchou; city fell May 19, 1938], enemy guerrilla activity within the Army's jurisdictional area increased markedly." U.S. Army, Forces in the Far East, *North China Area Operations Record, July 1937– May 1941* (Tokyo: Military History Section; Headquarters, Army Forces Far East, 1955), pp. 137–38. ["Japanese Monograph 178."] This document was written by Lt. Gen. Shimoyama Takuma, former staff officer, North China Area Army, and Lt. Gen. Hashimoto Gun, former Chief of Staff, First Army.

9. The term "peasant nationalism" was first used to describe the Chinese resistance by Professor George E. Taylor in his study of Japanese occupation policies. He wrote: "The peasants, as usual, stayed on their fields and the village headmen, local gentry, and even district magistrates failed to retreat with the Chinese armies. It was not that they welcomed the invader; they were merely unaccustomed to resisting by force the exchange of one tax collector for another. . . . The village was a collection of impoverished and leaderless farmers, at least at the beginning of the war. That the peasantry of North China did not prove such an easy problem in government, and later emerged as the chief obstacle to the extension of Japanese-sponsored administration, was due to the development of a peasant nationalism on a scale broad enough to constitute a political revolution. The main contribution of the Japanese to this development of peasant nationalism lay in their conduct of the war, but the chief responsibility rests with the Chinese leadership which emerged in the hinterland." *The Struggle for North China* (New York: International Secretariat, Institute of Pacific Relations, 1940), pp. 41–42.

10. Of China's total population in 1949, which has been estimated at 557,-010,000, village dwellers accounted for 480,720,000, or 89.65 per cent. *Gendai Chūgoku jiten*, p. 302.

11. Branko Lazitch, *Tito et la révolution yougoslave* (Paris, 1957), p. 65. (All translations from the French, as well as those from Chinese and Japanese, are by the author unless otherwise indicated.) In regard to the social composition of the Partisan units, Lazitch (Lazić) remarks (p. 63), "The Communist insurrection combined two forces: the members of the Party, who executed Moscow's directives, and the population, which wanted to help sustain the fight against the Germans and which had to defend itself against the extermination policy of the Independent State of Croatia. The former constituted the

leadership, and the latter *the bulk of the Partisans*. From the point of view of social origins, the former consisted largely of young intellectuals and the latter of *peasants*." Italics mine.

12. Milovan Djilas, *The New Class, An Analysis of the Communist System* (New York, 1957), pp. 174–75.

13. *The Theory of Social and Economic Organization*, Henderson and Parsons, trans. (Glencoe, Ill., 1947), p. 324.

14. Lucian W. Pye's distinctions among the various "appeals" of Communism are different from, but parallel to, the interpretation of Chinese Communism offered here. He records (1) a Communist appeal by the British and American parties to intellectuals alienated from the general society, and (2) an appeal by the French and Italian parties to the interests of distinct classes in the total society. His third type of "appeal" is that made by "People's Liberation Communism." "[In Asia] large numbers of people are losing their sense of identity with their traditional ways of life and are seeking restlessly to realize a modern way. . . . These people see the Communist organization as a stable element in their otherwise highly unstable societies. In modern times, these societies have generally been subjected to war and violence to an extreme degree. . . . The structure of Communism is something to which these people can hitch their ambitions. In the hierarchy of the party they can discover potentialities for advancement. They come to believe that in the structure of the party they can find a closer relationship between effort and reward than in anything they have known in either the static old society or the unstable, unpredictable, new one. . . . Communism also offers to such persons a means for understanding and explaining the social realities that have been disturbing them. Events and developments that they have had to accept as the workings of an unknown fate become comprehensible through Communism. The promise of knowledge is also a promise of action; a sense of futility can be replaced by the spirit of the activist. Thus, it seems that People's Liberation Communism can best be explained by the role it has assumed in an acculturation process involving whole societies." *Guerrilla Communism in Malaya* (Princeton, N.J., 1956), pp. 7–8. This role taken by Communism in Asian societies can equally well be understood as a species of nationalism.

15. *Marxism, An Historical and Critical Study* (London, 1961), p. 378.

16. Jules Monnerot, *Sociology and Psychology of Communism* (Boston: Beacon ed., 1960), p. 21. Italics mine. (Translation of Monnerot's *Sociologie du communisme*, Paris, 1949).

17. The authoritative study of precisely this question is Charles B. McLane, *Soviet Policy and the Chinese Communists 1931–1946* (New York, 1958). McLane (p. 9) finds that "The Fourth Plenum [January 1931] is primarily significant, not because it marked another change in the Party leadership, but because it is the last identifiable instance of outright Soviet intervention in the internal affairs of the Chinese Communist Party." Contacts between Mao and Stalin in this period were fragmentary, if they existed at all.

18. For a reappraisal of the Seventh Comintern Congress, see Kermit E. McKenzie, "The Soviet Union, the Comintern, and World Revolution: 1935,"

Political Science Quarterly, LXV (1950), 214–37. The most carefully reasoned analysis of the Sian Incident is Ishikawa Tadao, "Shian-jiken no ikkōsatsu; Mosukō to Chūgoku kyōsantō to no kankei ni tsuite" (An Inquiry into the Sian Incident: Concerning the Relations Between Moscow and the Chinese Communist Party), in his *Chūgoku kyōsantō shi kenkyū* (Studies in the History of the Chinese Communist Party) (Tokyo, 1959), pp. 217–45. As we shall see, the true significance of the Sian Incident lies not in its giving rise to the United Front, but in its compelling Chiang Kai-shek and his government to adopt an anti-Japanese policy.

19. "On 10 January 1933 the Chinese Red Army offered a united front to any armed force that would join it in battle against Japan." U.S. War Dept., "The Chinese Communist Movement," p. 2327. In the pre-1935 period, however, the united front propaganda of the CCP did not envisage collaboration with the *Kuomintang* against Japan. It was a call for a "popular front from below." Despite the existence of anti-Japanese sentiment in China, the Communists' anti-Japanese pronouncements from as early as April 1932 were dismissed by the public at large as transparent attempts to undermine the Kuomintang's anti-Communist campaign. The Chinese Communist attitude toward a KMT-led United Front was changed by the Seventh Comintern Congress (1935). The CCP acquiesced in Russian demands for a Sino-Russian alliance against Japan in response to the obvious Japanese threat to Russia's borders. (The Soviet Union and Nanking had re-established diplomatic relations in December 1932.) Thus, although Russian influence on United Front policy in China was important, the United Front cannot be understood wholly in terms of Comintern directives. For Chinese Communist United Front policy, see McLane, *Soviet Policy and the Chinese Communists,* pp. 62–63; and Ishikawa Tadao, "Kōsei soveto ki ni okeru kōnichi hantei tōitsu sensen no shomondai" (Various Questions Concerning the Anti-Japanese, Anti-Imperialist United Front in the Period of the Kiangsi Soviet), *Chūgoku kyōsantō shi kenkyū,* pp. 198–216. For an excellent discussion of the dangers of deducing all wartime actions of individual Communist parties from the Seventh Comintern Congress, see David T. Cattell, *Communism and the Spanish Civil War* (Berkeley, Calif., 1955), pp. 28–56 and *passim.*

20. "[The three-thirds] system supports the claims of the Communists that they are maintaining a democratic, united front government. But no real opposition toward the Communists could, it appears, develop from any other party or class or group, since the electoral vote is controlled by the masses and the masses are controlled by the Communists. Anyone is free to stand as a candidate, but in practice nearly all the candidates are proposed by the mass movement associations and the choice offered the electors is usually limited. . . . The Communists' control of (or loyalty from) the masses, combined with universal suffrage, is the chief cause of Communist power and political and military control." U.S. War Dept., "The Chinese Communist Movement," p. 2338.

21. Mary C. Wright, "The Chinese Peasant and Communism," *Pacific Affairs,* XXIV (1951), 258–59.

22. *Ibid.*, p. 257.

23. Sidney Klein, *The Pattern of Land Tenure Reform in East Asia After World War II* (New York, 1958), p. 142.

24. Mao Tse-tung, April 19, 1941, in *Selected Works*, IV, 11.

25. See the article "Hung Hsiu-ch'üan," by Teng Ssu-yü in A. W. Hummel, ed., *Eminent Chinese of the Ch'ing Period* (Washington, 1943), I, 362.

26. Franz Michael, "The Fall of China," *World Politics*, VIII (1956), 303.

27. The land problem in Kiangsi is fully discussed in Brandt, *et al., A Documentary History of Chinese Communism* (London, 1952), pp. 218–19; for agrarian policy in Kiangsi and during the Sino-Japanese war period, also see Chao Kuo-chun, *Agrarian Policy of the Chinese Communist Party 1921–1959* (Bombay, 1960), pp. 38–74. On April 19, 1941, Mao Tse-tung wrote, "In agrarian policy [in Kiangsi] we also made a mistake in repudiating the correct policy adopted in the earlier and middle periods of the Ten-year Civil War [the Chingkangshan period and after—late 1927 to the autumn of 1931], i.e., allotting the same amount of land to the landlords as to the peasants, so that the landlords could engage in farming and would not become displaced or turn to banditry to disturb peace and order." "Postscript to Rural Survey," *Selected Works*, IV, 10. Even this "correct policy" did not win a mass following for the Communist Party; that is one of the reasons why it was abandoned.

28. Brandt, *et al.*, pp. 275–76.

29. It might be argued that the peasants' subordination of economic interests to nationalism was only temporary, for they reverted to a violently anti-landlord policy in the land confiscations of 1947. However, an aspect of the postwar anti-landlord struggle that is commonly overlooked is its nationalistic coloration. The landlords were attacked not solely as rentiers, but also as collaborators with the enemy. Frank C. Lee has observed, "As a rule, most of the collaborationists were landlords, or, if not landlords originally, they had fared so well under the protection of the Japanese Army that they had accumulated large fortunes, mainly in land, at the expense of the local peasants." "Land Redistribution in Communist China," *Pacific Affairs*, XXI (1948), 22–23. Thus, the economic interests of the peasantry in these activities cannot be discounted, but neither can they be taken as the sole determinants.

30. Edward H. Carr, *Nationalism and After* (London, 1945), p. 2.

31. *Ibid.*, p. 18.

32. Carlton Hayes, *Nationalism: A Religion* (New York, 1960), p. 5.

33. Hayes: "In simplest terms, nationalism may be defined as a fusion of patriotism with a consciousness of nationality." *Ibid.*, p. 2.

34. *Nationalism and Social Communication, An Inquiry into the Foundations of Nationality* (New York, 1953), p. 2. Italics mine.

35. *Ibid.*, pp. 70–71.

36. *Ibid.*, p. 162.

37. Cf. Karl W. Deutsch, "Social Mobilization and Political Development," *American Political Science Review*, LV (1961), 493–514. In Deutsch's view, "Social mobilization can be defined . . . as the process in which major clusters of old social, economic, and psychological commitments are eroded or broken

and people become available for new patterns of socialization and behavior" (p. 494).

38. Eric J. Hobsbawm, *Social Bandits and Primitive Rebels, Studies in Archaic Forms of Social Movement in the 19th and 20th Centuries* (Glencoe, Ill., 1959), pp. 2–3.

39. Although he mistakenly regards joint action as the sole characteristic of nationalism, Ernest Renan stresses its importance as follows: "What constitutes a nation is not speaking the same tongue or belonging to the same ethnic group, but having accomplished great things in common in the past and the wish to accomplish them in the future." *Qu'est-ce qu'une nation?* (1882), quoted in Louis Snyder, *The Meaning of Nationalism* (New Brunswick, N.J., 1954), p. 14.

40. For the development of nationalism in Chinese intellectual circles, see Chow Tse-tsung, *The May Fourth Movement* (Cambridge, Mass., 1960); John De Francis, *Nationalism and Language Reform in China* (Princeton, N.J., 1950); Kiang Wen-han, *The Chinese Student Movement* (New York, 1948); Joseph R. Levenson, *Confucian China and its Modern Fate* (Berkeley, Calif., 1958); and Robert A. Scalapino and George Yu, *The Chinese Anarchist Movement* (Berkeley: Center for Chinese Studies, University of California, 1961).

41. The Boxer Rebellion could be compared to the Mau Mau uprising in Kenya in the early 1950's in the sense that both were pre-national, atavistic rebellions against aliens and their native followers.

42. Cf. Y. C. Wang, "Intellectuals and Society in China 1860–1949," *Comparative Studies in Society and History* (July 1961), pp. 395–426.

43. "The Nation," *From Max Weber: Essays in Sociology,* Gerth and Mills, eds. (New York: Oxford Galaxy ed., 1958), p. 174.

44. For a revealing illustration of the political backwardness of the peasantry in an area untouched by either the war or the Communist Party, see G. William Skinner, "Aftermath of Communist Liberation in the Chengtu Plain," *Pacific Affairs,* XXIV (1951), 61–76.

45. Cf. Salo Wittmayer Baron, *Modern Nationalism and Religion* (New York, 1960). On this point, Elie Kedourie observes, "Nationalist historiography operates, in fact, a subtle but unmistakable change in traditional conceptions. In Zionism, Judaism ceases to be the *raison d'être* of the Jew, and becomes, instead, a product of Jewish national consciousness. In the doctrine of Pakistan, Islam is transformed into a political ideology and used in order to mobilize Muslims against Hindus; more than that it cannot do since an Islamic state on classical lines is today an impossible anachronism. In the doctrine of the *Action Française* Catholicism becomes one of the attributes which define a true Frenchman and exclude a spurious one. This transformation of religion into nationalist ideology is all the more convenient in that nationalists can thereby utilize the powerful and tenacious loyalties which a faith held in common for centuries creates." *Nationalism* (London, 1960), p. 76. For an insight into Israeli national myth, see Alfred Kazin, "Eichmann and the New Israelis," *The Reporter* (April 27, 1961), pp. 24–25.

46. Henry Hatfield (professor of German at Harvard), "The Myth of

Nazism," in *Myth and Mythmaking,* Henry A. Murray, ed. (New York, 1960), p. 199.

47. The thirteen Communist states are Albania, Bulgaria, China, Czechoslovakia, East Germany, Hungary, Mongolia, North Korea, North Vietnam, Poland, Rumania, USSR and Yugoslavia. If Cuba is included, the number, of course, is fourteen.

48. Lichtheim, *Marxism,* p. 364, for example.

49. Thomas T. Hammond, "The Origins of National Communism," *Virginia Quarterly Review,* XXXIV (1958), 278.

50. Fitzroy Maclean, *Tito* (New York, 1957), p. 355.

CHAPTER TWO

1. Michael Lindsay, *North China Front* (London: H.M. Stationery Office and the China Campaign Committee, 1945), p. 9. With regard to the state of political consciousness in north China, Taylor observes, "North China, in fact, was a kind of political vacuum. The Japanese did not differ from the judgment of most observers in assuming that although there might not be any broad-faced political movement favorable to their ambitions upon which they could base their power, at least there would be no spontaneous organized opposition against it." *The Struggle for North China,* p. 29.

2. The agreement that paved the way for the East Hopei Autonomous Government was the Ho-Umezu Pact of June 1935. The Japanese Army commander in north China, General Umezu Yoshijirō, utilized anti-Japanese incidents in Tientsin and Kalgan to force the Chinese government to evacuate all Nationalist troops from the Hopei-Chahar area and to close all Kuomintang offices and organs. The Nationalist officer who agreed to these demands was General Ho Ying-ch'in.

3. Doihara was self-styled the "Lawrence of Manchuria." He was a true political general; his military leadership as commander of the 14th division in the battle for Lanfeng (Honan), May 24, 1938, almost resulted in the loss of his division. In the prewar period, Doihara served as adviser to Chang Tso-lin, played a key role (as Mayor of Mukden) in the Manchurian Incident, and was the Japanese officer most closely identified with the plan to establish the five northern provinces of China as an autonomous area. He was tried and executed as a war criminal after the war. The most thorough study of Japanese policies in China during the 1930's, and of the course of the war between 1937 and 1941, is Hata Ikuhiko, *Nitchū sensō shi* (History of the Sino-Japanese War) (Tokyo, 1961). However, Hata reports the conflict chiefly from the Japanese side.

4. Japan, Army Ministry, *Shina kyōsangun ni tsuite* (Concerning the Chinese Communist Army) (Tokyo: Rikugunshō shimbun-han, November 1936), 43 pp., plus a map of the Long March. Japanese apprehension about the trend of Chinese politics is further revealed in Military Attaché, Shanghai, *Kokkyō ryōtō kōnichi kyūkoku shuchō* (Anti-Japanese National Salvation Statements of the KMT and CCP), 1938 [T888].

5. Kusano Fumio, *Shina henku no kenkyū* (The Study of China's Border Regions) (Tokyo, 1944), p. 79. Kusano describes K'angta thoroughly, pp. 77–85; see also *Gendai Chūgoku jiten,* pp. 575–80. The contingent of youths that went to Yenan in 1937 entered K'angta in May of that year.

6. The "central authorities" comprised the Army and Navy General Staffs and the War and Navy Ministries. They exercised supreme command of the "China Incident" until the establishment of Imperial General Headquarters in Tokyo on November 17, 1937. For details on the reinforcements sent to Katsuki, see *North China Area Operations Record,* pp. 17–25.

7. For details of the descent into war in China, from Japanese perspectives, see the following: (1) Col. Matsui Gennosuke, "Hokushi no kinjō" (The Present Situation in North China), *Kaikōsha kiji,* No. 745 (October 1936), pp. 23–35. This is a detailed study of political conditions in Hopei, Shantung, Shansi, Chahar, and Suiyüan, the five provinces that were the immediate objects of Japanese interest in 1937. (*Kaikōsha kiji* was the monthly military review for officers of the Japanese Army. Although in the late 1930's it was increasingly given over to patriotic and fascist articles, it occasionally contained informed articles on such rarely discussed subjects as mopping-up and peace preservation in China.) (2) Kaikōsha Editorial Board, "Rokōkyō jiken no kaiko" (Recollections of the Marco Polo Bridge Incident), *Kaikōsha kiji,* No. 802 (July 1941), pp. 39–66. (3) Kaikōsha Editorial Board, "Shina jihen keika nisshi" (Daily Record of the China Incident), *ibid.,* pp. 73–80. (4) Richard Storry, *The Double Patriots, A Study of Japanese Nationalism* (Boston, 1957), p. 219.

8. Evans F. Carlson, *The Chinese Army, Its Organization and Military Efficiency* (New York, 1940), p. 68.

9. Chief of Staff, Tada Corps, *Chūgoku kyōsantō undō no kaisetsu* (Explanation of the Chinese Communist Party Movement) (n.p. [Peiping], February 17, 1941), p. 20. Evans Carlson mentions Lü Cheng-ts'ao as former commander of the 691st Regiment of the 53rd Army, but other sources cite the 683rd Regiment. See Evans F. Carlson, *Twin Stars of China* (New York, 1940), pp. 244–49. Lü Cheng-ts'ao's base is considered further in Chapter Four.

10. For details of this operation from a Japanese perspective, see U.S. Army, Forces in the Far East, *Central China Area Operations Record 1937–1941* (Tokyo, 1955), pp. 13–21. ["Japanese Monograph 179."] This document was written by Lt. Col. Ishihara Heizō, former Chief of the War Records Department, General Staff Headquarters. A military opinion on the Hangchow Bay landing is contained in Carlson, *Twin Stars,* p. 26.

11. Lt. Gen. Shimoyama Takuma and Lt. Gen. Hashimoto Gun, in *North China Area Operations Record,* p. 150. Italics mine.

12. *Ibid.,* pp. 151–52.

13. Printed in Hatano Ken'ichi, "Kokkyō masatsu ni kan suru chōsa," (An Inquiry Concerning KMT-CCP Friction), *Jōhō,* No. 31 (December 1, 1940), p. 9.

14. Sixteen mass organizations were disbanded by Chiang on August 20, 1938; the *Hsin-Hua jih-pao* was suspended from publication between August 21 and 24 because it had attacked the disbandment directives. Disputes between

the *Hsin-Hua jih-pao* and non-Communist papers such as the *Ta kung pao* and *Wu-han jih-pao* in Hankow were numerous; particularly notable was the argument of March 1938 concerning the "Trotskyism" of Ch'en Tu-hsiu, which was tolerated by the KMT because it infuriated the CCP. See Hatano Ken'ichi, "Saikin Chūkyō kankei nenpyō" (Recent Chronology of Chinese Communism [January 1938–April 1941]), *Jōhō*, No. 42 (May 15, 1941), pp. 74, 77.

15. The Ch'iung-Yai base was located in the hsien of Ch'iungshan and Yaihsien, the latter being part of what is today the Li and Miao Nationalities Autonomous Chou of Hainan. Information on the Japanese seizure of Hainan is contained in U.S. Army, Forces in the Far East, *South China Area Operations Record (1937–41)* (Tokyo, 1956), pp. 43–45, 101. ["Japanese Monograph 180."] See also Niijima Sunayoshi, "Liberated Areas," *Gendai Chūgoku jiten*, p. 47.

16. Itagaki Seishirō, Chief of the General Staff, Japanese Expeditionary Force in China, *Kokkyō sōkoku ni kan suru kansatsu* (Observations Regarding Kuomintang-Communist Rivalry), March 22, 1940 [T983], p. 2. Itagaki was a well-known Japanese "ultra." He was War Minister and President of the Manchurian Affairs Bureau from June 1938 to August 1939 in the first Konoye and Hiranuma cabinets. Between September 1939 and July 1941, he was Chief of Staff of the China Expeditionary Army. After the war, Itagaki was tried and found guilty by the International Military Tribunal on several counts, including that of "ordering, authorizing, or permitting atrocities" (count 54). He was hanged December 23, 1948.

17. "Saikin no Chūgoku kyōsantō" (Latest News of the Chinese Communist Party), *Jōhō*, No. 22 (July 15, 1940), p. 5.

18. "Kyōsangun ni okeru seiji kunren" (Political Training Within the Communist Army), *Jōhō*, No. 10 (January 15, 1940), p. 85.

19. Rivalries within the Japanese Army concerning the establishment of puppet governments are investigated in F. Hilary Conroy, "Japan's War in China: An Ideological Somersault," *Pacific Historical Review*, XXI (1952), 367–79. The subject of this article is the extensive revision required in Japanese ideological and propaganda pronouncements when the Japanese decided to support Wang Ching-wei as their chief puppet. Prior to 1940, the Japanese had stressed that their war in China was to save Chinese culture from the Westernized Kuomintang and from Communism, to bring about an "Asian Revival," and to exorcise the Western materialist devils. When they shifted to support one of the founders of the Kuomintang as a puppet and to re-establish the Kuomintang itself at Nanking (albeit the "orthodox Kuomintang—*junsei kokumintō*"), swift revisions of official ideology were required. Concerning rivalries between the three Japanese Army commands in China, see also John Goette, *Japan Fights for Asia* (New York, 1943), p. 61.

20. The changes in policy that were actually adopted by the Japanese in 1940 were summarized by Rear Admiral Tomioka Sadatoshi, former Chief of the Operations Section, Imperial General Headquarters, as follows: "The policy of the Japanese armed forces during this year gradually shifted from operations to

political strategy. The main points were as follows: (1) non-expansion of operations area, (2) promotion of pacification and peace preservation activities in the occupied areas, (3) cooperation in the growth of a new central government, (4) undermining of the fighting strength of Chiang Kai-shek's army through a tight sea blockade and effective interruption of Chiang's aid routes from Burma, northern French Indo-China, Hong Kong, and Kwangchowwan." U.S. Army, Forces in the Far East, *Political Strategy Prior to Outbreak of War*, Part II (Tokyo, 1953), pp. 4–5. ["Japanese Monograph 146."] The new China policy was decided upon at a cabinet meeting, January 8, 1940; the resulting policy statement is published in *ibid*. as "The Fundamental Principles for the Readjustment of Relations between Japan and China," Appendix I, pp. 37–41.

21. See the memoirs of Loo Pin-fei, one of the founders of the student sabotage units operating in Peiping and Shanghai, *It Is Dark Underground* (New York, 1946), pp. 98–99. Loo's unit was responsible for the attempted assassination of Wang K'o-min, the north China puppet, in early 1938. The Japanese erroneously credited this incident to the Communists. See Okabe Naosaburo, Chief of Staff, North China Area Army, *Hokushi ni okeru kyōsantō katsudō jōkyō no ken hōkoku* (Report on the General State of Communist Party Activities in North China), April 14, 1938 [T891, frame 22051].

For an example of Nanking's anti-British propaganda, see the treatment of the 100th anniversary of the Treaty of Nanking (ending the Opium War) in Shanghai, August 23–29, 1942, in U.S. Federal Communications Commission, Foreign Broadcast Intelligence Service, *Radio Report on the Far East*, No. 2 (August 31, 1942), p. D2. The *Radio Report* (hereafter *RRFE*) was a classified periodical of the U.S. Government. It presented intelligence on Far Eastern countries derived from radio sources. The editors of *RRFE* monitored such stations as Shanghai, Nanking, Hsinking, Peiping, Hong Kong, and XNCR Yenan (after September 1, 1944), as well as Tokyo and Chungking. *RRFE* was published from August 24, 1942 (No. 1), to August 25, 1945 (No. 80).

22. *RRFE*, No. 7 (November 10, 1942), p. J1. For a study of the Hsin Min Hui's attempts to put an ideological foundation under the Japanese occupation, see Lt. Col. Shigeda Mitsugi, "Chūka minkoku shinminkai no katsudō to sono jisseki" (The Activities and Accomplishments of the Chinese Republic's New Citizens' Association), *Kaikōsha kiji*, No. 788 (May 1940), pp. 73–96.

23. Dōmei, May 17, 1945; *RRFE*, No. 74 (June 1, 1945), p. E1.

24. "The Fundamental Principles for the Readjustment of Relations between Japan and China," in U.S. Army, *Political Strategy Prior to Outbreak of War*, Part II, pp. 39–40. Italics mine.

25. "Japanese Civilians in Occupied Asia," *RRFE*, No. 57 (October 27, 1944), p. A4.

26. "Labor Conscription in North China," *RRFE*, No. 32 (October 27, 1943), p. E7.

27. Supplement to *RRFE*, No. 51 (August 9, 1944), p. D2; and "Exploitation and Resistance in Shantung," *RRFE*, No. 56 (October 13, 1944), p. AA14.

28. Federated People's Republic of Yugoslavia, *Stenographic Record and*

Documents from the Trial of Dragoljub-Draza Mihailović (Belgrade, 1946), p. 204. One of the most incredible accounts of the predicament of the Chetniks in attempting to oppose the Communists and yet remain nationalists is contained in Major James M. Inks, *Eight Bailed Out* (New York, 1954). Inks, a USAAF officer, parachuted from his crippled airplane into Chetnik territory on July 28, 1944. He then spent the next ten months impersonating a Chetnik soldier as the Chetniks retreated in collaboration with retreating German columns. The group was subjected to continuous Anglo-American-Partisan attack, and Inks barely survived the German defeat. Curiously enough, his book is dedicated to Mihailović!

29. Cf. *RRFE,* No. 26 (August 3, 1943), p. B7. Mao formally accused the KMT of betraying the resistance in a *Chieh-fang jih-pao* ("Liberation Daily") editorial of October 5, 1943. He contends that the opposition of public opinion, domestic and foreign, is the only restraint preventing the KMT from launching the civil war. Finally Mao says to the KMT leaders, "The enemy of the nation has penetrated deep into our country, and the more actively you oppose the Communists and the more passively you resist the Japanese, the lower will the morale of your troops sink. If you fight so badly against the foreign enemy, then do you think that in the struggle against the Communists, against the people, your troops will suddenly become brave?" *Selected Works,* IV, 134.

30. There are numerous exceptions to this general statement. The following are examples:

(1) The appointment of Li Hsien-liang as the "Central Government Representative" in Tsingtao in 1945, even though he had cooperated with the Japanese for a long period of time. See *RRFE,* No. 80 (August 25, 1945), pp. CA6, CA9.

(2) The wartime collaboration between KMT guerrillas and puppets in Shantung. On this subject, see Lawrence Tipton, *China Escapade* (London, 1949), pp. 203–4, 223. Tipton, an English tobacco merchant in China, was interned at the Weihsien, Shantung, concentration camp, from which he escaped on June 9, 1943. He spent the rest of the war with a Nationalist guerrilla unit. On collaboration with the enemy by guerrillas, he remarks, "There was no doubt in our minds that their [the Communists'] policy left no room for compromise with the Japanese, as did that of certain so-called guerrillas" (p. 202). His eyewitness account is a valuable indication of the complexity of the resistance situation that existed in a given area.

(3) Direct contact between the CC Clique and the Japanese during the post-Hankow period of defeatism. See Yamada Corps (Headquarters, Central China Expeditionary Army), *Chūshi hakengun taikyō shisō kōsaku jisshi hōkoku* (Report on Actions Taken by the Central China Expeditionary Army Against Communist Thought), July 10, 1939 [T940], pp. 22–25. This report describes extensive contact between members of the KMT right wing and Japanese agents.

(4) The Kuomintang's exoneration of Chou Fu-hai, former Minister of Finance and Mayor of Shanghai in the Wang Ching-wei government, of treason;

and the hiring of the former Japanese Commander-in-Chief in China, General Okamura, as an adviser after 1945. See Graham Peck, *Two Kinds of Time* (Boston, 1950), p. 683; and "On Ordering the Reactionary Kuomintang Government to Re-arrest Yasuji Okamura, Former Commander-in-Chief of the Japanese Forces of Aggression in China, and to Arrest the Kuomintang Civil War Criminals—Statement by the Spokesman for the Communist Party of China, January 28, 1949," *Mao Tse-tung hsüan-chi,* IV (1960), 1397–1402. Okamura was returned to Japan by the KMT in 1949; see *ibid.,* pp. 1403–6.

31. Although Radio Tokyo once described Chiang as fast approaching the fate of Mihailović and Badoglio, he was never actually compromised as a nationalist leader. *RRFE,* No. 47 (June 9, 1944), pp. B3–B4.

32. Excellent and numerous samples of propaganda leaflets used by the Japanese against Nationalist troops and pro-Chungking populations are to be found in the Japanese Army archives. The constant theme of this propaganda is that Nationalist troops are the servants of Chiang Kai-shek's personal pretensions and that "peace, national construction, and anti-Communism" are what all Chinese and Japanese desire. See, for example, Aoki Shigemasa, Chief of Staff, "Ro" Group Army, *Senden bira sanpu jisshi no ken hōkoku* (Report on the Carrying Out of Propaganda Leaflet Distribution), November 23, 1939 [T969]. Item 4 in this collection is a cartoon showing Chiang Kai-shek riding across a field of spikes on the back of a near-skeleton labeled "the People"; Chiang holds in his hand a raised sword labeled "Protracted War." Other titles in the Army Archives series containing samples of pro-Nanking, anti-Chiang propaganda are T899, T932, T936, T942, T960, T961, T981, T990.

33. Dōmei, February 3, 1943; *RRFE,* No. 14, (February 16, 1943), p. C2. The north China regime also adopted a national flag at this time; the Hsin Min Hui had formerly had the Yin-Yang symbol as its emblem, but in February 1943 it changed to a white flag emblazoned with the character for Asia in crimson.

34. Defense Document 949, Exhibit 2609, in evidence at p. 22383, International Military Tribunal for the Far East, *Proceedings.* The IMTFE staff gives the title of this work in Japanese, i.e., *Dōsei kyōshi;* it was originally edited and published by General Headquarters, China Expeditionary Army. See also Wang Ching-wei, *Nihon to tazusaete* (Accompanied by Japan) (Osaka: Asahi Shimbun Co., 1941). The phrase "land-purifying" is a literal translation of *ch'ing hsiang,* which is more accurately rendered as "rural pacification."

35. Lindsay, *North China Front,* pp. 8, 10. Italics mine.

36. Taylor, *The Struggle for North China,* p. 116.

37. North China Area Army, *Hokushi sakusengun kōhō chiiki no gyōsei shidō yōryō no ken* (Outline of Administrative Directives on Administration of Areas Behind Battle Lines in North China), September 23, 1937 [T878].

38. The system of "Administrative Inspectors" *(hsing-cheng tu-ch'a chuan-yüan)* predated the Japanese invasion; the Inspector's office was a special supervisory organ intermediary between the hsien and the province, and its function varied from area to area—mainly in accordance with whether or not the Admin-

istrative Inspector was also a hsien magistrate. See Ch'ien Tuan-sheng, "Wartime Local Government in China," *Pacific Affairs,* XVI (1943), 444.

39. *North China Area Operations Record,* pp. 186–87. The withdrawal of forces for the battle of Hsüchou is described as the Communists' "golden opportunity" in another Japanese report. Simultaneously with the battle of Hsüchou, this report continues, the Communists "attacked our Army in all parts of Shansi; destroyed railroads, roads, and bridges; set up a large number of bases; and enlarged their guerrilla units by training and organizing the masses." "Chūgoku kyōsantō no kinjō" (Recent Facts Concerning the Chinese Communist Party), *Jōhō,* No. 7 (December 1, 1939), p. 36.

40. Chief of Staff, North China Area Army, *Chian iji jisshi yōryō no ken tsūchō* (Instruction on Principles for Carrying Out Peace Preservation), December 21, 1937 [T887].

41. See, for instance, Headquarters, Tada Corps, *Kahoku ni okeru shisōsen shidō yōryō* (Outline of Instructions Regarding Ideological Warfare in North China), April 20, 1940 [T986], pp. 35–36.

42. T. H. White and A. Jacoby, *Thunder Out of China* (New York, 1946), p. 54.

43. "Chūgoku kyōsantō no genkyō, dōkō narabi ni taisaku" (The Present Condition of the Chinese Communist Party: Trends and Countermeasures), *Jōhō,* No. 57 (January 1, 1942), p. 12.

44. *Ibid.,* pp. 13–14.

45. See Imperial General Headquarters, "General Order for 1939," in *North China Area Operations Record,* pp. 200–202.

46. The Japanese independent mixed brigade (*dokuritsu konsei ryodan*) was a special unit composed of five infantry battalions plus supporting units and generally commanded by a major general. According to the U.S. Army, "These brigades [were] used for border garrison, line of communication and *anti-guerrilla* duties. The strength of these brigades [varied] from 7,500 to 10,000." War Department, *Handbook on Japanese Military Forces,* September 21, 1942, pp. 38–39. Italics mine.

47. *North China Area Operations Record,* p. 208.

48. *Ibid.,* p. 228.

49. U.S. Office of War Information, Analysis and Research Bureau, General Intelligence Division, "The 18th Group Army: Training, Medical Care and Supply" (GID OPINTEL Report No. 324, December 15, 1944), p. 8. A collection of these reports is housed in the Documents Department, General Library, University of California, Berkeley.

50. Japanese Embassy, Peking, *Chūkyō dōkō jittai chōsa; Kahoku shō Hōteidō Ankokuken Daisanku Go-jin-kyō o chūshin to suru* (Investigation Of Chinese Communist Trends and Conditions: Focus on Wujench'iao, Third District, Ankuo hsien, Paoting tao, Hopei Province) (Peking: November 18, 1943), Introduction.

51. Ting Li, *Militia of Communist China* (Hong Kong, 1955), p. 73. Long probing rods were used to search for the dugouts. See also "Underground War-

fare," in Harrison Forman, *Report from Red China* (New York, 1945), pp. 138–44. Reports from Radio Tokyo later in the war indicated that the tunnels were still in full use. On April 2, 1944, the Japanese and puppet forces reportedly "chased the enemy into underground shelters" in the vicinity of Ts'ang hsien, south of Tientsin. On April 23, 1944, Dōmei described Japanese activities against guerrillas in Hsien hsien, an area of central Hopei "dotted with caves and underground caverns which are used by Communists as both fortresses and houses." This latter action resulted in the destruction of the office of the *Shengli pao* ("Victory News"), "a Communist four-page tabloid published in a cave headquarters" in a village of Hsien hsien. See compilation of Japanese-Communist encounters for the month of April 1944, *RRFE*, No. 45 (May 11, 1944), pp. B3–B6.

52. Fujita Masatsune, "Sankō seisaku," in *Gendai Chūgoku jiten*, pp. 209–10. "Sankō" means "three all" with "all" used in the sense of "exhaustive" (synonym: *nekosogi*). The three parts of the policy were: *sakkō* (*korosu*), *shōkō* (*yaku*), and *ryakkō* (*ubau*), i.e., "kill all, burn all, loot (or destroy) all." For a sensational treatment of the "three-all" policy, see Kanki Haruo, ed., *Sankō, Nihonjin no Chūgoku ni okeru sensō hanzai no kokuhaku* (The Three-All: Japanese Confessions of War Crimes in China) (Tokyo: Kōbunsha "Kappa" ed., 1957). This illustrated book was the subject of protests from Japanese veterans' organizations when it was first published. The material in the book is drawn from confessions made by Japanese soldiers to the Chinese Communists in the early 1950's before the Japanese prisoners were repatriated to Japan; the confessions were compiled by Mr. Kanki, the head of the well-known Japanese publishing house Kōbunsha. Mr. Kanki himself is a conservative. The Communist origins of these confessions and their propagandistic flavor suggest that the charges against *sankō* have been inflated. Nevertheless, the *sankō* did take place and was comparable to German anti-guerrilla practices in Yugoslavia and the USSR; the distinction between the ruthless execution of an admittedly brutal policy and the perpetration of atrocities depends upon the allegiance of the commentator.

For technical studies by Japanese officers on mopping-up operations, see Kaikōsha Editorial Board, "Shina ni okeru saikin no chian jōkyō" (The Recent Peace Preservation Situation in China), *Kaikōsha kiji*, No. 784 (January 1940), pp. 79–87; and Yaginuma Takeo, "Hokushi senbuhan no katsuyaku" (Activities of North China Pacification Squads), *Kaikōsha kiji*, No. 778 (July 1939), pp. 91–97. Cf. Professor Fujiwara Akira, *Gunjishi* (History of Military Affairs), a volume in the series *Nihon gendaishi taikei* (Outline of the Modern History of Japan) (Tokyo, 1961), p. 211.

53. Fujita Masatsune, *loc. cit.* For other examples of mass destruction of the civilian population in Hopei by the Japanese Army, see IMTFE, *Proceedings*, pp. 4619–35. The prosecution presented evidence on cases that occurred in the following areas: Chiaoho hsien, Kaoyang hsien, and Jench'iu. One village of 400 families near the city of T'angshan in east Hopei had only twenty inhabitants left alive and only one unburned home after an attack in the spring of

1943 (p. 4637). See also Exhibit 344 (Japanese text; in evidence at p. 4619) describing several attacks between July 1941 and May 1942 on a village in Jaoyang hsien. The scale of this destruction is comparable to the German reprisals at Kragujevać (6,000 killed) and Kraljevo (1,700 killed) in Yugoslavia. It is estimated that a total of 1,700,000 persons (one-tenth of the population) lost their lives in Yugoslavia during World War II. Nikola Kapetanović, *Tito et les partisans: ce qui s'est passé en réalité en Yougoslavie de 1941 à 1945* (Belgrade, n.d.), p. 18.

54. *North China Area Operations Record*, p. 218. Railroad defenses were described in a Tokyo German-language broadcast of September 22, 1943, in connection with a tour of Asia by a German citizen—one Dr. Erwin Wickert. Wickert noted that there were pillboxes along the railroad routes for the Japanese guards. Each pillbox had a bundle of straw in it, which was set on fire in case of attack. The next post, seeing the fire, lighted its bundle, and so on, until the alarm reached the larger stations from which reinforcements were sent. There were no telegraph lines along the route. On both sides of the track there was a ditch filled with water or a wall of mud. It was forbidden to grow certain varieties of millet along the railways, since these afforded good cover for the guerrillas. *RRFE*, No. 30 (September 28, 1943), p. D8. Taylor describes a railroad defense system whereby local villages were held responsible for the safety of the railroad in their sectors (p. 49). Speaking of the railroad between Peiping and Tientsin, Taylor notes that the Japanese claimed, on December 13, 1938, to have cleared a thirty-mile belt on either side of the tracks, but that in January 1939 the line was cut near Langfang (Antz'u) and a trainload of cotton burned up. "Considering that the attack came about 7:00 P.M., the guerrillas, although mounted, must have been well within the thirty-mile band before sunset." *The Struggle for North China*, p. 62. Lindsay observed, "The Pinghan railway between Paoting and Shihchiachuang is defended by a high wall and two ditches on either side, and by more than 90 forts and garrisons, over one per mile." *North China Front*, pp. 3–4. See also Loo Pin-fei, *It Is Dark Underground*, p. 49; and the report of a derailing in Shansi, January 17, 1945, *RRFE*, No. 68 (March 16, 1945), pp. E12–E13.

55. U.S. Office of War Information, "The Chinese 18th Group Army: Tactics and Achievements" (OPINTEL Report No. 325, December 15, 1944), p. 3. Eighteenth Group Army was Chungking's designation for the Communist Army.

56. U.S. War Dept., "The Chinese Communist Movement," p. 2366. This study calls the Hundred Regiments Offensive the largest Communist campaign of the war.

57. In May 1940, the Kōain's Central China Office itself drew attention to Chungking's weakening attitude toward the resistance and noted that anti-Communist elements within the Kuomintang were becoming very vocal. It listed four reasons for Chungking's pessimism about the future: (1) the European situation and its effect on Chungking's relations with the U.S. and the

USSR; (2) pessimism about the chances of eventual victory on the part of overseas Chinese who had supported the resistance strongly in the past; (3) worsening of Nationalist-Communist relations; and (4) development of support, particularly among intellectuals, for the Wang Ching-wei regime. See "Jūkei-seiken kōsen shiji no teichō-ka to kokkyō kankei no shin dōkō" (Weakening of Support for the Resistance War by the Chungking Government and New Trends in KMT-CCP Relations), *Jōhō*, No. 21 (July 1, 1940), pp. 31–32.

58. Fujita Masatsune, "Hyakudan taisen" (Hundred Regiments Offensive), in *Gendai Chūgoku jiten*, pp. 624–25; General Political Department, 18th Group Army, *K'ang-chan pa-nien-lai ti pa-lu-chün yü hsin-ssu-chün* (The Eighth Route Army and the New Fourth Army Through Eight Years of the Resistance War) ([Yenan], March 1945), pp. 103–12; *North China Area Operations Record*, pp. 316–20; OPINTEL Report No. 325; and Hata, *Nitchū sensō shi*, pp. 302–4.

59. *North China Area Operations Record*, pp. 316–17. There were actually two anthracite mining centers at Chinghsing; they were deveolped by German capital at the end of the nineteenth century. After World War I, the mines were operated by the Chinghsing Mining Department of Hopei province; the technicians, engineers, and managers were Germans. See Ke Han ["Correspondent of the *Sin Xua Rhboa*, Hankow-Chungking"], *The Shansi-Hopei-Chahar Border Region, Report 1, 1937–38* (Chungking: New China Information Committee, Bulletin No. 8, April 1940; printed in Manila), p. 57.

60. *Ibid.,* pp. 317–18.

61. Staff, Noboru Group Army, *Shō Kai-seki no kyōsangun tōbatsu narabi ni kokumintō no bōkyō taisaku no gaiyō* (Outline of Chiang Kai-shek's Suppression of the Communist Army and the Kuomintang's Defensive Measures Against Communism), February 1941 [T1000], p. 2.

62. According to Communist sources, by April 1941 the Japanese had 480 *li* of roads and 270 strongholds in the western Hopei plains alone. The most ambitious of the Japanese fortification schemes was a plan to build a wall 18 feet high and 16 feet wide from Paoting in central Hopei to Taming in the southern part of the province, in order to stop Communist infiltrations. The work was actually begun in Kuch'eng hsien, Chi hsien, and Ch'ingho hsien, all in southern Hopei; but on April 28, 1941, the south Hopei guerrilla base mobilized some 35,000 people and dismantled it. See Kao Yung, "The Destruction of the Great Wall," People's Republic of China, *Saga of Resistance to Japanese Invasion* (Peking: Foreign Languages Press, 1959), pp. 75–81. This fourth volume in the series issued by Peking on Chinese Communist military history contains some useful information, but is written in a soap-opera style: for example, we are told that on one occasion when the situation seemed hopeless, some men of the Eighth Route Army "set aside money for the last payment of Party dues" (p. 3).

63. Niijima Sunayoshi, "Kaihō-ku," in *Gendai Chūgoku jiten*, p. 47; Fujita Masatsune, "Hachirogun" (Eighth Route Army), *ibid.,* p. 611. In 1945, Yenan Radio claimed that during 1942 the Japanese carried out nine offensives against

Communist troops in north China, employing over 160,000 men. These figures are unconfirmed, but there is no doubt that the Japanese made a great effort. *RRFE,* No. 79 (August 11, 1945), pp. CB10–CB11.

64. C. Bobrowski, *La Yougoslave socialiste* (Paris, 1956), p. 37. The War Department analyzed the Chinese situation as follows: "The Japanese reply to guerrilla war was a policy of frightfulness. It drove the people into the arms of the Communists, because they undertook to organize the rural areas for defense after the regular Chinese armies had been defeated and fled. The people subscribed fully to the Communists' answer to those who doubted their ability to fight the superior Japanese forces: 'If we don't fight, what happens? The Japanese kill us anyway. If we fight, let's see what happens.'" U.S. War Dept., "The Chinese Communist Movement," p. 2337.

65. By the spring of 1944, Communist troop strength equaled 470,000; the militia comprised 2,000,000 men, and the population of the "liberated areas" had risen to 86 million. Niijima, in *Gendai Chūgoku jiten,* p. 47.

66. "Yūgekisen no dōkō" (Trends in Guerrilla Warfare), *Jōhō,* No. 58 (January 15, 1942), pp. 4–5.

67. For Shantung, see "Exploitation and Resistance in Shantung," *RRFE,* No. 56 (October 13, 1944), pp. AA1–AA12. For Hopei and Shansi, see *RRFE,* No. 55 (September 29, 1944), pp. C5–C6.

68. *RRFE,* No. 62 (January 5, 1945), pp. AB1–AB7. The military campaigns in central Shantung of November 6–27 and December 14–21, 1944, were reported by both Yenan and Tokyo radios; the former referred only to "the Eighth Route Army winter offensive," and the latter spoke of "Communist-suppression campaigns."

69. This order is given in full in *Central China Area Operations Record,* pp. 106–7. Italics mine.

70. Ch'ien Tuan-sheng, "Wartime Local Government in China," *Pacific Affairs,* XVI (1943), 449. Pao Chia was introduced in Honan, Hupeh, and Anhwei by the National Government on August 1, 1932; it was extended to all other areas under KMT control on November 7, 1934. Mao Tse-tung, *Selected Works,* IV, 345.

71. U.S. Navy Department, Office of the Chief of Naval Operations, *Civil Affairs Handbook, Japanese Administrative Organization in Taiwan (Formosa)* (Washington: August 10, 1944), pp. 8–9; for the Taiwanese precedent in using Pao Chia in the occupation of central China, see *Central China Area Operations Record,* p. 107, n.55. The thousand-year history of Pao Chia is surveyed in Robert Lee, "The Pao-chia System," *Harvard University Papers on China,* III, 193–224.

72. "Shinkokumin-seifu kanka no hokō seido" (The Pao Chia System Under the Jurisdiction of the New National Government), *Jōhō,* No. 22 (July 15, 1940), p. 37. The gist of the law of May 30, 1938, is given on pp. 44–48.

73. *Ibid.,* pp. 42–44.

74. Tipton describes the Pao Chia system enforced against "enemy aliens" in occupied Peiping in early 1942. All aliens were required to wear red arm

bands with characters indicating their nationality. In each *chia* of ten persons, one person was held responsible for the proper conduct of the remaining nine. *China Escapade,* p. 59. Taylor comments that the Pao Chia system was enforced "especially near the railways and in big towns." *The Struggle for North China,* p. 81.

75. See Kaikōsha Editorial Board, "Chūshi ni okeru seikyō kōsaku [*ch'ing-hsiang kung-tso*] ni tsuite" (Concerning the Rural Pacification Work in Central China), *Kaikōsha kiji,* No. 802 (July 1941), pp. 67–71. This article describes the organization of the Rural Pacification Movement within the Nanking Government and prints the most important directives.

76. The Eight-Point Program was broadcast by Dōmei, June 29, 1944. *RRFE,* No. 49 (July 7, 1944), pp. D4–D5. For a history of the Rural Pacification Movement, see *RRFE,* No. 18 (April 13, 1943), p. C9, and No. 42 (March 30, 1944), p. D9.

77. The term *pao an tui* is a source of constant confusion. It was the name of the local hsien militia units that existed under the National Government before the invasion and were retained by the Japanese to defend villages that did not have Japanese garrisons. *Pao an tui* was also the name given to the north China puppet army that was organized at the T'ungchou Officers' School outside Peiping in 1938. Our use of the term (usually in translation, "peace preservation units") is to refer to the local militia, not the puppet army. In speaking of the *pao an tui* in the sense of local self-defense forces, OPINTEL Report No. 1 (July 18, 1944) states that "the Japanese have stolen the name of this organization for their puppet troops" (p. 3). In Shantung, according to Tipton, "The Self-Protection Corps [*pao an tui*] was a regular feature of all villages in which soldiers were not stationed. The Corps was comprised of the able-bodied men of the village who guarded the gates and patrolled the walls armed with flint-locks or crude rifles." *China Escapade,* pp. 140–41. A history of the north China puppet army (*Pao An Tui*) is given in *RRFE,* No. 37 (January 13, 1944), p. D8.

78. Chiang-nan K'ang-Jih I-yung Chün; abbreviated Chiang-k'ang.

79. The two most useful studies on the Kiangnan Army are "Kōnan kōnichi giyūgun no enkaku to genjō" (The History of the Kiangnan Anti-Japanese Patriotic Army and Its Present Condition), *Jōhō,* No. 37 (March 1, 1941), pp. 37–43; and the relevant parts of Kōain, Central China Liaison Bureau, *Kaisan made no shinshigun* (The New Fourth Army to the Time of Its Dispersal) (Shanghai, October 1941), 204 pp. The term Teng-Hsi-Yü is an abbreviation for the hsien of Ch'angshu, Wuhsi, and Chiangyin. The Kiangnan Army is discussed further in connection with the New Fourth Army.

80. "Chūgoku kyōsantō no genkyō, dōkō narabi ni taisaku" (The Present Condition of the Chinese Communist Party: Trends and Countermeasures), *Jōhō,* No. 57 (January 1, 1942), pp. 2–3. See also the "Pacification Survey" published on the Third Anniversary of the Model Peace Zones, *RRFE,* No. 49 (July 7, 1944), p. D4.

81. *Central China Area Operations Record,* pp. 185–91.

82. For Shigemitsu's tour, see *RRFE*, No. 4 (September 28, 1942), p. D2. For the role of Model Peace Zones in the New China Policy, see U.S. War Dept., "The Chinese Communist Movement," pp. 2369–70.

83. *RRFE*, No. 49 (July 7, 1944), p. D4, gives their names, sizes, and dates of establishment.

84. See "Occupation and Resistance in Kiangsu," *RRFE*, No. 63 (January 19, 1945).

85. See *RRFE*, No. 39 (February 17, 1944), p. D5; *RRFE*, No. 41 (March 16, 1944), p. D6; and *RRFE*, No. 63 (January 19, 1945), p. AB6.

86. "Shinshigun kankei jōhō" (Intelligence Relating to the New Fourth Army), *Jōhō*, No. 51 (October 1, 1941), p. 70.

87. "Chūkyō kankei jutsugo-shū" (A Collection of Technical Terms Relating to Chinese Communism), *Jōhō*, No. 61 (March 1, 1942), pp. 78–79.

88. See "Reader on the Struggle Against Rural Pacification" (Fan ch'ing-hsiang tou-cheng tu-pen), *Jōhō*, No. 51, pp. 71–73.

89. U.S. War Dept., "The Chinese Communist Movement," p. 2370.

90. Loo Pin-fei, *It Is Dark Underground*, p. 177. It is interesting to note that Loo never refers to the guerrillas as "Communists," but only as "aroused peasants." He was in the Soochow sector at the time of the Model Peace Zone movement and testifies to its relative success.

91. For the establishment of the Kwangtung Rural Pacification Office, see *RRFE*, No. 35 (December 8, 1943), p. D5; for the use of Pao Chia in Kwangtung, see *RRFE*, No. 45 (May 11, 1944), p. D9.

92. *South China Area Operations Record*, p. 46.

93. *Ibid.*, p. 47.

94. For details of the operations in October 1939 and February 1940, see *ibid.*, pp. 62–65 and 97–101, respectively.

95. *RRFE*, No. 41 (March 16, 1944), p. D9.

96. *RRFE*, No. 55 (September 29, 1944), pp. C8, E2.

97. Tokyo: *RRFE*, No. 67 (March 2, 1945), p. C1. Yenan: *RRFE*, No. 69 (March 30, 1945), p. E3.

CHAPTER THREE

1. Eighteenth Group Army, *K'ang-chan pa-nien-lai*, p. 7. Similarly, Eighth Route Army Chief of Staff Yeh Chien-ying reported the figure of 45,000 to the Yenan press party on June 22, 1944. Office of War Information, GID OPINTEL Report No. 323 (December 15, 1944), p. 2. This figure is also accepted by L. M. Chassin, *L'Ascension de Mao Tse-tung (1921–1945)* (Paris, 1953), p. 149. The Japanese use a figure of 40,000 for the Eighth Route Army. See "Chūgoku kyōsantō no genkyō narabi ni taisaku" (The Present Condition of the Chinese Communist Party: Trends and Countermeasures), *Jōhō*, No. 57 (January 1, 1942), pp. 3–4.

2. Gaimushō Jōhō-bu (Foreign Office, Intelligence Department), *Chūgoku*

kyōsantō ichi-ku-san-roku nen shi (History of the Chinese Communist Party During 1936), Hatano Ken'ichi, ed. (Tokyo, February 1937), pp. 1–3; Snow, *Red Star Over China* (Modern Library ed.), p. 423; U.S. War Dept., "The Chinese Communist Movement," pp. 2327, 2332. In Edgar Snow's recent supplementary notes to *Red Star Over China,* he concludes from information given to him in 1936 that the size of the Red Army was 90,000 when the three front armies were combined. But, he states, "My guess would be that the present Red strength [1936] may not exceed 30,000 to 50,000 regulars, with no more than 30,000 rifles." He based this on the alleged propensity of Chinese military leaders to overestimate unit sizes. See "The Red Army Losses on the Long March," *Random Notes on Red China (1936–1945)* (Cambridge, Mass., 1957), pp. 100–102. Boyd Compton uses the figures of 80,000 (1937) and 910,000 (1945) for Communist regulars. *Mao's China, Party Reform Documents, 1942–1944* (Seattle, 1952), p. xxii.

3. "On Coalition Government," *Selected Works,* IV, 253–54.

4. It was not until October 2, 1943, that the Tung Chiang (East River, Kwangtung) Anti-Japanese Government "formally declared that it henceforth accepted full leadership from the Central Committee of the Chinese Communist Party at Yenan." Forman, *Report from Red China,* p. 124. Resistance in Kwangtung was led by General Tseng Sheng, a native of Kwangtung, who had previously been a university student and a merchant seaman. In his early life, Tseng lived with his father in Sydney, Australia, for six years. He was 27 when he organized a guerrilla unit in his native Huiyang hsien after the outbreak of the Sino-Japanese war. He became leader of the Tung Chiang Column in 1943 and was a member of the Kwangtung Provincial Government after 1949.

5. U.S. War Dept., "The Chinese Communist Movement," p. 2433. Fujita Masatsune gives an unsupported total of 1,028,893 for the Communist forces in 1945, a jump of more than 50 per cent over his 1944 figure of 507,620. *Gendai Chūgoku jiten,* p. 611. See also Greater East Asia Ministry, General Affairs Bureau, *Chūkyō gaisetsu* (Outline of Chinese Communism) (Tokyo, July 1944), pp. 16–17.

6. Kōain, Central China Liaison Bureau, *Kaisan made no shinshigun* (The New Fourth Army Down to Its Dispersal) ([Shanghai], October 1941), p. 1.

7. See Yuasa Seiichi, "Chūshi ni okeru kyōsantōgun jōsei" (The Communist Military Situation in Central China), *Jōhō,* No. 38 (March 15, 1941), p. 43; "Su Yü," in Kasumigaseki Society, *Gendai Chūgoku jinmei jiten* (Biographical Dictionary of Modern China) (Tokyo, 1957), p. 324; "Fang Chih-min," in *Men and Politics in Modern China (Preliminary),* H. L. Boorman, ed. (New York, 1960), pp. 49–51; and *China Weekly Review* (Shanghai), February 9, 1935, p. 355, and February 16, 1935, p. 386. Fang Chih-min, who had a reward of $80,000 posted for him, was captured on January 29 in the mountains of northeast Kiangsi. He and other Red Army troops were brought to Nanch'ang from Shangjao on February 2 in four armored cars; they were personally es-

corted by General Chao Kuan-t'ao, Garrison Commander for the Fukien-Che-kiang-Kiangsi-Anhwei Border Area. On February 7, Fang was put on display in a cage in the center of Nanch'ang.

8. Edgar Snow, *The Battle for Asia* (New York, 1941), pp. 132–33; Chassin, *L'Ascension de Mao Tse-tung,* p. 160. Hatano estimated the size of Hsiang's forces at the beginning of 1936 at 20,000 troops in the four provinces of Kiangsi, Fukien, Chekiang, and Hupeh. *Chūgoku kyōsantō ichi-ku-san-roku nen shi,* pp. 1–2.

9. "Chūkyō kankei jutsugo-shū," *Jōhō,* No. 61, p. 67; "Shinshigun," in *Gendai Chūgoku jiten,* pp. 304–5.

10. See Shen Tzu-min, "The Nanch'ang Uprising on August First," Shanghai *Ta kung pao,* July 31, 1952.

11. The Kōain estimates that there were only 4,000 Red Army veterans in the New Fourth Army. *Kaisan made no shinshigun,* pp. 7–8. Another official Japanese study states that the New Fourth Army regrouped only 5,000 of the original 30,000 Red troops left in south China. This latter study also states that there was an understanding between the Communists and the Government that the total strength of the Chinese Communist forces participating in the United Front would be 50,000 troops—i.e., 45,000 in the Eighth Route Army and 5,000 in the New Fourth Army. *Jōhō,* No. 57, p. 3. The standard figure of 12,000, which was announced by the Communists, is reported by Fujita Masatsune in *Gendai Chūgoku jiten,* p. 305; and in Forman, *Report from Red China,* p. 161. Yeh Chien-ying, Chief of Staff of the Eighth Route Army, told the Yenan press party in July 1944, "In December [1937] another 12,000 guerrillas of the Red Army were reorganized into the New Fourth Army of the National Revolutionary Force." OPINTEL Report No. 323, p. 2. See also U.S. War Dept., "The Chinese Communist Movement," p. 2352.

12. The Second Column was sworn into the New Fourth Army at Lung-yen, March 27, 1938. *Jōhō,* No. 42, p. 74. For the Minhsi Soviet, see Japan, Office of the General Staff (Sanbō Honbu), *Shina kyōsantō undō shi* (A History of the Chinese Communist Party Movement) (Tokyo, March 1931), pp. 301–2.

13. *Kaisan made no shinshigun,* pp. 7–8.

14. "Ko" Group Army, "Kita Shina hōmen kyōsangun gaikyō yōzu" (Outline Map of the Disposition of the Communist Army in North China), January 13–17, 1940 [T977].

15. *Jōhō,* No. 57, pp. 3–4. The U.S. Army compiled the following information on the New Fourth Army's growth: "As new areas were brought under its control, the New Fourth Army recruited more soldiers and began to arm the people. By 1939 its strength grew to 35,000. By May 1940, it had grown to over 100,000 troops. In addition, some 500,000 guerrillas and local militia were operating under its command on both sides of the lower Yangtze. By January 1941, the regular army numbered 125,000 troops according to one report." U.S. War Dept., "The Chinese Communist Movement," p. 2352. Chassin presents a series of growth figures that correlate closely with wartime estimates. These figures were supplied by Yeh Chien-ying, Chief of Staff of the Eighth Route Army.

YEAR	EIGHTH	NEW FOURTH	TOTAL
1937	80,000	12,000	92,000
1938	156,700	25,000	181,700
1939	270,000	50,000	320,000
1940	400,000	100,000	500,000
1941	305,000	135,000	440,000
1942	340,000	110,960	450,960
1943	339,000	125,892	464,892
1944	320,000	153,676	473,676

The drop in 1941 is explained by Japanese anti-guerrilla measures. Chassin, *L'Ascension de Mao Tse-tung*, p. 187. (Chassin gives 1944 total as 474,476.)

16. The type of work performed by the militia is illustrated by this report from a Berlin broadcast based on a north China Japanese newspaper article: "In their fighting methods characteristic of guerrilla warfare, Chinese Communists have the collaboration of the broad masses since the Reds have been working for the protection of mass interests in order to enlist their support. For instance, the greater part of road construction, mine planting, and similar work was being done by armed bodies of young peasants and not by the Communists themselves." *RRFE*, No. 32 (October 27, 1943), p. C4.

17. U.S. War Dept., "The Chinese Communist Movement," p. 2436. As a further indication of how widely guerrilla units fluctuated in size, here are figures on the New Fourth Army drawn from Japanese sources: "According to interrogations of New Fourth Army political personnel made prisoner by our [the Japanese] Army in its September 1940 mopping-up campaign north of the Yangtze, the standard sizes for units of column size and below are as follows: column, 4,000 men; regiment, 1,300 men; battalion, 400 men; company, 130 men; platoon, 40 men; squad, 12 men." Yuasa Seiichi, "Chūshi ni okeru kyōsantōgun jōsei" (The Communist Military Situation in Central China), *Jōhō*, No. 38 (March 15, 1941), p. 48.

18. Terauchi Corps, Chief of Staff, "Kyōsangun no seijibu ni tsuite" (Concerning the Political Department of the Communist Army), November 8, 1938 [T912, particularly frames 22428, 22429, and 22430].

19. Carlson, *Twin Stars*, p. 260.

20. Tada Corps, *Chūgoku kyōsantō*, p. 63.

21. Katherine M. Chorley, *Armies and the Art of Revolution* (London, 1943), pp. 197–99; Georg von Rauch, *A History of Soviet Russia* (New York, 1957), pp. 100–101.

22. F. F. Liu (Liu Chih-pu), *A Military History of Modern China, 1924–1949* (Princeton, N.J., 1956), pp. 19–20. For further information on political work in the KMT armies, see R. L. MacFarquhar, "The Whampoa Military Academy," *Harvard University Papers on China*, IX, 146–72.

23. "Hachirogun, 'shin senshi tokuhon'" (The Eighth Route Army's "New Soldier's Reader"), *Jōhō*, No. 59 (February 1, 1942), pp. 40–41. This is a translation of the Eighth Route Army's manual *Hsin chan-shih tu-pen*, made by the Kōain's Kalgan Office, October 28, 1941.

24. For a summary of Soviet practice, see Headquarters, Department of the Army, *Handbook on the Soviet Army* (Washington, 1958), pp. 10, 57; Leonard Schapiro, *The Communist Party of the Soviet Union* (New York, 1959), pp. 327ff., 421; and Zbigniew Brzezinski, "Party Controls in the Soviet Army," *The Journal of Politics*, XIV (1952), 565–91.

25. "The 18th Group Army: Training, Medical Care and Supply," OPINTEL Report No. 324, p. 1.

26. "Shinshigun no seiji kōsaku soshiki kōyō sōan" (The New Fourth Army's Draft Outline of the Organization of Political Work), *Jōhō*, No. 43 (June 1, 1941), pp. 19–45.

27. *Ibid.*, pp. 23–24.

28. These translations of *cheng-chih-pu, cheng-chih-ch'u,* and *cheng-chih chih-tao-yüan* are the same as those employed in U.S. War Dept., "The Chinese Communist Movement," pp. 2448ff.

29. Yuasa Seiichi, *Jōhō*, No. 38 (March 15, 1941), p. 61. Some Communist manuals indicate that propaganda and education were divided into individual sections in the political department.

30. *Jōhō*, No. 43, p. 26.

31. See, for example, the composition of the 3d Column Political Department of the New Fourth Army's North Kiangsu Command, in Kōain, Central China Liaison Bureau, *Sohoku kyōsan chiku jitsujō chōsa hōkokusho* (Investigation Report of the Current Situation in the North Kiangsu Communist Region) ([Shanghai]: June 16, 1941), p. 89. (The north Kiangsu area and the New Fourth Army are studied in detail in Chapter Five.) For the use of dramatic productions as propaganda vehicles by the Chinese Communists, see Forman, *Report from Red China*, pp. 93–96.

32. *Jōhō*, No. 43, p. 32.

33. *Ibid.*, p. 35. The political fighter usually had completed some schooling and he had a fair degree of political consciousness. He was selected from the platoon by the company political instructor and his selection was approved by a higher authority. "Kyōsangun nai ni okeru seiji kunren" (Political Training Within the Communist Army), *Jōhō*, No. 10 (January 15, 1940), p. 74; "Shinshigun no rentai seiji kōsaku" (Political Work at the Company Level in the New Fourth Army), *Jōhō*, No. 56 (December 15, 1941), pp. 94–95. (Note that whereas a *rentai* in the Japanese Army was a regiment, the same character, *lien*, was used by the Chinese to designate a company; the Chinese regiment was called a *t'uan*.)

34. Snow, *Red Star Over China*, pp. 308–11.

35. *Jōhō*, No. 43, pp. 35–37; *Jōhō*, No. 10, pp. 74–76; *Jōhō*, No. 56, p. 91.

36. Its Chinese title is: *Min-chung yün-tung kung-tso chiang-shou t'i-kang.* See Central China Liaison Office, Kōain, trans., "Shinshigun no minshū undō kōsaku kōju teikō" (The New Fourth Army's Teaching Guide for Mass Movement Work), *Jōhō*, No. 44 (June 15, 1941), pp. 1–52.

37. The terminology "war areas" and "guerrilla areas" varied somewhat between north and south China. Regions occupied by both Japanese and Chinese

Communist forces at the same time were uniformly called "guerrilla areas," but the base areas, which were evacuated only in the face of a Japanese assault, were known as "war areas," "base areas," "red areas," "liberated areas," and so forth. Regions so strongly garrisoned by the Japanese that only secret liaison and intelligence units of the Communist Army could exist in them were called "white areas." Cf. Research Section, Central Committee for the Extermination of Communism, *Satsunan henchi tainichi sekka kōsaku jittai chōsa hōkokusho* (Investigation Report on the Current Situation with Regard to Anti-Japanese Communizing Activities in the South Chahar Border Area), July 1940 [T993], p. 1.

38. *Jōhō*, No. 44, p. 10.

39. *Ibid.*, p. 34.

40. *Ibid.*, p. 37.

41. *Ibid.*

42. The U.S. War Department study comments: "A vast propaganda program was set in motion [by the Eighth Route Army in the guerrilla bases], utilizing mass meetings, propaganda posters, theatrical plays (probably the most effective method of indoctrinating the illiterate masses), and the dissemination of newspapers, magazines, and books. The central theme of this propaganda was anti-Japanism, but it also emphasized the meaning of the united front, democracy, and the struggle against imperialism and fascism." "The Chinese Communist Movement," p. 2335.

43. *Jōhō*, No. 44, p. 30.

44. *Ibid.*, pp. 30–31.

45. *Ibid.*, pp. 39–40.

46. *Ibid.*, pp. 12, 16–17.

47. *Nung-ts'un ch'ing-nien kung-tso ti chu-wen-t'i;* "Shinshigun no nōson seinen kōsaku" (New Fourth Army Work with Village Youths), *Jōhō*, No. 40 (April 15, 1941), pp. 73–81.

48. *Ibid.*, p. 73.

49. *Ibid.*, p. 75.

50. *Jōhō*, No. 44, p. 13.

51. The manual *Nung-ts'un ch'ing-nien kung-tso ti chu-wen-t'i* stresses the necessity of winning over popular "go-betweens" in mass-movement work. It states that "positive elements" might be found among intellectuals, schoolteachers, village chiefs, Pao Chia heads, etc. *Jōhō*, No. 40, p. 76.

52. *Jōhō*, No. 44, pp. 13–15.

53. *Ibid.*, pp. 14, 47–48.

54. *Ibid.*, p. 45.

55. For examples of the Communists' welcoming Japanese attacks on non-Communist guerrillas in Shantung, see Tipton, *China Escapade,* p. 202.

56. Chief of Staff, Sugiyama Corps, *Shina himitsu kessha gaikan* (General View of Chinese Secret Societies), August 25, 1939 [T952], pp. 31ff.

57. *Jōhō*, No. 44, p. 46.

58. *Ibid.*, pp. 46–47.

59. According to the Hong Kong *Ta kung pao,* December 8, 1950, some 82,300 persons voluntarily withdrew from the I-kuan-tao secret society in Shansi during 1950; 1,692 former members were forced to register; and 133 leaders of the society were imprisoned.

60. For a detailed treatment of mass associations based on work group, see "Yūgeki konkyochi ni okeru Chūkyō no kensetsu kōsaku" (Establishment Work by the Chinese Communists in the Guerrilla Bases), *Jōhō,* No. 18 (May 15, 1940), pp. 76–77.

61. Lindsay, *North China Front,* p. 15.

62. "The most spectacular, and in some ways the most permanent step toward an institutional basis for democracy has been the encouragement of mass organizations, most of them spontaneous in origin, particularly the Village Mobilization Committees, which carried on the work of civil government during the interregnum between Lukouchiao and the Fuping Conference [January 10–15, 1938, which established the Chin-Ch'a-Chi Government]. When normal administration was restored, they were abolished. On the other hand, the Farmers' Union, Merchants' Association, and Women's Association have been encouraged, and their growth has made it quite clear that the people are willing to take part in political life if given the chance. To these must be added the Workers', Teachers', and Youth Associations, which the Government hopes will confine themselves to executing Government policies and to purely anti-Japanese activities." Taylor, *The Struggle for North China,* p. 107.

63. Yuasa Seiichi, *Jōhō,* No. 38, p. 71. It is an undeniable fact that the modest tax relief instituted by Communist political workers added an economic motive to the peasants' support of the guerrillas. However, as we have seen, the Communists did not redistribute land or destroy titles. Japanese commentators often exaggerated Communist economic appeals, since the Japanese were not able themselves to admit that the primary cause of peasant mobilization and the spread of resistance was the presence of the Japanese Army.

64. *Ibid.,* pp. 71–72.

65. "Shinshigun kankei jōhō" (Intelligence Concerning the New Fourth Army), *Jōhō,* No. 51 (October 1, 1941), Item A, pp. 62–67.

CHAPTER FOUR

1. Karl W. Deutsch, "Social Mobilization and Political Development," *American Political Science Review,* LV (1961), 497–98.

2. Donald G. Gillin, "Portrait of a Warlord: Yen Hsi-shan in Shansi Province, 1911–1930," *Journal of Asian Studies,* XIX (1960), 289–306.

3. On the morning of September 25, 1937, at P'inghsingkuan, Lin Piao's 115th Division encircled and destroyed the rear guard of the crack Japanese Fifth Division, commanded by the famous Japanese nationalist Lt. Gen. Itagaki Seishirō. The Communist attack was carried out as Itagaki's division was passing along the difficult mountain road from Yühsien, Chahar, into Shansi. Lin's victory caused many Japanese casualties and gave large amounts of supplies to the Communists, but it did not materially influence the course of the Japanese

invasion of Shansi. It was nonetheless very useful ideologically for the Communists to be credited with a victory precisely at the time that the Nationalists were suffering defeats. See Li Tien-yu, "First Encounter at P'inghsingkuan Pass," in *Saga of Resistance to Japanese Invasion*, pp. 1–23; *North China Area Operations Record*, pp. 32–33; and an account by Chu Teh in Carlson, *Twin Stars*, pp. 70–71. For a description of the battle by Lin Piao (with journalistic embellishments not by Lin), see Haldore Hanson, *Humane Endeavour, the Story of the Chinese War* (New York, 1939), pp. 104–6. P'inghsingkuan is a pass midway between Fanchih and Lingch'iu in northeast Shansi. The battle has since been elevated by Communist propagandists to the level of a Stalingrad.

4. Tada Corps, *Chūgoku kyōsantō*, pp. 23–24.

5. *Ibid.*, p. 23.

6. "Shin-Satsu-Ki henku no jōkyō (The General Situation in the Chin-Ch'a-Chi Border Region), *Jōhō*, No. 35 (February 1, 1941), p. 2.

7. *Report from Red China*, p. 132.

8. Nohara Shiro, "Japan-China War," in *Gendai Chūgoku jiten*, p. 578; Carlson, *Twin Stars*, p. 236. Wut'aishan and Foup'ing are very different areas. Wut'aishan has within one of its valleys a famous Buddhist sanctuary made up of 65 temples. Before the fall of the Dynasty (1912), thousands of Mongols and Tibetans made pilgrimages to the mountain, and Wut'ai was regarded by all Chinese as a sacred area. Even during the period when Wut'aishan was a Communist base, there were special mass associations for monks and lamas—called the "Yellow Temple" and "Green Temple" National Salvation Unions—in addition to the usual peasants', workers', and women's mass associations. Ke Han, *The Shansi-Hopei-Chahar Border Region*, p. 50; Taylor, *The Struggle for North China*, p. 39. Foup'ing, on the other hand, was in a culturally backward area. *Jōhō*, No. 35, p. 72.

9. According to Hatano Ken'ichi, the Communist invading force may have amounted to as many as 27,000 men; *Chūgoku kyōsantō ichi-ku-san-roku nen shi* (A History of the Chinese Communist Party During 1936), pp. 3–6. Also see Snow, *Red Star Over China*, pp. 224–25. This general discussion of the origins of the Hsi Meng Hui follows Pacification Unit, Sugiyama Corps, *Sekishoku kōnichi kenseifu no kenchi gyōsei: Sanseishō Wajunken chihō kyōsan chiku jōkyō chōsa hōkokusho* (Hsien Administration by Red Anti-Japanese Hsien Governments: Report of an Investigation of the Situation in the Communist Areas in Hoshun, Shansi), June 5, 1939 [T934], pp. 1–6. The Hoshun investigation was carried out by Misaki Ryōichi. For an excellent military study of the Communists' invasion of Shansi on February 27, 1936, see "Sansei no botsuraku to kyōsangun" (The Collapse of Shansi and the Communist Army), *Kaikōsha kiji*, No. 742 (July 1936), pp. 197–201. A map of the campaign appears on p. 200.

10. *The Struggle for North China*, p. 165. Taylor does not cite the Kung Tao T'uan as the Hsi Meng Hui's predecessor, but he does mention Yen's having created a unit known as the Fan Kung T'uan (Anti-Communist Corps) to watch over the Hsi Meng Hui. The name Kung Tao T'uan is used by Misaki in his report for the Sugiyama Corps. Misaki (p. 2) emphasizes that the Kung

Tao T'uan was a poorly conceived organization that was subverted from within by the Hsi Meng Hui. (Taylor credits Mr. Aylwin Hogg as the source of his information on internal developments in Shansi in this period.) For a detailed study of the organization of the Kung Tao T'uan, although from a vociferously anti-Communist and Japanese nationalist point of view, see Fukada Yūzō, *Shina kyōsangun no gensei* (The Present Strength of the Chinese Communist Army) (Tokyo, 1939), pp. 336–61. Fukada also identifies Yen's mass organization as the Kung Tao T'uan.

11. Sung Shao-wen was arrested in 1936 for his participation in the anti-Japanese demonstrations. In 1948 he was a member of the North China People's Government, and in September 1949 he was a delegate from the north China "liberated areas" to the People's Political Consultative Conference. In September 1953, he was appointed Vice-Minister of Light Industry.

12. *Jōhō*, No. 35, pp. 13–14; and the biography of Sung Shao-wen, *ibid.*, p. 71. Also see Taylor, *The Struggle for North China*, pp. 164–67. The figure of 30,000 rifles delivered to the Dare-to-Die Corps is from Taylor.

13. After 1949, Hu Jen-k'uei served in the Communist government in the field of foreign trade; in January 1953, he was appointed Vice-Chief of the Maritime Customs Office.

14. *Jōhō*, No. 35, p. 14. Taylor gives a breakdown of the groups represented at Foup'ing, p. 35. The official title of the Foup'ing conference was *Chin-Ch'a-Chi pien-ch'ü tang-chün-cheng-min lin-shih tai-piao ta-hui* (Special Representative Congress of the Party, Army, Government, and People of the Chin-Ch'a-Chi [i.e., Shansi-Chahar-Hopei] Border Area).

15. Some sources also list Lü Cheng-ts'ao, Military Commander in central Hopei, and Lou Ning-hsien, Chief of the Administrative Committee's Secretariat, as members of the Border Region Administrative Committee. See *Jōhō*, No. 35, pp. 57ff. Also see U.S. War Dept., "The Chinese Communist Movement," p. 2405; and Kusano Fumio, *Shina henku no kenkyū* (Research on China's Border Regions), p. 8.

16. *Twin Stars*, p. 235. As for Foup'ing, he remarked, "Towards evening we reached Fup'ing [Foup'ing], but it was not the bustling city I had visited in January. The Japanese had captured the city in March, and half of the buildings had been burned. The population was half its normal size." *Ibid.*, pp. 233–34.

17. *Jōhō*, No. 35, pp. 68–69.

18. *Ibid.*, p. 8. Teng T'o was ousted from the editorship of the *People's Daily* in the "Hundred Flowers" debacle of 1957.

19. Ke Han, *The Shansi-Hopei-Chahar Border Region*, p. 42.

20. See Chou Erh-fu, "Dr. Bethune—Our True Friend," *China Reconstructs*, VIII, No. 11 (November 1959), pp. 26–28, a propagandistic but informative article.

21. Ke Han, *The Shansi-Hopei-Chahar Border Region*, p. 5.

22. OPINTEL Report No. 323, p. 6.

23. *Jōhō*, No. 35, p. 55. For a list of hsien included in each area in early 1940, see Ke Han, *The Shansi-Hopei-Chahar Border Region*, p. 6.

24. Research Section, Central Committee for the Extermination of Communism, *Dokuritsu daiichishi ni tsuite: Kisei hōkokusho no ni* (West Hopei Report: Concerning the First Independent Division), July 1940 [T996], pp. 1–2. Yang himself was a native of Fukien and from a rich-peasant background. He received a middle-school education and joined the Red Army in Kiangsi at about the age of 18. After the Long March, he was trained at K'angta and given command in Chin-Ch'a-Chi. His vice-commander and chief of staff were also graduates of K'angta; his political commissar, Lo Yüan-fa (reportedly the child of a beggar), was a graduate of the Red Army School in Kiangsi (*ibid.,* pp. 15–17).

25. Ke Han, *The Shansi-Hopei-Chahar Border Region,* pp. 81–82. With regard to the over-all impact of the war on P'ingshan, Ke remarks: "In the mountainous West of Hopei Province there is a small county town called P'ingshan. Locked in these inland mountains, it lived a secluded life undisturbed by national event [*sic*] until fairly recently. Today, however, it is enjoying a remarkably prosperous commerce because of its importance as a strategic base for operations of guerrilla warfare against the Japanese" (p. 78).

26. Research Section, Central Committee for the Extermination of Communism, *Kyōsangun naibu ni okeru butaiin narabi ni tōin no shojōkyō* (Situation Concerning Military and Party Personnel in the Communist Army), July 1940 [T997], pp. 1–25.

27. Ke Han, *The Shansi-Hopei-Chahar Border Region,* p. 6.

28. Research Section, Central Committee for the Extermination of Communism, *Kichū-ku chūbu chihō ni okeru Chūkyō no minshū kakutoku kōsaku jitsujō chōsa hōkoku* (Investigation Report on the State of Communist Efforts to Win the Masses in the Central Section of the Central Hopei Area), May 1940 [T999], pp. 7, 27. The area considered in this report is Hochien, Jench'iu, Wenan, Yungch'ing, and Tach'eng—i.e., the area located slightly to the south of the midpoint between Peiping and Tientsin. Lü Cheng-ts'ao's military headquarters was located at Jench'iu when Evans Carlson interviewed him in 1938. See *Twin Stars,* pp. 241–46. For the early mopping-up campaigns in central Hopei, see Eighteenth Group Army, *K'ang-chan pa-nien-lai,* p. 63.

29. Officers of the Japanese Self-Defense Force, War History Office, have indicated to me in conversation that the major objective and the chief accomplishment of anti-Communist measures by the North China Area Army was the elimination of the central Hopei base. In their opinion, Lü Cheng-ts'ao would not have been able to re-enter central Hopei were it not for the weakening of Japanese forces after the outbreak of the war with the United States and England.

30. Tada Corps, *Chūgoku kyōsantō,* p. 27.

31. For references to Hsü Fan-t'ing, see Hsü Yung-ying, *A Survey of Shensi-Kansu-Ninghsia Border Region; Part I, Geography and Politics* (New York: International Secretariat, Institute of Pacific Relations, 1945), p. 78; U.S. War Dept., "The Chinese Communist Movement," p. 2459; and Carlson, *Twin Stars,* p. 210. Carlson interviewed Hsü at K'olan in 1938. According to the War Department account, Hsü was a former member of the T'ung Meng Hui.

32. Taylor, *The Struggle for North China,* p. 166.

33. Hatano Ken'ichi, "Kokkyō masatsu ni kan suru chōsa" (An Inquiry Concerning Nationalist-Communist Friction), *Jōhō,* No. 31 (December 1, 1940), pp. 21–22; and Research Section, Central Committee for the Extermination of Communism, *Sanseishō seihokubu hijō chōsa hōkokusho* (Survey of Banditry in Northwest Shansi), July 1940 [T994], pp. 5–6. The latter Japanese investigation concludes (p. 17): "The intervention of Yen Hsi-shan was never really possible. The main instruments of mass mobilization in the surrendered areas were the Sacrifice League and the New Army. Therefore, control in the region evaded the grasp of the Shansi Army. The old Army was isolated from the masses."

34. T994, p. 16.

35. Harrison Forman visited the Shansi-Suiyüan base in 1944 and talked with Generals Lü and Ch'en Man-yüan. See *Report from Red China,* pp. 200–201.

36. Pacification Unit, Sugiyama Corps, *Sekishoku kōnichi kenseifu no kenchi gyōsei: Sanseishō Wajunken chihō kyōsan chiku jōkyō chōsa hōkokusho* (Hsien Administration by Red Anti-Japanese Hsien Governments: Investigation Report on the Situation in the Communist Areas of the Hoshun, Shansi, Area), June 5, 1939 [T934], pp. 1–6.

37. Pacification Unit, Sugiyama Corps, *Sanseishō Wajunken chihō kyōsan chiku jōkyō hōkokusho: minshū kōnichi kakudantai no naiyō oyobi kambu kyōiku* (Report on Communist Areas in Hoshun Hsien, Shansi: Anti-Japanese Mass Organizations and Leadership Education), August 8, 1939 [T944], p. 36. Rules of association, pp. 44–49.

38. *Ibid.,* pp. 50–52.

39. *Ibid.,* pp. 106–8.

40. Tada Corps, *Chūgoku kyōsantō,* p. 26. According to Carlson, Hsü entered south Hopei in April 1938 in response to a request of local representatives who came to 129th division headquarters from Hopei. *Twin Stars,* p. 250. These were presumably members of Yang Hsiu-feng's group. After 1949, Yang became governor of Hopei province, and later he joined the Education Ministry. He was elected a member of the Eighth Central Committee of the CCP in 1956.

41. *North China Area Operations Record,* p. 329.

42. *Ibid.,* p. 337. For a brilliant treatment of the political and social implications of the KMT defeat in Chungt'iaoshan, see Peck, *Two Kinds of Time,* pp. 235–96.

43. OPINTEL Report No. 323, p. 8; U.S. War Dept., "The Chinese Communist Movement," p. 2433.

44. *RRFE,* No. 75 (June 15, 1945), p. 66; Fujita Masatsune, "Eighth Route Army," in *Gendai Chūgoku jiten,* p. 611.

45. Goette, *Japan Fights for Asia,* p. 153. Goette's account of the war in China is pro-Japanese, but it is also of great value because of the author's close personal contact with Japanese officers.

46. Hanson, *Humane Endeavour,* pp. 109–15.

47. Hatano Ken'ichi, "Chūkyō san-hachi-nen shi" (A History of Chinese Communism in 1938), Part III, *Jōhō*, No. 67 (June 1, 1942), p. 69. This study, in three parts (see Bibliography), is an annotated collection of Chinese Communist accounts of the establishment of guerrilla bases in north China. It is a very valuable source. With regard to the east Shantung region, one account recalls (p. 69), "After the collapse of Han's authority, all the regional bureaucrats fled. The whole province fell into a state of anarchy. Traitors and bandits flourished. It was only in the midst of this disorder that the people formed the Shantung Eighth Route Army."

48. *Ibid.,* p. 76. Swamps were also common sites for Soviet partisan bases during World War II. See Edgar M. Howell, *The Soviet Partisan Movement, 1941–1944* (Washington: Department of the Army, 1956).

49. Hatano Ken'ichi, in *Jōhō*, No. 67, p. 76.

50. *Ibid.,* pp. 76–77.

51. *Ibid.,* p. 81; students from Peiping-Tientsin, pp. 85–86. Another valuable (although Communist) source on the resistance in Shantung is Wang Yu-chuan, "The Organization of a Typical Guerrilla Area in South Shantung," in Carlson, *The Chinese Army,* pp. 84–130. With respect to armaments, Wang writes (p. 97): "During the disorderly retreat of Han Fu-ch'ü to the south, a large amount of rifles and ammunition were [*sic*] discarded. Some were sold by Han's defeated soldiers, some were picked up by the people, and all eventually fell into the hands of the land-owners and the peasants. This store was further added to after the battle of T'aierhchuang, when great quantities of arms were abandoned by both sides. Even machine guns were found left in the fields after this great battle."

52. This discussion of Fan Chu-hsien's operations relies on several articles written by Communists in Hatano's collection, *Jōhō*, No. 67, pp. 75–86. See also Carlson's description of Fan, whom he met at Liaoch'eng in 1938, in *Twin Stars,* pp. 261–62.

53. For Ch'i Hsieh-yüan, see Taylor, *The Struggle for North China,* pp. 24–25.

54. Tada Corps, *Chūgoku kyōsantō,* p. 24.

55. *Ibid.* One account (*Jōhō*, No. 67, p. 79) states that Ch'en's unit reached Liangshan moor in January 1939, but this is not confirmed by other sources.

56. Tada Corps, *Chūgoku kyōsantō,* p. 22.

57. The "Fan Chu-hsien Column" is referred to in Liao Kuan-hsien, "Cavalry on the Plains," *Saga of Resistance to Japanese Invasion,* pp. 39–40. Liao Kuan-hsien led a 129th division cavalry unit into the Liaoch'eng-Yangku-Tunga area of western Shantung in August 1939. His account maintains that Fan Chu-hsien was killed in January 1938 (p. 40, n.1), but this is obviously mistaken; the Japanese had barely entered Shantung at that time.

58. The estimate of "several thousand" was given to Taylor by a Communist source in the summer of 1938. *The Struggle for North China,* p. 58.

59. Tada Corps, *Chūgoku kyōsantō,* p. 21; *Jōhō*, No. 42, p. 76; *Jōhō*, No. 67, p. 61; "Kitō chiku ni okeru kōnichi-gun" (Anti-Japanese Army in the East Hopei Region), *Jōhō*, No. 3 (October 1, 1939), pp. 56–62. The last source indi-

cates that many members of the Communist East Hopei Expeditionary Force (approximately 300) were Manchurians under a former officer of the Tungpei Army—one T'ang Chü-wu. T'ang was killed in July 1939 in a village of Lulung hsien in east Hopei (pp. 59–60).

60. Taylor, *The Struggle for North China*, p. 58.

61. Tada Corps, *Chūgoku kyōsantō*, p. 21.

62. "Chūkyō Kahoku saikō kanbu rinji kinkyū kaigi" (Extraordinary Conference of High CCP Leaders in North China), *Jōhō*, No. 9 (January 1, 1940), p. 35. On the subject of political work in the east Hopei area, see Taylor, *The Struggle for North China*, pp. 78, 102–4.

63. Headquarters, Tada Corps, *Kyōsan hachirogun no Kitō chiku ni okeru kōnichi kakusaku jōkyō* (Anti-Japanese Policy of the Communist Eighth Route Army in East Hopei), November 27, 1939 [T970], pp. 1–2.

64. *Ibid.*, p. 3.

65. Lindsay, *North China Front*, p. 5.

66. See First Patrol Regiment, North China Special Patrol Garrison, *Kitō tōbu chiku dai ikki sakusen sentō shōhō* (First Phase Battle Report: Eastern Area of East Hopei), September 6, 1943–June 10, 1944, *Kita Shina tokubetsu keibitai hōkoku*, No. 1 [T1249]. For other detailed reports of fighting in north China and east Hopei at the end of the war, see T1250, T1251, T1252, T1253, T1254, T1255.

67. Tipton, *China Escapade*, p. 148. Wang Yu-min's Fifteenth Mobile Brigade was independent until late in the war when it was contacted by the American O.S.S. (p. 205) and by General Tai Li in Chungking (p. 207).

68. Hatano Ken'ichi, "Kokkyō masatsu ni kan suru chōsa" (An Inquiry Concerning Nationalist-Communist Friction), *Jōhō*, No. 31 (December 1, 1940), p. 8. Hatano notes in his introduction to this detailed list of incidents that some 200 cases of KMT-CCP friction occurred during the period 1937–41, but that only 45 were sufficiently well documented to be discussed in this article. Of Hatano's 45, we have used only those that were armed clashes in the rear areas. See also Hatano Ken'ichi, "Saikin Chūkyō kankei nempyō" (Chronological Table Concerning Recent Chinese Communism), *Jōhō*, No. 42 (May 15, 1941), p. 75.

69. Taylor, *The Struggle for North China*, p. 167.

70. *Jōhō*, No. 31, pp. 12–13.

71. Hatano (*ibid.*) gives both versions; another Japanese study accepts the version that the Nationalists attacked the Communists with the intent of eliminating all CCP organs in Hopei. See "Kokkyō ryōgun no sōkoku ni tsuite" (Regarding the Clashes Between the Nationalist and Communist Armies), *Jōhō*, No. 13 (March 1, 1940), pp. 7–8. The December 16 battle is called the "Ankuo Incident."

72. *Jōhō*, No. 31, p. 13; *Jōhō*, No. 13, p. 7.

73. *Jōhō*, No. 31, p. 14.

74. *Ibid.*, pp. 15–16, 21. A KMT version of the destruction of Chang Yin-wu's People's Army can be found in U.S. War Dept., "The Chinese Commu-

nist Movement," p. 2347. Not only did Lu Chung-lin clash with Lü Cheng-ts'ao in central Hopei; he also fell out with Yang Hsiu-feng in southern Hopei. Compton reviews the situation in the south as follows: "A typical clash came in southern Hopei when the Kuomintang dispatched Lu Chung-lin to act as governor in an area already organized behind Japanese lines by a Peking professor, Yang Hsiu-feng. Lu immediately proposed changes in administration and policy which Yang could not accept, then proceeded to set up a parallel administration of his own. Through the middle of 1939 two governments worked side by side—one Kuomintang, the other drawing closer and closer to Communist policy and the red military forces operating in the area. The issue was finally decided when a section of Lu's troops went over to the Japanese and his government disintegrated." Boyd Compton, *Mao's China*, p. xviii. This southern Hopei disagreement did not, however, lead to military action between the two rivals.

75. The East Kansu Incident arose from a small clash between Eighth Route Army troops that were being transferred and KMT peace preservation units. The respective commanders came to the aid of their troops, and large-scale fighting resulted. Mao Tse-tung sent a telegram to Chiang Kai-shek charging that the incident was a prearranged attack by Nationalist forces on the Communists in Ch'ingyang, Hoshui, Chenyüan, and Ning hsien of eastern Kansu. See *Jōhō*, No. 31, p. 19; *Jōhō*, No. 13, pp. 4–6; and "Kokkyō masatsu mondai ni kan suru shiryō" (Materials Concerning the Problem of Nationalist-Communist Friction), *Jōhō*, No. 15 (April 1, 1940), pp. 45–48.

CHAPTER FIVE

1. Ku Chu-t'ung's Third War Zone included southern Kiangsu, Chekiang, eastern Kiangsi, and southern Anhwei. For further details on the origins of the New Fourth Army, see Chapter Three.

2. Eighteenth Group Army, *K'ang-chan pa-nien-lai*, p. 53; Kōain, Central China Liaison Bureau, *Kaisan made no shinshigun* (The New Fourth Army to the Time of Its Dispersal) ([Shanghai], October 1941), pp. 9–10.

3. *Kaisan made no shinshigun*, pp. 14–15; "Shinshigun no kaisan oyobi senkō shojijō" (The Dispersal of the New Fourth Army and All Preceding Events), *Jōhō*, No. 36 (February 15, 1941), pp. 36–38; *Jōhō*, No. 31, pp. 23–24. The authoritative Communist work on the Communist clashes with Li P'in-hsien and other aspects of New Fourth Army policy prior to the New Fourth Army Incident is "Freely Expand the Anti-Japanese Forces; Resist the Attack of the Anti-Communist Die-hards," *Selected Works of Mao Tse-tung*, III, pp. 204–10.

4. The Japanese account of the "Three Rivers Operation" (the Yangtze, the new bed of the Yellow River, and the Grand Canal) contains a curiously frank admission that there were insufficient forces to garrison the conquered areas.

"In the area north of the Yangtze River, particularly in the area between the Tientsin-Pukow railway, the Tayün Ho [Grand Canal], the New Huang Ho [Yellow River], and the Yangtze River, Communist guerrillas were very active and although the necessity for destroying these forces was fully recognized, the 13th Army in its weakened condition [it had sent most of its main force to participate in the Ichang Operation, May 1–June 29, 1940, in the area west of Hankow] was unable to undertake the operation. However, about the middle of July, with the return of the units which had participated in the Ichang Operation, the Army began preparations for the destruction of these forces." *Central China Area Operations Record,* pp. 184–85. The Three Rivers Operation was carried out between September 4 and September 17, 1940; the area mopped up was between Liuho and Kaoyu. The 13th Army's headquarters were at Shanghai.

5. *Kaisan made no shinshigun,* pp. 8, 15.

6. *Ibid.,* p. 15. Evans Carlson met P'eng Hsüeh-feng in December 1937 in southern Shansi, where P'eng headed a guerrilla school. Although Carlson says that P'eng was 45 years old at the time (*Twin Stars,* p. 62), he was actually born in 1905. P'eng participated in the May 30th Movement in Shanghai in 1925, and joined the Communist movement at that time. He was instrumental in enlarging the Communist areas in Honan in 1944 when the KMT retreated in the face of Hata's offensive. P'eng died in battle in September 1944. For the dispatch of Eighth Route Army troops to central China, also see Mao Tse-tung, *Selected Works,* III, 207.

7. *Jōhō,* No. 36, p. 15; Yuasa Seiichi, *Jōhō,* No. 38, pp. 84ff.

8. See Yuasa Seiichi, *Jōhō,* No. 38, p. 50. For a complete list of the hsien held by Li Hsien-nien, see Ch'en Yi and Liu Shao-ch'i, "Kannan jiken ato ni okeru shinshigun jōkyō" (The Situation of the New Fourth Army After the New Fourth Army Incident), *Jōhō,* No. 53 (November 1, 1941), p. 94.

9. Yuasa Seiichi, *Jōhō,* No. 38, p. 83; Hatano, *Jōhō,* No. 31, p. 18; *Jōhō,* No. 36, p. 14. The last-named source states that the KMT attack on P'ingchiang was carried out by the 117th Group Army, whereas Hatano cites the 27th Group Army as the attacker.

10. The characters normally romanized as *chiang-nan* (meaning "south of the river," i.e., south of the Yangtze) are written here as Kiangnan in deference to usage.

11. "Daitōasen to Chūkyō no Kōso ni okeru katsudō" (The Activities of the Chinese Communists in Kiangsu and the Greater East Asia War), *Jōhō,* No. 66 (May 15, 1942), p. 41.

12. Tai Li's official title was Chief of the Statistical and Investigation Office of the Military Affairs Commission; in fact, he directed the military police and supervised one aspect of rear-area affairs, namely the clandestine activities of the Chungking government. He did not, however, have exclusive control over all Kuomintang-affiliated guerrillas. As the Japanese show, Ch'en Li-fu's CC Clique was also quite active in and around Shanghai. For a list of all Chungking-affiliated organizations with offices in the Shanghai concessions, see *ibid.,*

p. 44. For a useful summary of factions within the wartime Kuomintang, including the position of Tai Li, see "Memorandum by the Counselor of the Embassy in China to the Ambassador in China, July 22, 1942," U.S. Department of State, *Foreign Relations of the United States, Diplomatic Papers, 1942, China* (Washington, 1956), pp. 212–26.

13. See *Jōhō*, No. 66, p. 43.

14. *Ibid.*, pp. 44–45, 47–48. Also see *Kaisan made no shinshigun*, p. 12; and "Kōnan kōnichi giyūgun no enkaku to genjō" (The History of the Kiangnan Anti-Japanese Volunteer Army and Its Present Condition), *Jōhō*, No. 31 (March 1, 1941), p. 37.

15. *Jōhō*, No. 31, p. 37.

16. Forman, *Report from Red China*, p. 166. Forman interviewed Ch'en Yi in Yenan in 1944. Ch'en had come up to Yenan from Kiangsu via Shantung and the T'aihang mountains. Along with some useful information, Forman's report of the discussion includes a preposterous statement by Ch'en Yi to the effect that the Red Army was not driven out of south China in 1934, but "voluntarily gave up its bases in Kiangsi in the interests of internal peace, in the face of the growing threat of Japanese aggression" (p. 163). Ch'en must have smiled when he saw the visiting American reporter write that one down.

17. Ch'en Yi and Liu Shao-ch'i, *Jōhō*, No. 53, p. 95; Forman, *Report from Red China*, p. 165.

18. *Kaisan made no shinshigun*, pp. 12–13; *Jōhō*, No. 31, pp. 37–38; and *Jōhō*, No. 66, pp. 45, 49, 54–55.

19. *Jōhō*, No. 31, pp. 38–39.

20. *Jōhō*, No. 66, pp. 56–58. See also *Jōhō*, No. 31, pp. 39–43, and *Kaisan made no shinshigun*, p. 13.

21. *Ibid.*, pp. 11–12, 16; *North Kiangsu Report*, pp. 3, 72–73 (see note 23 below); biography of Kuan Wen-wei in Kasumigaseki Society, *Gendai Chūgoku jinmei jiten* (Biographical Dictionary of Modern China). Kuan Wen-wei is described in all accounts as "an old member of the Communist Party." He was a normal-school graduate and an elementary-school teacher before the war.

22. "Land Concentration in North Kiangsu," *Agrarian China, Selected Source Materials from Chinese Authors* (London: Institute of Pacific Relations, 1939), pp. 11–14.

23. Kōain, Central China Liaison Bureau, *Sohoku kyōsan chiku jitsujō chōsa hōkokusho* (Investigation Report on the Current Situation in the North Kiangsu Communist Region) (Shanghai: June 16, 1941, "Secret"), p. 29; hereafter cited as *North Kiangsu Report*. This long report (484 pp.), written by the Political Department, Central China Liaison Bureau, Kōain, in March 1941, constitutes the main source for the following discussion of the north Kiangsu base. It is one of the most thorough studies on a large Communist area to be found in the Japanese archives.

24. "Occupation and Resistance in Kiangsu," *RRFE*, No. 63 (January 19, 1945), p. AB3.

25. The Battle of Shanghai in the autumn of 1937 did not extend above the

Yangtze River, but Japanese forces did advance from the south into north Kiangsu after the defeat at T'aierhchuang and during the T'ungshan Operation. The Central China Expeditionary Army undertook operations against T'ungshan in the period April 23–May 20, 1938, to support the main Japanese drive on T'ungshan from the north. These operations secured the entire length of the Tientsin-Pukow railroad. Also, on May 20, a Japanese landing force captured the city of Lienyünkang, the eastern terminus of the Lunghai railroad. However, after June 1938, the Japanese continued to hold only strong points on the Lunghai railroad in the extreme northern part of the province and left but three infantry battalions south of Tungt'ai to garrison the area just above the Yangtze.

26. Technically, Han was Governor of Kiangsu from 1938 until 1944, when he was replaced by Wang Mao-kung (*RRFE*, No. 63, p. AB1). Actually, Han was a New Fourth Army prisoner from late 1941, and was in exile in Kweiyang, Kweichow province, from September 1943 until the end of the war.

27. *North Kiangsu Report*, pp. 30, 116, 135; Ch'en Yi and Liu Shao-ch'i, *Jōhō*, No. 53, p. 95.

28. *Jōhō*, No. 36 (February 15, 1941), pp. 14–15, 39; *North Kiangsu Report*, p. 30.

29. On Kuan Wen-wei's raid, see *North Kiangsu Report*, pp. 30–31; on Eighth Route Army reinforcements, see "Shinshigun jiken kyūmei no shoshiryō" (Various Materials for an Investigation of the New Fourth Army Incident), *Jōhō*, No. 45 (July 1, 1941), p. 57.

30. *North Kiangsu Report*, p. 31.

31. "Sohoku kokkyō shōtotsu ni kan suru shinshigun tsūden" (New Fourth Army Telegram Concerning the KMT-CCP Clash in North Kiangsu), *Jōhō*, No. 30 (November 15, 1940), pp. 53–55.

32. For the defeat of Han Te-ch'in at Huangch'iao, see *Kaisan made no shinshigun*, pp. 8, 16; *Jōhō*, No. 45, pp. 59–60; *North Kiangsu Report*, pp. 31–32. One Japanese study reprints a letter addressed to a "known person" by someone living in north Kiangsu, dated October 17, 1940. This letter states in part, "The present situation in this area has changed suddenly. The KMT and CCP armies clashed at Huangch'iao. The result is that the 89th Army's Commander, Li Shou-wei [Han Te-ch'in's forces], and the Independent Sixth Brigade's Commander, Weng, are both dead in battle and 20,000 to 30,000 [KMT] troops are in disorderly flight and appear unable to regroup." *Kaisan made no shinshigun*, p. 69.

33. For accounts of the Eighth Route Army reinforcements, see *Jōhō*, No. 45, pp. 55–57 (information based on Communist newspapers of August 1940 that were captured in the Japanese "Three Rivers" mopping-up campaign); Yuasa Seiichi, *Jōhō*, No. 38, pp. 79–81; Tada Corps, *Chūgoku kyōsantō*, p. 25; and *North Kiangsu Report*, pp. 31, 41.

34. Ch'en Yi and Liu Shao-ch'i, *Jōhō*, No. 53, p. 94.

35. U.S. War Dept., "The Chinese Communist Movement," p. 2352.

36. With regard to the New Fourth Army's change of policy in 1940 and the strength of the Kuomintang reaction, see *Kaisan made no shinshigun,* pp. 11–12.

37. U.S. War Dept., "The Chinese Communist Movement," p. 2349.

38. For the First Detachment's transfer, see *North Kiangsu Report,* p. 3; for the Third Detachment, see *Kaisan made no shinshigun,* p. 11.

39. U.S. War Dept., "The Chinese Communist Movement," p. 2351.

40. "Shinshigun," *Gendai Chūgoku jiten,* pp. 304–5; *Jōhō,* No. 61, pp. 67–69. The semi-official Japanese (Kōain) version contends that the New Fourth Army was ordered to cross at Fangch'ang and T'ungling, and that when Yeh T'ing led his forces from Ching hsien toward south Kiangsu, in the opposite direction, the Nationalists attacked. See "Shinshigun no kaisan oyobi senkō shojijō" (The Dispersal of the New Fourth Army and All Preceding Events), *Jōhō,* No. 36 (February 15, 1941), pp. 16–17.

Another extremely interesting account is that prepared by the CCP Tunglu Committee (the Tunglu Committee was made up of the upper echelons of the Kiangsu, Chekiang, and Anhwei provincial Party committees plus the Shanghai Special Committee) to explain the New Fourth Army Incident to Shanghai mass organizations. It contends that the New Fourth Army obeyed the order to cross at Fangch'ang but was prevented from doing so by the presence of Japanese soldiers and a shortage of ammunition. The attack on the New Fourth Army is portrayed as part of a general conspiracy by the KMT to capitulate to the Japanese and to reopen the civil war; the Tunglu Committee explained that the incident would have come regardless of the New Fourth Army's moves. See "Shinshigun jiken to Chūkyō 'tōro' no dōkō" (The New Fourth Army Incident and Trends in the CCP "Tunglu" Committee), *Jōhō,* No. 37 (March 1, 1941), pp. 31–32.

For a valuable study that utilizes the numerous propaganda pamphlets published in English by both sides concerning the incident, as well as other Chinese materials, see Paul H. Kreisberg, "The New Fourth Army Incident and the United Front in China" (unpublished master's thesis in political science, Columbia University, 1952). See also the biography of Hsiang Ying in Boorman, ed., *Men and Politics in Modern China (Preliminary),* pp. 55–58.

41. Yeh T'ing remained in custody until March 4, 1946, when he was released from prison in Chungking. He died April 8, 1946, in an airplane crash while flying to Yenan.

42. The official statements from the Communists and the KMT charging each other with treason and insubordination, respectively, are contained in L. K. Rosinger, *China's Wartime Politics 1937–1944,* 2d ed. (Princeton, N.J., 1945), pp. 111–21.

43. Nohara Shiro, in *Gendai Chūgoku jiten,* p. 579. The title of this law was *Chih-hsien i-tang huo-tung pien-fa.*

44. *North Kiangsu Report,* pp. 40–41; Chiang Ke-fu, "The War of Resist-

ance to Japanese Aggression," *China Reconstructs,* VIII, No. 8 (August 1959), p. 31; and Hong Kong *Ta kung pao,* September 29, 1951, in U.S. Consul General, Hong Kong, *Survey of China Mainland Press,* No. 185, pp. 16–17.

45. Liu's article was dated March 20, 1941. It was written in the form of instructions to Ch'en P'i-hsien, secretary of the Central Kiangsu Area Party Committee; Su Yü, commander of the New Fourth Army's First Division after reorganization; Liu Yen, political commissar of the First Division; and Kuan Wen-wei, head of the North Kiangsu Administrative Committee. The article is translated by the Japanese as "Sochū mokuzen no keisei to ninmu" (Present Conditions and Tasks in Central Kiangsu), *Jōhō,* No. 53 (November 1, 1941), pp. 72–90. Ch'en P'i-hsien is a native of Fukien and served in Kiangsu throughout the war. In 1949 he was a member of the East China Military Administrative Committee, and he has served ever since as a high official in the Shanghai Party Committee. He was named an alternate member of the Eighth Central Committee in September 1956.

46. *North Kiangsu Report,* pp. 32, 143, 176; *Kaisan made no shinshigun,* p. 9. T'ao Yung is a native of Ssu hsien, Anhwei, on the north Kiangsu border. He served in the New Fourth Army until 1946, when he was assigned to the North Kiangsu Sea Defense Command. In 1952, he transferred to the People's Liberation Navy. He was appointed a vice-admiral in June 1956.

47. Chi Fang, b. 1894, is a graduate of Paoting Military Academy, and served as an instructor at Whampoa and as Chief of the Organization Section, General Political Department, during the Northern Expedition. He joined Li Ch'i-shen's Fukien People's Government in 1933, but went to Shanghai after it failed. During the Sino-Japanese war, he served in Kiangsu and Chekiang as a representative of Li Ch'i-shen. After joining with the New Fourth Army, he became a vice-chairman of the North Kiangsu Special Administrative Committee. In September 1949, he participated in the Chinese People's Political Consultative Conference as a representative of the "East China Liberated Area." In October 1949, he was appointed Vice-Minister of Communications. Since February 1955, he has held a high post in the Kiangsu Provincial Government.

48. *North Kiangsu Report,* pp. 32–36, 174.

49. *Ibid.,* pp. 7–8.

50. *Kaisan made no shinshigun,* p. 69.

51. *Jōhō,* No. 45, pp. 79–80; and Hong Kong *Ta kung pao,* September 29, 1951, *loc. cit.* (note 44).

52. Most of the command personnel of the reorganized New Fourth Army either remained in the People's Liberation Army or received comfortable bureaucratic positions after the Communists came to power in 1949. Chang Yün-i (native of Hainan Island, graduate of Paoting, and participant in the Northern Expedition and the Nanch'ang Rebellion) became chairman of the Kwangsi Provincial Government. He was a member of the Seventh and Eighth Central Committees. Su Yü remained in the Army, as did Huang K'o-ch'eng. Both men were alternate members of the Seventh Central Committee (1945) and became full members of the Eighth (1956). P'eng Hsüeh-feng died in Sep-

tember 1944, in the course of resisting the Japanese campaign against U.S. air bases in central China. Li Hsien-nien, a member of both the Seventh and Eighth Central Committees, remained in the Army. T'an Chen-lin, also a member of both Central Committees, became chairman of the Chekiang Provincial Government; and Chang Ting-ch'eng received the Provincial Chairmanship of Fukien. Chang was also a member of both the Seventh and Eighth Central Committees.

53. See U.S. War Dept., "The Chinese Communist Movement," p. 2434.

54. The Chinese Communists changed their designations of various parts of Kiangsu province at the time of the reorganization. Previously, Supei referred to all of the province north of the Yangtze, and Sunan meant south Kiangsu. In February 1941, the term Suchung was introduced to refer to central Kiangsu between Huaian and the Yangtze. Sunan retained its original meaning, but Supei was now restricted to the extreme northern part of the province. "Chūkyō kankei jutsugoshū" (A Collection of Technical Terms Relating to Chinese Communism), *Jōhō*, No. 61 (March 1, 1942), p. 88.

55. The North Huai Administrative Committee—the highest civilian governmental agency in this base area—came into being on August 23, 1941. This region was the most inaccessible to Japanese forces stationed in the Shanghai area, and it served as a sanctuary for Communist forces in north Kiangsu during the 1941 mopping-up. "Kaihoku-So-Kan henku gyōsei kōsho no setchi" (Establishment of the North Huai-Kiangsu-Anhwei Border Region Administrative Office), *Jōhō*, No. 60 (February 15, 1942), pp. 19–22.

56. U.S. War Dept., "The Chinese Communist Movement," p. 2434. Another guerrilla region was opened in east Chekiang in 1942, reportedly by Eighth Route Army troops, but no information is available on operations in this area.

57. *North Kiangsu Report*, p. 170. Li Ch'ang-chiang became Commander of Nanking's First Group Army.

58. The U.S. War Department offers an unconfirmed account of Han's final humiliation: "Chinese sources at Sian stated that while in Kiangsu, General Han Te-ch'in had been taken prisoner by units of the New Fourth Army following a clash late in 1941. He had subsequently been released and arrived at Sian in September 1943. Communist sources in Chungking confirm this, adding that General Han Te-ch'in had been released after he had signed an agreement to withdraw his troops from eastern Kiangsu north of the Yangtze River." "The Chinese Communist Movement," p. 2358.

59. *Jōhō*, No. 57 (January 1, 1942), pp. 2–3. See also *Jōhō*, No. 61, p. 68 (s.v. *"ch'ing-hsiang yün-tung,"* rural pacification movement). It should be noted in passing that virtually all the Kōain's data on the New Fourth Army in north Kiangsu, which constitute the basis of the present study, were captured during the two mopping-up campaigns of 1941.

60. Liu Shao-ch'i, "Present Conditions and Tasks in Central Kiangsu," *Chiang-Huai jih-pao* (Yench'eng), March 22, 1941, *Jōhō*, No. 53, p. 77.

61. *Ibid.*, p. 78.

62. *Ibid.*, p. 82.

63. *Ibid.*, p. 83.

64. A report delivered by Mao on October 12, 1938; it amplifies his three-stage war theory introduced in *On the Protracted War*. A useful edition of Mao's wartime works in Japanese is Gaimushō, Investigation Bureau, 5th Section, *Mō Taku-tō shuyō genronshū* (A Collection of the Important Speeches of Mao Tse-tung) (Tokyo, November 1948), 550 pp., with editorial introductions. *On the New Stage* is included, pp. 167–252.

65. Liu Shao-ch'i, *Jōhō*, No. 53, pp. 83–84.

66. *Ibid.*, pp. 84–85.

67. *Ibid.*, p. 85.

68. Particularly *North Kiangsu Report*. It should be noted that "Fourth District" does not imply that there were four or more subdivisions to the Suchung area. The Fourth Administrative District of Kiangsu (Chiang-su-sheng Ti-ssu Hsing-cheng-ch'ü) was the regional designation for the area served by the Fourth District's Administrative Inspector (Hsing-cheng Tu-ch'a Chuan-yüan) under the Kuomintang government. These administrative districts were similar to the provincial *chuan ch'ü* under the present Communist government. The wartime Suchung area included only one subdivision, the Fourth District; the relationships between Suchung headquarters at Yench'eng and Fourth District Headquarters at Chüehchiang were similar to those between Wut'ai-shan and central Hopei.

69. *North Kiangsu Report*, pp. 35, 240, 273–90.

70. *Ibid.*, p. 102.

71. Yuasa Seiichi, *Jōhō*, No. 38, pp. 66, 69. For other examples of Communist literacy training cards, together with a discussion of their anti-Japanese content, see Fukada Yūzō, *Shina kyōsangun no gensei* (The Present Strength of the Chinese Communist Army) (Tokyo, 1939), pp. 72–77. Fukada's book is an extremely valuable study of Communist operations in the early part of the war and of Chiang Kai-shek's anti-Communist campaign in Kiangsi. It is, however, written from a strongly nationalistic point of view (it is dedicated to the heroes of Yasukuni Shrine).

72. *North Kiangsu Report*, pp. 308–10. The romanization system used was the "Latinxua Sin Wenz" created by Ch'ü Ch'iu-pai and Wu Yü-chang in 1931. See People's Republic of China, *Reform of the Chinese Written Language* (Peking: Foreign Languages Press, 1958), p. 49.

73. *North Kiangsu Report*, p. 311. Newspapers and magazines are discussed on pp. 311–16. For a complete list of the names of the journals published by the six detachments of the New Fourth Army prior to the New Fourth Army Incident, see *Kaisan made no shinshigun*, pp. 61–62. This source also discusses several local papers published in the Fifth Detachment's territory that were seized during the "Three Rivers" mopping-up campaign.

74. *North Kiangsu Report*, pp. 315–16. "Sanmin-ism" is of course a reference to Sun Yat-sen's Three People's Principles (San-min-chu-i).

75. *Ibid.*, pp. 194, 247.

76. For the background of the Fifth Branch of K'angta, see *ibid.*, p. 294, and *Kaisan made no shinshigun*, p. 45. It would appear that former Eighth Route Army troops were the guiding influence in central China cadre education; the Sixth Detachment (P'eng Hsüeh-feng's Fourth Division after February 18, 1941) established a Fourth Branch of K'angta at Pengpu, Anhwei, on July 22, 1940. P'eng's troops were originally from the Eighth Route Army. For the Fourth Branch, see *Kaisan made no shinshigun*, pp. 47–48. For information on the original K'angta, see Kusano Fumio, *Shina henku no kenkyū*, pp. 77ff. The Second Branch of K'angta was located in Chin-Ch'a-Chi.

77. *Kaisan made no shinshigun*, p. 43.

78. *North Kiangsu Report*, pp. 294–95.

79. *Ibid.*, pp. 248, 295.

80. See *ibid.*, pp. 248–50, 298–99; *Kaisan made no shinshigun*, p. 48.

81. *North Kiangsu Report*, pp. 47–50.

82. "Occupation and Resistance in Kiangsu," *RRFE*, No. 63 (January 19, 1945), p. AB3.

83. *Ibid.*, pp. AB1–AB9.

84. Analyzed in great detail in *North Kiangsu Report*, pp. 53–61.

85. *Ibid.*, pp. 54, 58, 61. Of the 210 cadres in the Third Column, 130 were members of the Communist Party. Of these, 18 joined the Party in 1936 or earlier, 11 in 1937, 24 in 1938, 46 in 1939, and 26 in 1940; five are unaccounted for. The statistics on occupation immediately prior to entering the New Fourth Army are inconclusive, since a large number (53) were apparently KMT soldiers. However, 44 (the second highest total) described themselves as "students" before joining the Army, which was also the typical background of Yugoslav Partisan leaders.

CHAPTER SIX

1. Robert Lee Wolff, *The Balkans in Our Time* (Cambridge, Mass., 1956), pp. 195–99; Kapetanović, *Tito et les partisans*, p. 5; and Nicholas Halasz, *In the Shadow of Russia, Eastern Europe in the Post-War World* (New York, 1959), chap. 4. Standard Serbocroatian orthography is employed in this study with the exceptions of č, š, and ž, which are rendered ch, sh, and zh, respectively.

2. Ernst Kris, Hans Speier, *et al.*, *German Radio Propaganda* (London: Oxford University Press, 1944), p. 321.

3. *Ibid.*, p. 317.

4. Stephen Clissold, *Whirlwind, An Account of Marshal Tito's Rise to Power* (New York, 1949), pp. 1–15 (Clissold was a member of the British Military Mission to the Partisans); Ernst Halperin, *The Triumphant Heretic, Tito's Struggle Against Stalin* (London, 1958), pp. 14–15. It should be noted that parts of the Catholic clergy and of the Muslim population of the Independent State of Croatia were accomplices to the Ustashe murders (see Halasz, *In the Shadow of Russia*, pp. 128–29). The chief victims of the Ustashe were

Serbs, although other nationalities also were persecuted on occasion. Pavelić's policies were analogous to the anti-Jewish measures instituted by the Germans in other parts of Europe. Pavelić himself fled Zagreb on May 4, 1945, and died in Madrid in January 1960, of bullet wounds received three years earlier from an assassin. The number of Ustashe victims has been conservatively estimated at 800,000.

5. See Jasper Rootham (Major, British Army), *Miss Fire, The Chronicle of a British Mission to Mihailovich 1943–1944* (London, 1946), p. 21, who observed White Russians in eastern Serbia during the war. He notes that White Russians, wearing German uniforms, were used by the German command for occupation and police purposes and for punitive expeditions against guerrillas. In the east Serbia region Rootham also observed Russian prisoners of war from the Eastern Front being used by the Germans in Yugoslavia, although they often went over to the Chetniks (p. 127).

6. Wolff, *The Balkans in Our Time*, p. 204; Clissold, *Whirlwind*, p. 56; Evgueniyé Yourichitch, *Le Procès Tito-Mihailovitch* (Paris, 1950), p. 27 (on Zbor); and Kapetanović, *Tito et les partisans*, p. 19 (on Nedić).

7. See *Trial of the Major War Criminals Before the International Military Tribunal* (Nuremberg, 1947), XIV, 523–24, for Special SS Division "Prinz Eugen." According to Halperin, there were half a million German Yugoslavs before the war, but only 55,000 were left in 1948. *The Triumphant Heretic*, p. 3.

8. Branko Lazitch (Lazić), *La Tragédie du Général Draja Mihailovitch, Le conflit Mihailovitch-Tito et la politique des Alliés* ([Paris]: Editions du Haut-pays, n.d.).

9. *Trial of the Major War Criminals Before the International Military Tribunal* (Nuremberg, 1947), VII, 552; Clissold, *Whirlwind*, p. 66.

10. Rootham, *Miss Fire*, p. 31.

11. Clissold, *Whirlwind*, p. 57; Basil Davidson, *Partisan Picture* (Bedford, England, 1946), pp. 82–93 (Davidson was an English liaison officer to the Partisans who was parachuted into central Bosnia, August 16, 1943); Halperin, *The Triumphant Heretic*, p. 18; Rootham, *Miss Fire*, p. 57. Overseas propaganda concerning Mihailović in the early years of the war greatly exaggerated his accomplishments and his following. It was comparable in this respect to overseas propaganda concerning Chiang Kai-shek in the same period. An example both of this exaggeration and of Serbian nationalism is found in K. St. Pavlowitch, *The Struggle of the Serbs* (London, 1943): "It should be realized that the Serbs never fought for hegemony, nor are they doing so now. Their central position among Southern Slavs, however, demands that they should be strong because a strong Yugoslavia is impossible without a powerful Serbia" (p. 3). The Foreword to this pamphlet is written, significantly, by Field Marshal Lord Milne, the commander at Salonika during World War I. The Preface states that "All author's profits on the sale of this book will be given to General Mihailović's Fund for National Defense."

12. Membership statistics are from Branko Lazitch, *Les Partis communistes d'Europe, 1919–1955* (Paris, 1956), p. 149. Also see Lazitch, *Tito et la révolution yougoslave* (Paris, 1957), pp. 9–15.

13. The standard biographies of Tito are Vladimir Dedijer, *Tito Speaks* (London, 1953), and Fitzroy H. Maclean, *Tito* (New York, 1957; published in England under the title *Disputed Barricade, The Life and Times of Josip Broz-Tito, Marshal of Jugoslavia*). Dedijer was official historian of the YCP until after the denunciation of Djilas (January 1954), whom Dedijer supported. Before the war, Dedijer was a correspondent for the Belgrade newspaper *Politika*. For a list of Yugoslav leaders who were liquidated between 1936 and 1938, see Lazitch, *Les Partis communistes d'Europe,* pp. 146–49.

14. Halperin, *The Triumphant Heretic,* p. 9. Lazitch comments further: "These students did not come from the big bourgeoisie or from the large urban centers, for neither the one nor the other existed; they came from the small towns and villages." *Tito et la révolution yougoslave,* p. 29. See also pp. 18, 36–37.

15. Lazitch, *Tito et la révolution yougoslave,* p. 24; *Les Partis communistes d'Europe,* p. 145.

16. *Tito et la révolution yougoslave,* pp. 65–66; Halperin, *The Triumphant Heretic,* p. 190.

17. Lazitch, *Tito et la révolution yougoslave,* p. 25. The Partisan cadres were not, of course, *all* from Belgrade University or trained in Spain, nor were they all Communists. Arso Jovanović, a former regular officer in the Royal Yugoslav Army, was the Partisans' chief of staff in over-all command of military operations; and Tito's personal staff included a Serbian Orthodox priest, Father Vlado Zechević, who had left the Chetniks to join the Partisans. See Fitzroy Maclean, *Escape to Adventure* (Boston, 1950), p. 228. (Brigadier Maclean headed the English military mission to Tito's headquarters, September 1943–March 1945.)

18. Lazitch, *Tito et la révolution yougoslave,* p. 43.

19. Kapetanović, *Tito et les partisans,* p. 11.

20. Kardelj is the Yugoslav Liu Shao-ch'i, both in the sense of his interest in Marxist theory and in that, during the war, he was in command in Slovenia—a relatively separated area analogous to the New Fourth Army's zone of operations. He was in the USSR from November 1934 to January 1937 as a student and later as a teacher at the Comintern school. On November 29, 1943, he was named Vice-President of the Provisional Government set up at Jajce, and on April 6, 1951, he acquired the additional post of Minister of Foreign Affairs.

21. Kapetanović, *Tito et les partisans,* p. 34.

22. Wolff, *The Balkans in Our Time,* pp. 208–9; and Bobrowski, *La Yougoslave socialiste,* p. 35.

23. Clissold, *Whirlwind,* pp. 65–67; and Vladimir Dedijer, *With Tito Through the War, Partisan Diary, 1941–1944* (London, 1951), pp. 42–45.

24. Davidson actually compares the Partisans' evacuation into Bosnia with "the famous march of the Chinese Eighth Route Army." *Partisan Picture,* p. 94.

25. Dedijer, *With Tito Through the War,* p. 42.

26. *Ibid.,* pp. 67–68. On this same point, Dedijer quotes a speech made by Djilas at a Party meeting at Focha, March 10, 1942: "We must not allow anybody to force us into a class war—that is what the invaders want—we are

carrying on, and must do so, a national people's liberation war" (p. 75). One should note carefully what Djilas is, in effect, saying: class warfare (i.e., Marxism) is a policy of defeat, since it plays into the hands of the Germans; only a policy of nationalism can succeed. And Djilas is a Communist.

27. Dedijer himself was occasionally struck by the similarities between Partisan operations and certain events in China about which he knew. On March 6, 1943, faced with a difficult crossing of the River Neretva, Dedijer recalls the crossing of the Tatu (he calls it Tata) by the Red Army on the Long March (p. 285), and on another occasion (pp. 145–46) he writes, "Daddy Mosha (Piyade) has issued stern instructions to all brigades how to behave when passing through any village. The honor of the Partisans must be preserved. 'The people are water, a partisan is a fish; fish cannot live without water.' That principle of the Chinese partisans holds here too." Piyade was a Party intellectual who spent most of the 1920's and 1930's in prison, where, incidentally, he studied Chinese; he also translated Marx into Serbian. For other comparisons with China by a high-ranking Yugoslav Communist leader, see Svetozar Vukmanović, *How and Why the People's Liberation Struggle of Greece Met with Defeat* (London: Yugoslav Information Service, 1950), pp. 16, 29; and also Bobrowski, *La Yougoslave socialiste*, p. 35.

28. Rootham, *Miss Fire*, pp. 123, 183–84.

29. *Ibid*, pp. 112, 152–53; Maclean, *Escape to Adventure*, p. 309.

30. Wolff, *The Balkans in Our Time*, p. 213.

31. Winston S. Churchill, *Closing the Ring* (Vol. V of *The Second World War*) (Boston, 1951), p. 463.

32. Lazitch, *Tito et la Révolution yougoslave*, p. 95.

33. Federated People's Republic of Yugoslavia, *Stenographic Record and Documents from the Trial of Dragoljub-Draza Mihailović*, pp. 350–51. Punctuation slightly modified.

34. Dedijer, *With Tito Through the War*, p. 257. For the offensives in general, see Armija Vojno-istoriski Institut, Yugoslavia (The Military-Historical Institute of the Federated People's Republic of Yugoslavia), *The War Effort of Yugoslavia, 1941-1945* (Belgrade, n.d. [ca. 1955]), *passim*. Tito himself commented on the German assaults: "Far from intimidating our people and our fighters, the great attacks which the troops of occupation launched against the main body of our forces had a stimulating effect. Feats of mass heroism performed in these battles will buttress our peoples' pride for many centuries to come." J. B. Tito, *The Yugoslav Peoples Fight to Live* (New York: The United Committee of South-Slavic Americans, 1944), p. 27.

35. Kapetanović, *Tito et les partisans*, p. 51.

36. Clissold, *Whirlwind*, p. 166.

37. Kapetanović, *Tito et les partisans*, p. 37, n.21.

38. Bobrowski, *La Yougoslave socialiste*, p. 38, n.6.

39. Dedijer, *With Tito Through the War*, p. 68.

40. For size of the Youth Organization, see *ibid.*, p. 251 (entry of December 28, 1942); on the Youth Organization and the Pioniri, see Clissold, *Whirlwind*, pp. 182–83. The Youth Organization was founded on the nucleus of the League

of Communist Youth (SKOJ); with the outbreak of war this society was transformed into a united-front mass organization with the title "United Alliance of Yugoslav Anti-Fascist Youth" (USAOJ).

41. Halperin, *The Triumphant Heretic*, p. 30.

42. Wolff, *The Balkans in Our Time*, pp. 210–12; Clissold, *Whirlwind*, pp. 177–80; and Dedijer, *With Tito Through the War*, p. 234.

CHAPTER SEVEN

1. For the relation between Kao's ouster and subsequent suicide, on the one hand, and Soviet policy in Manchuria, on the other, see Kuo Ping-chia's analysis in *China, New Age and New Outlook*, rev. ed. (London, 1960), pp. 150–51.

2. "Yugoslav Communist Theory," *The American Slavic and East European Review*, XIX (1960), 44.

3. Thomas T. Hammond, "The Origins of National Communism," *Virginia Quarterly Review*, XXXIV (1958), 282.

4. Karl W. Deutsch, "Social Mobilization and Political Development," *American Political Science Review*, LV (1961), 494.

5. For a fascinating insight into the actual act of creating a national myth for areas in which social mobilization is occurring, see James Baldwin, "Princes and Powers," in *Nobody Knows My Name* (New York, 1961), pp. 13–55. Baldwin, one of America's leading novelists and essayists, reports on the Congress of Negro-African Writers and Artists (Le Congrès des Ecrivains et Artistes Noirs), Paris, September 19–22, 1956.

6. For a study of the continuing acumen of allegedly "brainwashed" intellectuals, see Roderick MacFarquhar, ed., *The Hundred Flowers Campaign and the Chinese Intellectuals* (New York, 1960); and my "An Intellectual Weed in the Socialist Garden: The Case of Ch'ien Tuan-sheng," *China Quarterly*, April–June 1961, pp. 29–52.

7. *Mao's China, Party Reform Documents, 1942–1944*, p. xxxix.

8. Brandt, *et al.*, *A Documentary History of Chinese Communism*, p. 374.

9. Compton, *Mao's China*, pp. 12–13.

10. Persons familiar with the academic controversy in America concerning Maoism may be surprised at my contention that Maoism flowered during the Sino-Japanese war. Thus, in order to avoid confusion, the following points should be mentioned:

(1) Most studies of Maoism have concentrated upon its earliest manifestations—the rural-base Red Army policy of the Kiangsi period—and have ignored the major divide in CCP history represented by the Long March. They overlook the fact that the wartime Communist-peasant alliance, *which actually brought the CCP to power*, bore no relation to the earlier policy of "land to the peasants."

(2) There has been considerable discussion about Mao's "originality" in the Kiangsi period and later. A near-perfect precedent for Mao's Kiangsi alliance with the peasantry may be found in Lenin (see Adam Ulam, *The Unfinished Revolution, An Essay on the Sources of Influence of Marxism and Communism*

(New York, 1960), pp. 182, 184). However, even if Mao has no objective claim to originality, the discussion of his originality has overlooked the more significant fact that the Chinese themselves hail him as an innovator. In order to understand this development, Maoism should be regarded in terms of Chinese national myth.

(3) Part of the confusion about the origins of Maoism reflects an uncritical acceptance of the CCP's own *ex post facto* apotheosis of Mao. Party ideologists began publishing Mao's works after 1949 and extending backward in time his title to the position of Marxist-Leninist sage. This is in accordance with the Stalinist tradition of making the leader always appear to be "correct," and it strengthens Maoist ideology as national myth. But in order to make Mao a sage, Party history has had to be rewritten for the period before 1935, when Mao became undisputed leader of the Party. See "Appendix: Resolutions on Some Questions in the History of Our Party," adopted by the Seventh Congress, April 20, 1945, in *Selected Works of Mao Tse-tung*, IV, 171–218.

For an example of fully developed Maoism in its role as state ideology, see the handbook *Hsüeh-hsi Mao Tse-tung ssu-hsiang* (Study the Thought of Mao Tse-tung) (Hong Kong, 1960), containing articles by Ch'en Po-ta, Chiang Wei-ch'ing, Su Hsing, Li Fu-ch'un, Shu T'ung, and others on how to study and understand Mao's works. For the controversy on Maoism, see K. A. Wittfogel, "The Legend of Maoism," *China Quarterly,* January–March 1960, pp. 72–86, and April–June 1960, pp. 16–34; and B. I. Schwartz, "The Legend of the 'Legend of Maoism,'" *ibid.* (April–June 1960), pp. 35–42. The most important point in any discussion of Maoism is that without the Japanese invasion it would always have remained irrelevant.

11. Josip Broz Tito, *Tito Speaks* (London: The United South Slav Committee, June 28, 1944), p. 14 (speech delivered at the Second Meeting of AVNOJ, Jajce, November 29, 1943).

12. See Mosha Piyade, member of the YCP politburo, *About the Legend that the Yugoslav Uprising Owed Its Existence to Soviet Assistance* (London: Yugoslav Information Service, 1950).

13. *Yugoslavia's Way, The Program of the League of Communists of Yugoslavia* (adopted by the Seventh Congress of the League of Communists of Yugoslavia, Ljubljana, April 22–26, 1958), trans. Stoyan Pribechevich (New York: All Nations Press, 1958), p. xxi, 230. For a complete study of Yugoslav national Communism, see F. W. Neal, *Titoism in Action, The Reforms in Yugoslavia After 1948* (Berkeley, Calif., 1958).

14. See my "Civilian Loyalties and Guerrilla Conflict," *World Politics*, XIV (1962), pp. 646–61.

15. *Mao Tse-tung on Guerrilla Warfare*, S. B. Griffith, trans. (New York, 1961), p. 44.

16. "The Present Situation and Our Tasks," *Selected Works* (Peking, 1961), IV, 162. This is the official English translation of Volume IV of Mao's works, and must be distinguished from the *four*-volume translation, published in London, of the first *three* Chinese volumes.

Bibliography

Bibliographical information is supplied under the following headings:

I. JAPANESE ARCHIVES
(arranged chronologically)

A. Army Ministry (Rikugunshō) (Library of Congress)

North China Area Army. *Hokushi sakusengun kōhō chiiki no gyōsei shidō yōryō no ken* (Outline of Administrative Directives on Administration of Areas behind Battle Lines in North China), September 23, 1937, *Rikushi mitsu dai nikki*, Vol. 8, 1937, No. 99 [T878].

North China Area Army, Chief of Staff. *Chian iji jisshi yōryō no ken tsūchō* (Instruction on Principles for Carrying out Peace Preservation), December 21, 1937, *Rikushi mitsu dai nikki*, Vol. 15, 1938, No. 2 [T887].

Military Attaché, Shanghai. *Kokkyō ryōtō kōnichi kyūkoku shuchō* (Anti-Japanese National Salvation Statements of the KMT and CCP), *Rikushi mitsu dai nikki*, Vol. 15, 1938, No. 138 [T888].

Okabe Naosaburo, Chief of Staff, North China Area Army. *Hokushi ni okeru kyōsantō katsudō jōkyō no ken hōkoku* (Report on the General State of Communist Party Activities in North China), April 14, 1938, *Rikushi mitsu dai nikki*, Vol. 18, 1938, No. 177 [T891].

Terauchi Corps, Chief of Staff. *Kyōsangun no seijibu ni tsuite* (Concerning the Political Department of the Communist Army), November 8, 1938, *Rikushi mitsu dai nikki*, Vol. 64 (of 73 volumes), 1938, No. 3 [T912].

Sugiyama Corps, Pacification Unit. *Sekishoku kōnichi ken seifu no kenchi gyō-*

sei: Sanseishō Wajunken chihō kyōsan chiku jōkyō chōsa hōkokusho (Hsien Administration by Red Anti-Japanese Hsien Governments: Report of an Investigation of the Situation in the Region of Hoshun Hsien, Shansi), June 5, 1939, *Rikushi ju mitsu dai nikki,* Vol. 35, 1939, No. 86 [T934].

Central China Expeditionary Army, Headquarters. *Chūshi hakengun taikyō shisō kōsaku jisshi hōkoku* (Report on Actions Taken by the Central China Expeditionary Army Against Communist Thought), July 10, 1939, *Rikushi ju mitsu dai nikki,* Vol. 48, 1939, No. 54 [T940].

Sugiyama Corps, Pacification Unit. *Sanseishō Wajunken chihō kyōsan chiku jōkyō hōkokusho: minshū kōnichi kakudantai no naiyō oyobi kambu kyōiku* (Report on Communist Areas in Hoshun hsien, Shansi: Anti-Japanese Mass Organizations and Leadership Education), August 8, 1939, *Rikushi ju mitsu dai nikki,* Vol. 53, 1939, No. 107, Part IV of Book IV [T944].

Sugiyama Corps, Chief of Staff. *Shina himitsu kessha gaikan* (General View of Chinese Secret Societies), August 25, 1939, *Rikushi ju mitsu dai nikki,* Vol. 60, 1939, No. 34, Part IV [T952].

Central Committee for the Extermination of Communism, Kasahara Yukio, Chairman. *Hokushi mekkyō iinkai kitei* (Rules of the North China Communist Extermination Committee), September 26, 1939, *Rikushi ju mitsu dai nikki,* Vol. 66, 1939, No. 71 [T957].

Tada Corps, Headquarters. *Kyōsan hachirogun no Kitō chiku ni okeru kōnichi kakusaku jōkyō* (Anti-Japanese Policies of the Communist Eighth Route Army in East Hopei), November 27, 1939, *Rikushi ju mitsu dai nikki,* Vol. 74, 1939, No. 183, Part IV [T970].

"Ko" Group Army. *Kita Shina hōmen kyōsangun gaikyō yōzu* (Outline Map of the Disposition of the Communist Army in North China), January 13–17, 1940, *Rikushi mitsu dai nikki,* Vol. 2, 1940, No. 133 [T977].

Itagaki Seishirō, Chief of the General Staff, Japanese Expeditionary Force in China. *Kokkyō sōkoku ni kan suru kansatsu* (Observations Regarding Kuomintang-Communist Rivalry), March 22, 1940, *Rikushi mitsu dai nikki,* Vol. 13, 1940, No. 86 [T983].

Tada Corps, Headquarters. *Kahoku ni okeru shisōsen shidō yōryō* (Outline of Instructions Regarding Ideological Warfare in North China), April 20, 1940, *Rikushi mitsu dai nikki,* Vol. 18, 1940, No. 150 [T986].

Central Committee for the Extermination of Communism, Research Section. *Satsunan henchi tainichi sekka kōsaku jittai chōsa hōkokusho* (Investigation Report on the Current Situation with Regard to Anti-Japanese Communizing Activities in the South Chahar Border Area), July 1940, *Rikushi mitsu dai nikki,* Vol. 40, 1940, No. 137, Part IV [T993].

―――. *Sanseishō seihokubu hijō chōsa hōkokusho* (Report on Investigation of Bandit Situation in Northwest Shansi), July 1940, *Rikushi mitsu dai nikki,* Vol. 40, 1940, No. 138, Part IV [T994].

―――. *Dokuritsu daiichishi ni tsuite: Kisei hōkokusho no ni* (Concerning the First Independent Division: West Hopei Report), July 1940, *Rikushi mitsu dai nikki,* Vol. 40, 1940, No. 140 [T996].

Central Committee for the Extermination of Communism, Research Section. *Kyōsangun naibu ni okeru butaiin narabi ni tōin no shojōkyō* (Situation Concerning Military and Party Personnel in the Communist Army), July 1940, *Rikushi mitsu dai nikki,* Vol. 40, 1940, No. 141, Part IV [T997].

———. *Kichū-ku chūbu chihō ni okeru Chūkyō no minshū kakutoku kōsaku jitsujō chōsa hōkoku* (Investigation Report on the State of Communist Efforts to Win the Masses in the Central Section of the Central Hopei Area), May 1940, *Rikushi mitsu dai nikki,* Vol. 40, 1940, No. 142, Part IV [T999].

Noboru Group Army, Staff. *Shō Kai-seki no kyōsangun tōbatsu narabi ni kokumintō no bōkyō taisaku no gaiyō* (Outline of Chiang Kai-shek's Suppression of the Communist Army and the Kuomintang's Defensive Measures Against Communism), February 1941, *Rikushi mitsu dai nikki,* Vol. 8, 1941 [T1000].

First Patrol Regiment, North China Special Patrol Garrison. *Kitō tōbu chiku dai ikki sakusen sentō shōhō* (First Phase Battle Report: Eastern Area of East Hopei), September 6, 1943–June 10, 1944, *Kita Shina tokubetsu keibitai hōkoku No. 1* (North China Special Police Unit Report No. 1) [T1249].

B. *Asia Development Board (Kōain)* (*East Asiatic Library, University of California, Berkeley*)

Kōain, Central China Liaison Bureau. *Sohoku kyōsan chiku jitsujō chōsa hōkokusho* (Investigation Report of the Current Situation in the North Kiangsu Communist Region). [Shanghai]: June 16, 1941.

———. *Kaisan made no shinshigun* (The New Fourth Army to the Time of its Dispersal). Shanghai: October 1941.

Kōain, Political Affairs Bureau. "Kitō chiku ni okeru kōnichigun" (Anti-Japanese Army in the East Hopei Region), *Jōhō,* No. 3 (October 1, 1939), pp. 59–62.

———. "Chūgoku kyōsantō no kinjō" (Recent Facts Concerning the Chinese Communist Party), *Jōhō,* No. 7 (December 1, 1939), pp. 31–49.

———. "Chūkyō Kahoku saikō kanbu rinji kinkyū kaigi" (Extraordinary Conference of High CCP Leaders in North China), *Jōhō,* No. 9 (January 1, 1940), pp. 31–44.

———. "Kyōsangun nai ni okeru seiji kunren" (Political Training Within the Communist Army), *Jōhō,* No. 10 (January 15, 1940), pp. 65–87.

———. "Daihachirogun no yurai to honshitsu" (Origins and Essential Qualities of the Eighth Route Army), *Jōhō,* No. 11 (February 1, 1940), pp. 19–41.

———. "Kokkyō ryōgun no sōkoku ni tsuite" (Regarding the Clashes Between the Nationalist and Communist Armies), *Jōhō,* No. 13 (March 1, 1940), pp. 3–8.

———. "Kokkyō masatsu mondai ni kan suru shiryō" (Materials Concerning the Problem of Nationalist-Communist Friction), *Jōhō*, No. 15 (April 1, 1940), pp. 1–48.

Kōain, Political Affairs Bureau. "Yūgeki konkyochi ni okeru Chūkyō no kensetsu kōsaku" (Establishment Work by the Chinese Communists in the Guerrilla Bases), *Jōho*, No. 18 (May 15, 1940), pp. 73–77.

———. "Jūkei seiken kōsen shiji no teichō-ka to kokkyō kankei no shin dōkō" (Weakening of Support for the Resistance War by the Chungking Government and New Trends in KMT-CCP Relations), *Jōhō*, No. 21 (July 1, 1940), pp. 31–32.

———. "Saikin no Chūgoku kyōsantō" (Latest News of the Chinese Communist Party), *Jōhō*, No. 22 (July 15, 1940), pp. 5–16.

———. "Shinkokumin seifu kanka no hokō seido," (The Pao Chia System Under the Jurisdiction of the New National Government), *Jōhō*, No. 22 (July 15, 1940), pp. 37–48.

———. "Sohoku kokkyō shōtotsu ni kan suru shinshigun tsūden" (New Fourth Army Telegram Concerning the KMT-CCP Clash in North Kiangsu), *Jōhō*, No. 30 (November 15, 1940), pp. 53–55.

———. Hatano Ken'ichi. "Kokkyō masatsu ni kan suru chōsa" (An Inquiry Concerning KMT-CCP Friction), *Jōhō*, No. 31 (December 1, 1940), pp. 1–29.

———. "Shin-Satsu-Ki henku no jōkyō" (The General Situation in the Chin-Ch'a-Chi Border Region), *Jōhō*, No. 35 (February 1, 1941), pp. 1–72.

———. "Shinshigun no kaisan oyobi senkō shojijō" (The Dispersal of the New Fourth Army and All Preceding Events), *Jōhō*, No. 36 (February 15, 1941), pp. 13–100.

———. "Shinshigun jiken to Chūkyō 'tōro' no dōkō" (The New Fourth Army Incident and Trends in the CCP "Tunglu" Committee), *Jōhō*, No. 37 (March 1, 1941), pp. 31–32.

———. "Kōnan kōnichi giyūgun no enkaku to genjō" (The History of the Kiangnan Anti-Japanese Patriotic Army and Its Present Condition), *Jōhō*, No. 37 (March 1, 1941), pp. 37–43.

———. Ho Lung. "Shinseihoku no konjaku" (Past and Present in Northwest Shansi), *Jōhō*, No. 38 (March 15, 1941), pp. 31–39.

———. Yuasa Seiichi. "Chūshi ni okeru kyōsantōgun jōsei" (The Communist Military Situation in Central China), *Jōhō*, No. 38 (March 15, 1941), pp. 41–84.

———. "Shinshigun no nōson seinen kōsaku" (New Fourth Army Work with Village Youths), *Jōhō*, No. 40 (April 15, 1941), pp. 73–81.

———. Hatano Ken'ichi. "Saikin Chūkyō kankei nenpyō" (Recent Chronology of Chinese Communism), *Jōhō*, No. 42 (May 15, 1941), pp. 73–83.

———. "Shinshigun no seiji kōsaku soshiki kōyō sōan" (The New Fourth Army's Draft Outline of the Organization of Political Work), *Jōhō*, No. 43 (June 1, 1941), pp. 19–45.

———. "Shinshigun no minshū undō kōsaku kōju teikō" (The New Fourth Army's Teaching Guide for Mass Movement Work), *Jōhō*, No. 44 (June 15, 1941), pp. 1–52.

Kōain, Political Affairs Bureau. "Shinshigun jiken kyūmei no shoshiryō" (Various Materials for an Investigation of the New Fourth Army Incident), *Jōhō*, No. 45 (July 1, 1941), pp. 55–80.

————. "Shinshigun kankei jōhō" (Intelligence Relating to the New Fourth Army), *Jōhō*, No. 51 (October 1, 1941), pp. 62–73.

————. Liu Shao-ch'i. "Sochū mokuzen no keisei to ninmu" (Present Conditions and Tasks in Central Kiangsu), *Jōhō*, No. 53 (November 1, 1941), pp. 72–90.

————. Ch'en Yi and Liu Shao-ch'i. "Kannan jiken ato ni okeru shinshigun jōkyō" (The Situation of the New Fourth Army After the South Anhwei Incident), *Jōhō*, No. 53 (November 1, 1941), pp. 91–97.

————. "Shinshigun no nōson kōsaku senden kyōiku zairyō" (Propaganda and Educational Materials for New Fourth Army Work in Villages), *Jōhō*, No. 55 (December 1, 1941), pp. 73–85.

————. "Shinshigun no rentai seiji kōsaku" (Political Work at the Company Level in the New Fourth Army), *Jōhō*, No. 56 (December 15, 1941), pp. 89–97.

————. "Chūgoku kyōsantō no genkyō, dōkō narabi ni taisaku" (The Present Condition of the Chinese Communist Party: Trends and Countermeasures), *Jōhō*, No. 57 (January 1, 1942), pp. 1–16.

————. "Yūgekisen no dōkō" (Trends in Guerrilla Warfare), *Jōhō*, No. 58 (January 15, 1942), pp. 1–24.

————. "Hachirogun 'shin senshi tokuhon' " (The Eighth Route Army's "New Soldier's Reader"), *Jōhō*, No. 59 (February 1, 1942), pp. 28–52.

————. "Kaihoku-So-Kan henku gyōsei kōsho no setchi" (Establishment of the North Huai-Kiangsu-Anhwei Border Region Administrative Office), *Jōhō*, No. 60 (February 15, 1942), pp. 19–22.

————. "Chūkyō kankei jutsugo-shū" (A Collection of Technical Terms Relating to Chinese Communism), *Jōhō*, No. 61 (March 1, 1942), pp. 67–90.

————. "Shinshigun daigoshi no hanseigō kōsaku" (Anti-Peace Movement Work of the Fifth Division, New Fourth Army), *Jōhō*, No. 64 (April 15, 1942), pp. 25–27.

————. "Daitōasen to Chūkyō no Kōso ni okeru katsudō" (The Greater East Asia War and the Activities of the CCP in Kiangsu), *Jōhō*, No. 66 (May 15, 1942), pp. 41–59.

————. Hatano Ken'ichi. "Chūkyō san-hachi-nen shi" (A History of Chinese Communism in 1938), Part I: *Jōhō*, No. 64 (April 15, 1942), pp. 72–98; Part II: *Jōhō*, No. 66 (May 15, 1942), pp. 82–110; Part III: *Jōhō*, No. 67 (June 1, 1942), pp. 61–87.

————. "Chūkyō Kitō chiku gyōsei kikō" (Administrative Structure of the Chinese Communist East Hopei Area), *Jōhō*, No. 68 (June 15, 1942), pp. 102–4.

C. Kaikōsha kiji (Bōeichō senshishitsu, Tokyo)

Col. Matsui Gennosuke. "Hokushi no kinjō" (The Present Situation in North China), *Kaikōsha kiji*, No. 745 (October 1936), pp. 23–35.

Yaginuma Takeo. "Hokushi senbuhan no katsuyaku" (Activities of North China Pacification Squads), *Kaikōsha kiji*, No. 778 (July 1939), pp. 91–97.

Kaikōsha Editorial Board. "Shina ni okeru saikin no chian jōkyō" (The Recent Peace Preservation Situation in China), *Kaikōsha kiji*, No. 784 (January 1940), pp. 79–87.

Lt. Col. Shigeda Mitsugi. "Chūka minkoku shinminkai no katsudō to sono jisseki" (The Activities and Accomplishments of the Chinese Republic's New Citizens' Association), *Kaikōsha kiji*, No. 788 (May 1940), pp. 73–96.

Kaikōsha Editorial Board. "Rokōkyō jiken no kaiko" (Recollections of the Marco Polo Bridge Incident), *Kaikōsha kiji*, No. 802 (July 1941), pp. 39–66.

————. "Chūshi ni okeru seikyō kōsaku ni tsuite" (Concerning the Rural Pacification Work in Central China), *Kaikōsha kiji*, No. 802 (July 1941), pp. 67–71.

————. "Shina jihen keika nisshi" (Daily Record of the China Incident), *Kaikōsha kiji*, No. 802 (July 1941), pp. 73–80.

D. Other Archives (East Asiatic Library, University of California, Berkeley)

Army Ministry, Office of the General Staff. *Shina kyōsantō undō shi* (History of the Chinese Communist Party Movement). Tokyo: March 1931.

Army Ministry. *Shina kyōsangun ni tsuite* (Concerning the Chinese Communist Army). Tokyo: Rikugunshō shimbun-han, November 1936.

Gaimushō (Foreign Ministry), Intelligence Department. *Chūgoku kyōsantō ichi-ku-san-roku nen shi* (History of the Chinese Communist Party During 1936). Hatano Ken'ichi, ed. Tokyo: February 1937.

————, Investigation Department, Fifth Section. *Mō Taku-tō shuyō genron-shū* (A Collection of Important Speeches of Mao Tse-tung). Tokyo: November 1948.

Tada Corps, Chief of Staff. *Chūgoku kyōsantō undō no kaisetsu* (Explanation of the Chinese Communist Party Movement). [Peiping]: February 17, 1941.

Japanese Embassy, Peking. *Chūkyō dōkō jittai chōsa; Kahoku shō Hōteidō Ankokuken Daisanku Go-jin-kyō o chūshin to suru* (Investigation of Trends and Conditions in Chinese Communism: Focus on Wujench'iao, Third District, Ankuo Hsien, Paoting Tao, Hopei Province). Peking: November 18, 1943.

Greater East Asia Ministry, General Affairs Bureau. *Chūkyō gaisetsu* (Outline of Chinese Communism). Tokyo: July 1944.

II. OTHER CHINESE AND JAPANESE SOURCES

Chūgoku Kenkyū-sho (China Research Institute). *Gendai Chūgoku jiten* (Dictionary of Modern China). Tokyo: Iwasaki Shoten, October 1959.

Ch'en Ts'ung-i. *Wan-nan shih-pien ch'ien-hou* (Before and After the South Anhwei Incident). Shanghai: Hua-tung jen-min ch'u-pan-she (East China People's Publishing Co.), 1950.

Eighteenth Group Army, General Political Department. *K'ang-chan pa-nien-*

lai ti pa-lu-chün yü hsin-ssu-chün (The Eighth Route Army and the New Fourth Army Through Eight Years of the Resistance War). [Yenan]: March 1945.

Fujiwara Akira. *Gunjishi* (History of Military Affairs). Tokyo: Tōyō keizai shinbōsha, 1961.

Fukada Yūzō. *Shina kyōsangun no gensei* (The Present Strength of the Chinese Communist Army). Tokyo: Kaizōsha, 1939.

Hata Ikuhiko. *Nitchū sensō shi* (History of the Sino-Japanese War). Tokyo: Kawade shobō shinsha, 1961.

Ishikawa Tadao. *Chūgoku kyōsantō shi kenkyū* (Studies in the History of the Chinese Communist Party). Tokyo: Keiō University Press, 1959.

Kanki Haruo, ed. *Sankō, Nihonjin no Chūgoku ni okeru sensō hanzai no kokuhaku* (The Three-All Policy: Japanese Confessions of War Crimes in China). Tokyo: Kōbunsha, 1957.

Kasumigaseki Society. *Gendai Chūgoku jinmei jiten* (Biographical Dictionary of Modern China). Tokyo: Kōnan shoin, 1957.

Kusano Fumio. *Shina henku no kenkyū* (The Study of China's Border Regions). Tokyo: Kokuminsha, 1944.

Mao Tse-tung. *Mao Tse-tung hsüan-chi* (Selected Works of Mao Tse-tung). Volume IV. Peking: Jen-min ch'u-pan-she, 1960.

Sano Manabu. *Kyōsanshugi sensōron; Marukusu-Renin-Mō Taku-tō no sensōkan no bunseki* (Communist Theory of War: Analyses of the Views of Marx, Lenin, and Mao Tse-tung on War). Tokyo: Aoyama shoin, 1952.

Wang Ching-wei. *Nihon to tazusaete* (Accompanied by Japan). Osaka: Asahi shimbun, 1941.

III. WESTERN WORKS

A. General

Baron, Salo W. *Modern Nationalism and Religion.* New York: Meridian, 1960.

Boorman, H. L., ed. *Men and Politics in Modern China (Preliminary).* New York: Columbia University Press, 1960.

Brandt, Conrad, *et al. A Documentary History of Chinese Communism.* London: Allen and Unwin, 1952.

Brzezinski, Zbigniew. "Party Controls in the Soviet Army," *The Journal of Politics,* Vol. XIV (1952), No. 4.

Carleton, William G. "The New Nationalism," *Virginia Quarterly Review,* Vol. XXVI (1950), No. 3.

Carlson, Evans F. *The Chinese Army.* New York: Institute of Pacific Relations, 1940.

———. *Twin Stars of China.* New York: Dodd, Mead, 1940.

Carr, Edward H. *Nationalism and After.* London: Macmillan, 1945.

Chang, C. M. "Communism and Nationalism in China," *Foreign Affairs,* Vol. XXVIII (1950), No. 4.

Chao Kuo-chun. *Agrarian Policy of the Chinese Communist Party, 1921–1959.* Bombay: Asia Publishing House, 1960.

Chassin, Lionel Max. *L'Ascension de Mao Tse-tung (1921–1945).* Paris: Payot, 1953.
——. *La Conquête de la Chine par Mao Tse-tung (1945–1949).* Paris: Payot, 1952.
Chiang Ke-fu. "The War of Resistance to Japanese Aggression," *China Reconstructs,* Vol. VIII (1959), No. 8.
Ch'ien Tuan-sheng. "Wartime Local Government in China," *Pacific Affairs,* Vol. XVI (1943), No. 4.
Chorley, Katherine M. *Armies and the Art of Revolution.* London: Faber and Faber, 1943.
Chou Erh-fu. "Dr. Bethune—Our True Friend," *China Reconstructs,* Vol. VIII (1959), No. 11.
Compton, Boyd. *Mao's China, Party Reform Documents, 1942–1944.* Seattle: University of Washington Press, 1952.
Conroy, R. Hilary. "Japan's War in China: An Ideological Somersault," *Pacific Historical Review,* Vol. XXI (1952), No. 4.
Chu, Samuel. "The New Life Movement, 1934–1937," *Researches in the Social Sciences in China,* John E. Lane, ed. New York: Columbia University East Asian Institute Studies No. 3, 1957.
Clubb, O. Edmund. "Chiang Kai-shek's Waterloo: The Battle of the Hwai-Hai," *Pacific Historical Review,* Vol. XXV (1956), No. 4.
Deutsch, Karl W. *Nationalism and Social Communication.* New York: Wiley (for Massachusetts Institute of Technology), 1953.
——. "Social Mobilization and Political Development," *American Political Science Review,* Vol. LV (1961), No. 3.
Djilas, Milovan. *The New Class, An Analysis of the Communist System.* New York: Praeger, 1957.
Forman, Harrison. *Report From Red China.* New York: Holt, 1945.
Fuller, Francis F. "Mao Tse-tung: Military Thinker," *Military Affairs,* Vol. XXII (1958), No. 3.
Gillin, Donald G. "Portrait of a Warlord: Yen Hsi-shan in Shansi Province, 1911–1930," *Journal of Asian Studies,* Vol. XIX (1960), No. 3.
Goette, John. *Japan Fights for Asia.* New York: Harcourt Brace, 1943.
Hammond, Thomas T. "The Origins of National Communism," *Virginia Quarterly Review,* Vol. XXXIV (1958), No. 2.
Hanson, Haldore. *Humane Endeavour, The Story of the Chinese War.* New York: Farrar and Rinehart, 1939.
Hayes, Carlton. *Nationalism: A Religion.* New York: Macmillan, 1960.
Hobsbawm, Eric J. *Social Bandits and Primitive Rebels, Studies in Archaic Forms of Social Movement in the 19th and 20th Centuries.* Glencoe: The Free Press, 1959.
Hsü Yung-ying. *A Survey of Shensi-Kansu-Ninghsia Border Region: Part I, Geography and Politics.* New York: International Secretariat, Institute of Pacific Relations, 1945.
Institute of Pacific Relations. *Agrarian China, Selected Source Materials from*

Chinese Authors. London: Institute of Pacific Relations, and Allen and Unwin, 1939.

International Military Tribunal for the Far East. *Proceedings.* Tokyo: April 29, 1946–November 12, 1948.

Ke Han. *The Shansi-Hopei-Chahar Border Region, Report 1, 1937–38.* Chungking: New China Information Committee, Bulletin No. 8, April 1940. Printed in Manila.

Kedourie, Elie. *Nationalism.* London: Hutchinson, 1960.

Klein, Sidney. *The Pattern of Land Tenure Reform in East Asia After World War II.* New York: Bookman, 1958.

Kreisberg, Paul H. "The New Fourth Army Incident and the United Front in China." Unpublished master's thesis in political science, Columbia University, 1952.

Kuo, Ping-chia. *China, New Age and New Outlook.* London: revised Penguin edition, 1960.

Lee, Frank C. "Land Redistribution in Communist China," *Pacific Affairs,* Vol. XXI (1948), No. 1.

Li Ting. *Militia of Communist China.* Hong Kong: Union Research Institute, 1955.

Lichtheim, George. *Marxism, An Historical and Critical Study.* London: Routledge and Kegan Paul, 1961.

Lindsay, Michael. *North China Front.* London: H. M. Stationery Office and the China Campaign Committee, 1943.

Liu, F. F. (Liu Chih-pu). *A Military History of Modern China 1924–1949.* Princeton: Princeton University Press, 1956.

Loo Pin-fei. *It Is Dark Underground.* New York: Putnam's, 1946.

MacFarquhar, R. "The Whampoa Military Academy," *Harvard University Papers on China,* Vol. IX, 1955.

McKenzie, Kermit E. "The Soviet Union, the Comintern, and World Revolution: 1935," *Political Science Quarterly,* Vol. LXV (1950), No. 2.

McLane, Charles B. *Soviet Policy and the Chinese Communists 1931–1946.* New York: Columbia University Press, 1958.

Magnenoz, Robert [pseud. for Robert Jobez, former Chef de la Sûreté, French Concession, Tientsin]. *De Confucius à Lénine, la montée au pouvoir du parti communiste chinois.* Saigon: Editions France-Asie, 1951.

Mao Tse-tung. *Selected Works.* London: Lawrence and Wishart, 1956. Four volumes.

———. *Selected Works.* Peking: Foreign Languages Press, 1961. Vol. IV.

Michael, Franz. "The Fall of China," *World Politics,* Vol. VIII (1956), No. 2.

Mitrany, David. *Marx Against the Peasant.* Chapel Hill: University of North Carolina Press, 1951.

Monnerot, Jules. *Sociology and Psychology of Communism.* Boston: Beacon Press ed., 1960. (Translation of Monnerot's *Sociologie du communisme,* Gallimard, 1949.)

Muramatsu Yuji. "Nationalism and Communism in China," *Asian Affairs* (Tokyo), Vol. I (1956), No. 4.

Murray, Henry A., ed. *Myth and Mythmaking.* New York: Braziller, 1960.

Peck, Graham. *Two Kinds of Time.* Boston: Houghton Mifflin, 1950.

People's Republic of China. *Saga of Resistance to Japanese Invasion.* Peking: Foreign Languages Press, 1957.

Pye, Lucian W. *Guerrilla Communism in Malaya.* Princeton: Princeton University Press, 1956.

Rosinger, L. K. *China's Wartime Politics 1937–1944.* Princeton: Princeton University Press, 1945. 2d edition.

Schapiro, Leonard. *The Communist Party of the Soviet Union.* New York: Random House, 1959.

Skinner, G. William. "Aftermath of Communist Liberation in the Chengtu Plain," *Pacific Affairs,* Vol. XXIV (1951), No. 1.

Snow, Edgar. *Red Star Over China.* New York: Modern Library edition, 1938.

———. *The Battle for Asia.* New York: Random House, 1941.

———. *Random Notes on Red China (1936–1945).* Cambridge, Mass.: Harvard University, 1957.

Snyder, Louis. *The Meaning of Nationalism.* New Brunswick, N.J.: Rutgers University Press, 1954.

Storry, Richard. *The Double Patriots, A Study of Japanese Nationalism.* Boston: Houghton Miffln, 1957.

Taylor, George E. *The Struggle for North China.* New York: International Secretariat, Institute of Pacific Relations, 1940.

Tipton, Lawrence. *China Escapade.* London: Macmillan, 1949.

Weber, Max. *The Theory of Social and Economic Organization.* Henderson and Parsons, trans. Glencoe: Free Press, 1947.

———. "The Nation" in *From Max Weber: Essays in Sociology.* Gerth and Mills, eds. New York: Oxford Galaxy edition, 1958.

White, T. H. and A. Jacoby. *Thunder out of China.* New York: Sloane, 1946.

Wright, Mary C. "The Chinese Peasant and Communism," *Pacific Affairs,* Vol. XXIV (1951), No. 3.

Young, John. *Checklist of Microfilm Reproductions of Selected Archives of the Japanese Army, Navy, and other Government Agencies, 1868–1945.* Washington: Georgetown University Press, 1959.

B. Works on Yugoslavia

Bobrowski, C. *La Yougoslave socialiste.* Paris: Cahiers de la Fondation Nationale des Sciences Politiques; Librairie Armand Colin, 1956.

Churchill, Winston S. *Closing the Ring.* Boston: Houghton Mifflin, 1951. Vol. V of *The Second World War.*

Clissold, Stephen. *Whirlwind: An Account of Marshal Tito's Rise to Power.* New York: Philosophical Library, 1949.

Davidson, Basil. *Partisan Picture.* Bedford, England: Bedford Books, 1946.

Dedijer, Vladimir. *With Tito Through the War: Partisan Diary, 1941–1944.* London: Alexander Hamilton, 1951.

———. *Tito Speaks.* London: Weidenfeld and Nicolson, 1953.

Halasz, Nicholas. *In the Shadow of Russia: Eastern Europe in the Post-War World.* New York: Ronald, 1959.

Halperin, Ernst. *The Triumphant Heretic: Tito's Struggle Against Stalin.* London: Heinemann, 1958.

Inks, James M. *Eight Bailed Out.* New York: Norton, 1954.

International Military Tribunal. *Trial of the Major War Criminals Before the International Military Tribunal.* Nuremberg: 1947.

Kapetanović, Nikola. *Tito et les partisans: ce qui s'est passé en réalité en Yougoslavie de 1941 à 1945.* Belgrade: Jugoslovenska Knjiga, n.d.

Kris, E. and Hans Speier, *et al. German Radio Propaganda.* London and New York: Oxford University Press, 1944.

Lazitch (Lazić), Branko. *Tito et la révolution yougoslave.* Paris: Fasquelle, 1957.

———. *Les partis communistes d'Europe 1919–1955.* Paris: Les Iles d'Or, 1956.

———. *La Tragédie du Général Draja Mihailovitch.* Paris: Editions du Haut-pays, n.d.

Maclean, Fitzroy. *Escape to Adventure.* Boston: Little, Brown, 1950.

———. *Tito.* New York: Ballantine, 1957.

Neal, Fred Warner. *Titoism in Action: The Reforms in Yugoslavia After 1948.* Berkeley and Los Angeles: University of California Press, 1958.

———. "Yugoslav Communist Theory," *The American Slavic and East European Review,* Vol. XIX (1960), No. 1.

Piyade, Mosha. *About the Legend That the Yugoslav Uprising Owed Its Existence to Soviet Assistance.* London: Yugoslav Information Service, 1950.

Pavlowitch, K. St. *The Struggle of the Serbs.* London: 1943.

Pribechevich, Stoyan, trans. *Yugoslavia's Way: The Program of the League of Communists of Yugoslavia.* New York: All Nations Press, 1958.

Rootham, Jasper. *Miss Fire: The Chronicle of a British Mission to Mihailovich 1943–1944.* London: Chatto and Windus, 1946.

Tito, Josip Broz. *The Yugoslav Peoples Fight to Live.* New York: The United Committee of South-Slavic Americans, 1944.

———. *Tito Speaks.* London: The United South Slav Committee, June 28, 1944.

Wolff, Robert L. *The Balkans in Our Time.* Cambridge, Mass.: Harvard University Press, 1956.

Yourichitch, Evgueniyé. *Le Procès Tito-Mihailovitch.* Paris: Société d'Editions Françaises et Internationales, 1950.

Yugoslavia, Federated People's Republic. *Stenographic Record and Documents from the Trial of Dragoljub-Draza Mihailović.* Belgrade: 1946.

———, Military Historical Institute. *The War Effort of Yugoslavia 1941–1945.* Belgrade: n.d. [ca. 1955].

C. U.S. Government Documents

U.S. Army, Forces in the Far East. *North China Area Operations Record July 1937–May 1941.* Tokyo: Military History Section; Headquarters, Army Forces Far East, 1955. Japanese Monograph 178.

————. *Central China Area Operations Record 1937–1941.* Tokyo: Japanese Monograph 179, 1955.

————. *South China Area Operations Record 1937–1941.* Tokyo: Japanese Monograph 180, 1956.

————. *Political Strategy Prior to Outbreak of War,* Part II. Tokyo: Japanese Monograph 146, 1953.

————. *Japanese Preparations for Operations in Manchuria, January 1943–August 1945.* Tokyo: Japanese Monograph 138, 1954.

————. *Record of Operations Against Soviet Russia on Northern and Western Fronts of Manchuria, and in Northern Korea (August 1945).* Tokyo: Japanese Monograph 155, 1954.

U.S. Central Intelligence Agency. *China, Provisional Atlas of Communist Administrative Units.* Washington: Department of Commerce, 1959.

U.S. Federal Communications Commission, Foreign Broadcast Intelligence Service. *Radio Report on the Far East.* Washington: August 24, 1942–August 25, 1945.

U.S. Navy Department, Office of the Chief of Naval Operations. *Civil Affairs Handbook, Japanese Administrative Organization in Taiwan (Formosa).* Washington: August 10, 1944.

U.S. Office of War Information, Analysis and Research Bureau, General Intelligence Division. *GID OPINTEL Reports.*

U.S. State Department. *Foreign Relations of the United States, Diplomatic Papers, 1942, China.* Washington: Government Printing Office, 1956.

U.S. War Department, Military Intelligence Division. "The Chinese Communist Movement, 5 July 1945," U.S. Senate, 82nd Congress, 2nd Session, Committee on the Judiciary, *Institute of Pacific Relations Hearings,* Part 7A, Appendix II, pp. 2305–2474. Washington: Government Printing Office, 1952.

————. *Handbook on Japanese Military Forces.* Washington: Technical Manual TM 30-480, September 21, 1942.

Index

SINKIANG

KANSU

NING

CHINGHAI

TIBET

SIKANG

Lhasa

YUNNAN

Kunming

To Paot'ou

Kalgan

Huailai

Nank'ou

Tat'ung

Yühsien

Peiping

Lingchiu

Pinghsingkuan

Fanchih

Ihsien

Ningwu

Tai

Laiyüan

Wut'aishan

Mancheng

Fouping

Paoting

Wut'ai

T'anghsien

Chienping

Pingshan

Shihchiachuang

Tinghsiang

T'aiyüan

Chinghsing

Yütz'u

To Fenglingtu

To Hankow

Chin-Ch'a-Chi
Border
Region